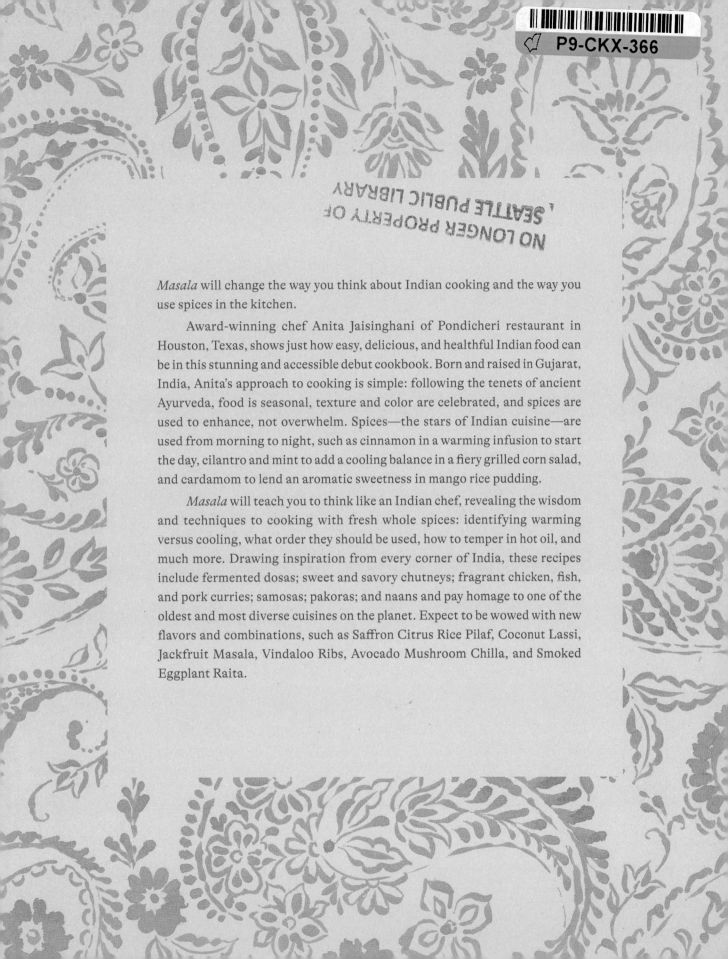

Masala will change the way you think about Indian cooking and the way you use spices in the kitchen.

Award-winning chef Anita Jaisinghani of Pondicheri restaurant in Houston, Texas, shows just how easy, delicious, and healthful Indian food can be in this stunning and accessible debut cookbook. Born and raised in Gujarat, India, Anita's approach to cooking is simple: following the tenets of ancient Ayurveda, food is seasonal, texture and color are celebrated, and spices are used to enhance, not overwhelm. Spices—the stars of Indian cuisine—are used from morning to night, such as cinnamon in a warming infusion to start the day, cilantro and mint to add a cooling balance in a fiery grilled corn salad, and cardamom to lend an aromatic sweetness in mango rice pudding.

Masala will teach you to think like an Indian chef, revealing the wisdom and techniques to cooking with fresh whole spices: identifying warming versus cooling, what order they should be used, how to temper in hot oil, and much more. Drawing inspiration from every corner of India, these recipes include fermented dosas; sweet and savory chutneys; fragrant chicken, fish, and pork curries; samosas; pakoras; and naans and pay homage to one of the oldest and most diverse cuisines on the planet. Expect to be wowed with new flavors and combinations, such as Saffron Citrus Rice Pilaf, Coconut Lassi, Jackfruit Masala, Vindaloo Ribs, Avocado Mushroom Chilla, and Smoked Eggplant Raita.

Masala

Anita Jaisinghani

Masala

Recipes from India, the Land of Spices

Photographs by Johnny Autry

Illustrations by Julie Keselman

TEN SPEED PRESS
California | New York

Contents

I wish to dedicate this book to
my late mother, Kamala, from whom I inherited
my passion for food and who gave me the love
and confidence only a mother can.

Recipes

Pancakes and Eggs

Street Foods

Vegetables

Legumes

Seafood and Meat

Introduction

Given my insatiable appetite for all matters related to food, my daughter, Ajna, often joked with me, "If I dressed up as a lamb chop, would I get more attention from you?" My cooking journey launched at the dawn of my teenage years; however, a career in food was not considered respectable in India in those days, I was ushered into science. Science came easy, and I learned a lot, but my senses kept pulling me toward the kitchen. My cooking style initially was largely influenced by the cuisine of Sindh, the lost homeland of my parents, and by the food of Gujarat, the state I was born and raised in. When I arrived in Canada as a young bride, a whole new world of food opened for me. By day, I worked as a microbiologist, but by night, I was stalking grocery and international food stores discovering new foods from around the world. I later immigrated to the United States. Fascinated by the new world I was in, yet pining for the culture I came from, I turned my husband and two young children into unsuspecting subjects of my relentless cooking experiments. Annual trips to India to visit family, where I carried tubs of peanut butter and cardamom cookies for my father, punctuated with stops in Europe opened my eyes to a better way of cooking.

I became a stay-at-home-mom-run restaurant, regaling my kids with daily changing breakfasts—scones for Ajna today, a paratha tomorrow, Nutella crepes or pancakes for my son, Virag, a rotating variety of naan sandwiches for school lunches, and fresh smoothies and cookies when they would arrive home from school. I found out years later that sometimes Ajna would trade her sandwiches for test answers, and Virag for what he deemed "normal food." To get over their Monday school blues, I would deliver them piping-hot lunches.

Seeing how poorly represented Indian food was in Canada and the United States during the eighties and nineties, I resolved to showcase the subcontinent's foods in a better way. I had set the intention; the path would follow. Eventually, I found my way into a career in food, first by catering meals for friends and family, then making fresh chutneys and selling them to Whole Food Markets in Houston. This was followed by a brief stint at the prestigious Annie Café, after which I went on to open two successful restaurants, Indika and Pondicheri.

Despite decades of exhaustive cooking with nonstop experimentation, I still have a tremendous sense of curiosity, and every single day, I wake up excited to walk into Pondicheri. Restaurant cooks are some of the toughest people to cook for, but they became my testing ground, and the first time I made pani poori, a quintessential street snack of India, I knew I had a winner on my hands when I would watch them sneak pooris in their mouths —they were intrigued by the flavors and textures! I am at my happiest in the kitchen, and being an intuitive cook, I almost never use recipes and seldom cook the same thing twice, always tinkering with a better way to make it. My philosophy about cooking is that the only way to get better is to keep cooking and get comfortable being in a kitchen. I made a fair amount of not-so-tasty food to arrive at good food. Bound neither by tradition nor a pursuit for authenticity, I use my years of prolific cooking to adjust age-old ideas into today's world.

With *Masala*, I am sharing with you stories of creativity and courage, about blending colonial ingredients with ancestral techniques. While it is hard to distill a culture this vast and diverse into a few recipes, I offer you my best renditions. My recipes are meant to be guides, so take the ideas, move them around, dream up your own versions. After a lifelong love affair with spices, I am here to share the love. And to convince you to add spices to your daily repertoire—this could be as simple as adding a stick of cinnamon into your rice to popping mustard seeds into your favorite soup to creating your own masala. The tiny bit of wisdom I have gleaned from years of being a student of yoga and Ayurveda, I offer you with hope that you will explore further. My dream for this book is that it finds a permanent place in your kitchen and the pages gradually fill up with stains of turmeric, ghee, and such. Happy cooking!

A Brief History of India and its Food

The history of food in India can be traced back for millennia, and many conquests, rulers, and expansions and subtractions of the country's border helped shape the cuisine of this nation and its provinces today. At a time when England was still unknown and lost in the cold gray mists of the ocean, ships sailed from India's sunny shores, and caravans wound through sandy desserts, laden with spices, silk, and jewels. Yet little was known of the land of gold and black pepper, peacocks and emeralds. Besides the merchants who grew rich from the trafficking, few journeyed to India. Only after the invasion of India by Alexander the Great in 326 BCE into the state of Punjab has the West known something of this wonderful land of the East. Alexander brought fennel, fenugreek, and fragrant herbs to the cuisine of India and introduced saffron and rice to the West. At this time, the Mauryan Empire flourished in India under one of the greatest emperors of its time, Ashoka. With a revulsion for warfare and deeply influenced by Buddhism, King Ashoka banished hunting in the royal households and put into place a moral political economy and an equitable society where the rule of law was to live in harmony with all living creatures. The history of vegetarianism in India can be traced back to the influence wielded by King Ashoka.

Fast forward to the seventh century, and the first foray of Muslim explorers and soldiers entered Sindh, a province west of Gujarat and Rajasthan, through the Indus River on a looting expedition. Sindh, the land my parents came from, now in present-day Pakistan, is home to Mohenjo-daro, meaning "Mound of the Dead." Discovered in the nineteenth century, it is one of the oldest, most advanced, and sophisticated Indus Valley civilizations built in the twenty-sixth century BCE. After the seventh century, for over half a millennium, a parade of invaders from lands as far as Persia, Uzbekistan, Afghanistan, and Turkey pillaged Sindh and the surrounding land's rich resources. This was followed by several full-scale invasions into the province of Punjab, culminating in the establishment of the Delhi Sultanate in 1206 CE. Despite internal struggles among rebellious and ambitious nobles, the Delhi Sultanate was the center of the entire Muslim world, and many historians argue that it contributed to India becoming the multicultural and cosmopolitan nation that it is today. These conquerors and their descendants left the social fabric of India almost intact while causing religious, political, and economic upheavals. The repeated invasions of foreign powers and their influence led to a subtle shift in the culture of India, from food to architecture to language.

The sixteenth century marked a significant change with the arrival of Babur, a descendant of Tamerlane and Genghis Khan. Babur, a great soldier and a skilled organizer, founded the Mughal Empire. The relationship between Hindus and Muslims never ceased to be tense; however, there were decades of exceptional harmony under the reign of Akbar in the sixteenth century. Akbar maintained an equanimity toward all religions, married a princess from Rajasthan, and abolished the hated tax that all non-Muslims had to pay. His spirit was eclectic and conciliatory, while his intention was part of a larger design of tolerance and compassion. It was during Akbar's rule that a fusing of the two cultures happened, and with the advent of the tandoor, open-fire cooking, naans, and kebabs became cuisine du jour. His successor, Jahangir, despite aesthetic leanings and political skill, loved pleasure and wine too much and left governance to his twentieth wife, the beautiful and intelligent Nur Jahan. Nur Jahan was a strong, charismatic, and well-educated woman who was more decisive and proactive than her husband. She enjoyed his absolute confidence, and she remains unique under the annals of the Mughal Empire for the tremendous political influence she wielded. It was under Nur Jahan's rule that the khichri, the age-old Indian rice and lentil stew, and the Persian pulao, a rice and meat dish, were married to create biryani, a layered rich and decadent rice and meat or vegetable dish.

Jahangir was succeeded by Shah Jahan, who, in the tradition of the dynasty, took power after assassinating his brother and other relatives desirous of the throne. It was a period of artistic splendor ending in tragedy, when his fourteenth and favorite wife, Mumtaz Mahal, died in childbirth and in whose memory he built the Taj Mahal. His overindulgence in opium weakened his character and united his four sons against him. A war of succession erupted, and one brother, Aurangzeb, killed the other three and seized control of the throne. One of the slain princes, Dara Shikoh, bears mention, as he was Shah Jahan's favorite son and was destined to succeed him. Neither a politician nor a soldier but more of a humanitarian and intellectual, he held the same interests in other cultures as his great-grandfather Akbar. In 1657, Dara Shikoh translated the Vedas, the ancient scriptures of India, into Persian. A French traveler specializing in Oriental studies, Anquetil-Duperron, made a Latin version of Dara's translation. That version was the one that Schopenhauer read, and the philosophic influence of that translation was enormous: on one side, Nietzsche, and the other, Emerson.

Aurangzeb turned out to be a religious fanatic, and the decline of the Mughal Empire began with him, with a series of terrible mistakes, senseless wars, and useless victories. Under him, the breach between Hindus and Muslims became unsurmountable. He restored taxation on locals, razed temples, and built mosques on their foundations. The internecine struggles between the Mughals, the new Sikh powers from the north, and Marathas from the west weakened the country and the empire as a new protagonist appeared. Around the year 1600, the British East India Company arrived, looking for land, with their hearts set not on the religious conversion of the infidels but on economic and political domination. At the outset the activities of the company, the first-ever publicly traded corporation in the world, were essentially commercial, but economics is inseparable from politics, and in a short time, it became a military and political superpower. India next lived through a century of British anarchy and civil wars when its global GDP fell from over 30 percent to 3 percent and the GDP of Britain skyrocketed. Shiploads and shiploads of jewels, ornate furniture, and other valuables were shipped off to England. By the mid-1700s, the East India Company accounted for 50 percent of the world's trade. New research by renowned economists drawing on nearly two centuries of records has estimated that from 1765 to 1938, Britain drained an estimated $45 trillion from India through various forms of devious tax and trade schemes. Not only this, but millions of Indians also died unnecessarily in famines, revolts, and wars. One can only imagine what a different country India would be today without the parade and pillage of foreign invasions. In 1857, the Church of England, eyeing India as the jewel in their crown, abolished the East India Company and seized control. Queen Victoria granted religious freedom to the Indians and the next era of divide and rule British Raj colonialism was born. This right was the seed for the future independence of India. After more than a thirty-year struggle of civil disobedience and ahimsa (nonviolence), Mahatma Gandhi led India to its true modern-day freedom in 1947.

At the beginning of independence, as a country, India was unsure of itself and its identity, like children stumbling in the dark, beaten down by the abuse of so many generations of foreign rule. After unimaginable post-traumatic stress over generations of invaders tearing the country apart with religious persecution, economic dominance, rampant robbing of its wealth and rich resources from the Mughals to the British, India had to learn how to stand on her own feet, take care of her rich land, and appreciate her heritage and scriptures. India's ancestors were designers and architects who built dozens of intricate forts and temples and other architectural marvels, yet as a young independent country, India had to relearn how to invest in itself.

At the time, in 1947, my parents, as young teens, were residing in the idyllic northern state of their homeland, Sindh. My maternal grandfather was a lawyer in Karachi with his own practice and a brood of twelve. My father's

family were mostly lawyers and landowners from Jacobabad, a small town in northern Sindh. For millennia, Hindus and Muslims had lived in relative harmony as neighbors in the northern states of Sindh and Punjab. But right after independence in 1947, in a final swift stroke of political travesty, India was split up into two. Sindh remained entirely in the neighboring Pakistan, and most Hindu Sindhis, like my parents, were urged to escape to India, and most Muslims were urged to move to Pakistan. Pakistan became the predominantly Muslim country, and India predominantly Hindu.

Given continuing unrest in Pakistan, I have never had a chance to visit my homeland province of Sindh. My mother, Kamala, born and raised in Karachi, recounted in hushed, pained tones many horror stories about innocent people getting massacred on streets and train stations at the time of Partition. Despite lofty promises by Lord Mountbatten, then the viceroy of India, and in a spectacular failure of governance and oversight, almost two million people died during the partition of India and Pakistan and about thirty million were displaced and forced to migrate. My mother as a young woman was one of those refugees who, with a few of her siblings, equipped with just the clothes on her back, fled Karachi, escaping fatal atrocities one early morning in December 1947 aboard a train to Bangalore, India. My father and his entire family were forced to abandon their properties in Jacobabad and do the same.

After my parents were married a few years later, my father got a job with the state government of Gujarat. Gujarat is home to some of the most successful industrialists of India and, more important, it is also the birthplace of peace-loving Mahatma Gandhi, who spearheaded the end of the British colonial rule in India, and where his main ashrams now reside. Gujarat is a small but powerful western state in India that borders Rajasthan, the Arabian Sea, and the Sindh province of Pakistan. I was born in a sleepy coastal town called Mandvi in the Kutch region of Gujarat.

Gujarat has the honor of being the state with the highest number of vegetarians in India and maybe the world. As a child growing up in Gujarat, I did not know much about the local food, since all we ate at home was Sindhi food. My mother was an amazing cook—whether it was the way she finished dal with fragrant cumin seeds or labored over a biryani, she was famous for her magic fingers (or the siri, which stands for love and taste in equal measure). Only when I was able to go over to friends' houses did I appreciate the nuanced, simple, but highly flavorful vegetarian Gujarati cuisine. I admired their delicate touch with spices, with hints of asafetida and mustard seeds, and myriad ways of preparing vegetables with a lingering sweetness of jaggery, and I relished the innumerable irresistible snacks made with chickpea flour and lentils.

Sindhi food shares the heartiness and complexity of other North Indian cuisines, like Punjabi and Kashmiri, but has a lighter tone. One of the best memories of my mother's cooking was sayel goat, a rustic stew with lots of onions, ginger, and the lingering fragrance of freshly crushed green carda-mom. Walking up the street from school, the aroma would hit and quicken my pace. It was also a smell that relegated us to meat-eating Sindhi barbarians by our gentle Gujarati neighbors. Growing up as a Sindhi in India was like being an outsider in my own country, so coming to America was a relatively easy transition for me. I assimilated the best I could, picking up some good and bad American habits, while trying to maintain most of my Indian roots.

Today, India is on an exciting quest to reclaim and reinvent its culinary heritage. Despite Western fast-food chains proliferating across larger cities, successful street vendors are setting up brick-and-mortar booths with locals lining up to try new-fangled chaats, the immensely popular humble snacky street food. Single-origin native spices and herbs are being carefully studied, preserved, and documented for posterity. Food historians are digging deep into the many varieties of rice native to India (thirty-two and counting) and studying the history of ancient supergrains, like ragi (a red finger millet) and sorghum. The government has set up tea, spice, and grain boards across the nation to document and preserve the many varieties native to India. My hope is that India, rather than looking to the West for inspiration, digs deep into the wealth of knowledge in its own Vedas and Ayurveda, adapts it to define a better way to eat, live, and be, and becomes a model for the rest of the world to follow.

coming to america

Despite being an impossible, diverse, incredible, extraordinary, and madden-ing country, I am hopelessly in love with the culture and history of India. The longer I have stayed away, the more I want to learn about it. It would take me living in the West for decades to reconcile the treasures I gave up in India and to lean into them to better understand myself and the culture I come from. When I arrived in North America in the early 1980s as a young girl, I was starstruck on my first trip to a grocery store, where I spent hours admiring the beautiful, neatly stacked fruits and vegetables. I found delight in the newness of the culture: the stores with glittering window displays, people with dif-ferent skin colors, the massive malls, restaurants with cuisines from all over the world, the wide landscapes and concrete highways, and roads with lanes. At the grocery store, I was like a kid in a candy store. I had never seen such enormous, perfectly sculpted bananas with even, golden-yellow unblemished skins. I made myself believe that this had to taste better than the pockmarked fruit I grew up eating. It took me a few trips back and forth to India to real-ize that those small spotty bananas had an intense sweetness missing in the sculpted fruits of the West.

What Is
Indian Food?

Early in my days as an adult cook in America, I would bristle and snap when my cooking was called "fusion." *They just don't know the home and street cooking of India*, I would console myself. They've never experienced an explosion of pani poori flooding their mouths with joy, nor have they healed themselves with a fragrant warming khichri to bring life back into their bodies. Disappointed that red-stained chicken (tandoori chicken, so they called it) and creamy frozen spinach (a sorry excuse for palak paneer) were America's impression of Indian food, I had a gnawing urge to transform this sad portrayal of my homeland's food. I was intuitively cooking foods I grew up with, sometimes in new and inventive ways, picking up ideas from frequent trips to India via Europe, using local seasonal ingredients, but I certainly was not bringing the cuisine of another culture into my fold. I opened my first restaurant, Indika, to multiple accolades in Houston, Texas, in 2001, and it had a glorious fifteen-year run until we closed it in 2016. A few months after opening Indika, I patiently explained to a local food writer, "Asking me to cook Indian food in America without using local ingredients is like asking me to live here but not breathe the air." Of course, I am going to use brussels sprouts and asparagus when they are in season and cook with local red snapper rather than trying to locate hilsa, a fish I grew up eating in India.

Little did I understand that authenticity can be a myth, and almost all cuisines, in some way, have an element of fusion, whether it is a result of multiple influences of foreign invasions like in India, human migrations across continents for survival, primitive tribes exchanging valuable techniques, or specialties like spices and other exotics traveling in ships around the globe to faraway lands. Take, for example, pasta, inspired by noodles brought into Italy during the thirteenth century by Italian explorer Marco Polo from his travels to China. Cacio de pepe, considered one of Italy's authentic pasta dishes, has copious amounts of black pepper, which grew native in the forests of Kerala. Every country and region in the world has been influenced by trade, travel, or migration. Given the wide-ranging confluences on India by the occupation of Greeks, Turks, Mongols, Portuguese, and British combined with the local bounty of spices, Indian food may just be the ultimate fusion food and, as a delicious consequence, one of the most exciting cuisines in the world. Naans and samosas, two of the most popular foods in Indian restaurants, are Afghan and Persian imports, and without them, Indian food would not be what it is today. The Portuguese brought chiles to India less than five hundred years ago, yet today it is impossible to imagine Indian food without chiles to balance the flavors. Even Ayurvedic physicians, who rarely incorporated foreign foods into the cosmic world of health and healing, embraced chiles wholeheartedly to help rekindle the digestive fire.

Fast-forward to almost twenty years later, on the eve of the tenth anniversary of my second restaurant, Pondicheri, also in Houston, where I seek to highlight the street and home cooking of India and I unabashedly borrow ideas from other cultures. When my Colombian friend Emmy introduced me to boronia, a delicious smoked plantain and eggplant dish, I immediately incorporated smoked plantains into our Punjabi smoked eggplant. Good cooking is and should be a constant flow of evolving ideas with one eye on history and another on the future, constantly retouched by creative minds. Today, Indian food continues to be an evolving, freewheeling, unregimented cuisine, a cuisine in eternal flux—of which I hope to remain a permanent student—where almost nothing is sacrosanct yet all is held together by the magical use of spices.

Food as Medicine

Food as medicine is not a new idea; it's been around for thousands of years, and with its surging popularity, it may be the ideal footprint to follow, how life should be for humanity. This thinking has radically changed the way I look at food and cook. Everything I put on a plate, whether it is for myself, my family, or the restaurant, must have value or purpose. Knowing the power of phytochemical-loaded brassicas, I sneak a small mound of marinated local cabbage on every lunch bowl we serve at Pondicheri. We continue tweaking our plates to incorporate locally grown vegetables, add mashed sweet potato in naan doughs to reduce the white flour, and add grated carrots or vegetable peels and cuttings into roti doughs.

Food is one of the greatest, if not *the* greatest, joy in life, and nature's bounty is all around us—we just need to notice and feel. I can sense the warm rush of carotene coursing through my bloodstream when I devour a bunch of freshly picked crunchy purple carrots on my way home from the farmers' market. Or the incredible joy I feel when I rest my eyes on my daughter Ajna's glowing face as I hand her a bowl of her favorite fresh, nourishing sautéed local greens—be it spinach, chard, or kale—spiked with cumin seeds and ginger. Or the simple emotional pleasure I experience when my pastry chef and dear friend Alexa and I settle on a cot outside Pondicheri on Sundays to review the week and nibble on sweet potato fries dusted with tangy spices.

It's ironic that Western medicine as we know it, being less than two hundred years old, is regarded as mainstream medicine, and ancient holistic practices, like Ayurveda or traditional Chinese medicine, which are more than four thousand years old, are thought of as alternative. Modern medicine has provided us with plenty of miracles, from eradicating endemic diseases like cholera and polio to the debt of gratitude I owe a brilliant young surgeon in Bombay for performing open-heart surgery to save my father's life in the mid-eighties. However, there is huge cause for concern in its systemic, formulaic, localized approach. It overlooks the fundamental fact that the human body is a complex synergy of mind, body, and spirit and, most important, pays no attention to the true root cause of disease, thereby marginalizing thousands of years of ancient wisdom. Modern medicine came into practice in the nineteenth century, around the same time pharmaceutical companies came into existence. In the intervening years, both associations turned into powerful businesses with a goal to turn medicine into a money-making machine. A partnership was forged to set sky-high prices and unprecedented profits yet woefully ignore side effects, like nutrient deficiencies, mental disorders, and allergies caused by these very drugs.

Historians argue that famous seventeenth-century French philosopher René Descartes had tremendous influence on the thinking of Europeans. Descartes believed that the world was divided into two: educated men, mostly white men, were the only intelligent sentient beings, and the rest, from rocks to rivers, animals and amoebas, and indigenous people, people of color, and women were extended, inferior, and sometimes unnecessary matter. In complete opposition to holistic conclusions from thousands of years before that everything is connected, from the leaf on a tree to a small bug crawling in the dirt to the air we breathe, Descartes purported that human bodies are like machines and separate from our minds, and we have long suffered the reckless consequences of such thinking.

ancient wisdom

Whether it's traditional Chinese medicine or cures mentioned in holy scriptures from the Bible to the Koran, the ultimate goal of most ancient practices is to restore balance with the assistance of food and movement exercises to help the body do its own healing. Focusing on prevention over cure, Ayurveda recommends practices, like meditation, diet, and yoga, to help us connect with the cosmic intelligence that went into creating everything in nature from a blade of grass to humans. These practices are designed to help the human body on a deeper level by curing diseases from the inside out, thereby elevating the human body and spirit.

As early as 2000 BCE, ancient Middle Eastern healers, Mayan cultures, and Ayurvedic practitioners knew that mental and spiritual well-being affected our physical well-being, an idea later embraced by Hippocrates and other Greek physicians. Through years of trial and error, these gentle healers crafted powerful cures and medicines using roots, herbs, and spices combined with simple techniques of yoga, tai chi, and chi gong and spending time in nature. In the Bible, Proverb 17:22, King Solomon says: "A joyful heart is good medicine but a broken and depressed spirit dries up the bones." While Western medicine has made many advances and saved lives, its spectacular failure in embracing or at least consulting ancient practices is astounding.

I felt the presence of Unani medicine, Reiki, and Ayurveda reverberate around me in India as a kid and young adult but was too wrapped up in myself to pay attention. Reiki is a Japanese alternative form of energy healing, and Unani medicine is a system of herbal, dietary, and alternative healing that originated

in Greece and was practiced in the Muslim culture of Southeast Asia. I had heard rumors about these practices going underground due to colonial suppression, but they had started to make a strong comeback by the seventies. I remember a daily line forming outside the clinic of a famous Unani healer that my father frequented in our neighborhood. My mother had her own personal Reiki master who would come to our house to do energy-healing sessions with her. Hiring a massage therapist to come to our home was not considered a luxury but a necessary part of maintaining good health. I would witness my parents careening off to an Ayurvedic resort for an annual panchakarma, a systematic lengthy rejuvenating cleanse to get rid of toxins and excess negative energy. However, after I moved West in the early eighties, I dove straight into assimilating with a new culture and left those practices far behind.

When I was studying microbiology during the late seventies, most bacteria were considered pathogens. Today, microbiome studies are proving that our gut is the second brain, and bacteria and other trillion-plus microorganisms that cohabitate in our body are necessary and actually help take care of us. Antibiotics may have been heralded as miraculous, but recent studies are showing that in many cases, the damage done by them to our gut flora may overshadow the benefits. There is no doubt in my mind that the future of human health lies in integrating ancient practices, like Ayurveda, with modern medicine, and it all begins with food.

ayurvedic perspective

Ayurveda, meaning "the knowledge of life," is a holistic living philosophy promoting a malleability that changes and evolves with seasons, our needs, and stages in life. Instead of seeing our body just as a collection of cells, tissues, and organs, Ayurveda sees it as a silent flow of intelligence created and controlled by bubbling impulses. At the quantum level, anything in our body can be changed with a flick of an intention. With neither dogma nor a strict doctrine, Ayurveda simply shows us a better way to live. What's most fascinating about it is that thousands of years ago, without the help of microscopes or modern technologies, the rishis, or bards, of ancient India culled the knowledge from the cosmos through deep, long, silent meditation and contemplation. They manifested profound, intricate, and exceedingly detailed life knowledge into Vedic scriptures. For millennia, this knowledge was tested in real time with millions of people while continuing to be passed down by oral tradition, eventually honed and transcribed into the Vedas, which give detailed information about healing, surgery, and longevity. Hushed for hundreds of years due to foreign occupation, it had to be dusted off, reexamined, and reinterpreted. It was this knowledge that subconsciously informed many of Indian people's

daily habits, from drinking room-temperature water to doing a headstand every morning upon waking, as my uncle did, to the reverence and empathy most of us experienced toward the plants and animals around us. Gandhi's philosophy of nonviolence, or ahimsa, was rooted in our scriptures.

I am no expert on the vast subject of Ayurveda; however, attempting to understand it has changed my perspective on how I cook, eat, and live. My first decade in the United States was spent trying to assimilate to the local culture, and modern medicine became the key to all health problems, whether it was popping a pill for a headache or casually taking antibiotics for mild infections. Eventually, when I understood that I needed to reach deeper, regular yoga practices led me to Ayurveda. The first time I visited an Ayurvedic healer, she asked me what I had eaten for lunch. Slightly embarrassed, I explained that after a busy lunch service at the restaurant, I had inhaled a quick sandwich while standing over a trash can to catch the juices so I didn't even have to use a plate. Looking at her expression, I knew right then that I needed to change my eating patterns, and this marked the beginning of a journey to attempt to understand Ayurveda.

Over years of practice, Ayurveda has inspired me to listen to my body and nurture my mind-to-body connection. I've trained myself to breathe slower and deeper to relieve anxiety and stress, take barefoot walks on grass to feel grounded to the earth, and listen to my body before I put something in my mouth. (Well, not always, and certainly not when my pastry chef Alexa, hands me a delicious sweet laddu to taste.)

Ayurveda is the pursuit of balance, a daily practice, and just like most people, I get it right about half the time. Beginning my day with breathing practices accompanied by a glass of warm water infused with fresh turmeric root and a squeeze of lemon (see page 44) is a start. I have learned to eat my biggest and most satisfying meal between noon and 2 p.m., when my digestive fire with the help of the sun is at its strongest. It is on the days when I maintain this discipline that I feel my strongest and most balanced. However, this is not always possible when sharing evening meals with my family, and I am learning how to navigate my needs with those of my family and friends.

Ayurveda is a science of preventative health and healing that rarely treats symptoms but rather attempts to cure us by removing the cause of disease and showing us a better way to be. Disease can come from transgressing against nature or our own instinctive wisdom and improper eating. Or from ignoring the cycles of seasons or our age, engaging in excessive pursuit of sensual pleasures, or a karmic burden we bear from a previous birth. Ayurveda teaches us that disease can often begin at the change of major seasons, from fall to winter or spring to summer, when the body is the most vulnerable, and the first seed of any disease is sown in the gut. Therefore, we are urged to cross the seasonal junctions gently and with care. When our digestive fire is obstructed, unprocessed and undigested food turns into toxins. The seed of disease may start out as general malaise, tiredness, or lack of clarity, and if left unchecked can spread beyond the site of origin via the bloodstream into other parts of the body, leading to complications such as headache, nausea, indigestion, or diarrhea. This could take years or decades to manifest, but these are vital signals our body is sending us to warn us to take charge before that seed finds a weak spot in our body, concentrating in specific tissues or organs and creating conditions like heart disease, arthritis, and cancer. Ayurveda considers chronic and clinical full-blown disorders a culmination of disease, which requires much more work to cure. We could take charge of our health better if we could only train ourselves to look for those vital signs.

In Ayurveda, it is believed that everything we eat, say, do, think, see, and feel affects our overall state of balance. The body, nothing short of a miracle, can withstand extensive abuse and trauma yet has tremendous capacity to self-correct. Keeping in tune with the environment, we can heal our body by staying connected and bringing it back into balance by simple home practices. Health is not just the absence of disease, a separate pursuit of the perfect body, a forging of an intellectual mind, or even austere practices of the spirit. It is self-defeating and burdensome to try to maintain a perfect body, life, or health, and the demands of such striving, sometimes using desperate measures, steal the vital force from life. Ayurveda's genius lies in balancing our bodies with nature, accepting that both are in constant flux. It's the guiding star that reminds us to not take ourselves too seriously, to hold on to the simple joys of life, like walking on a beach or running through a meadow to feel the wind. Accomplishing peace of mind can remove disease and years of aging. Immortality is maintained in the present, without moments or minutes; this is the foundation of holistic health. A life of balance has no extremes, with minimal fragmentation. Acceptance of ourselves as we are is the greatest health of all.

Growing up around Ayurveda, I suspect that some of its tenets became engrained in the DNA of Indians over millennia. This is why Indians add turmeric, the antioxidant blockbuster spice, to most foods but also use it as an antiseptic to dab on a cut. Instinctively knowing that cold water dampens our digestive fire, almost every Indian asks for "water, no ice" in a restaurant. When I was growing up, seeing a doctor for small ailments, like a cold or stomachache, was unheard of. Fevers were met with cold compresses and hot clear soups while the body's immune response did its job to get rid of an infection. I would inhale eucalyptus steam to get rid of colds, plant black peppercorns way back on my tongue to calm a persistent cough, and sip brews made with ginger, fennel, and ajwain for stomachaches. I have a visceral memory of a doctor coming to our home only once during my childhood. I contracted a persistent bout of malaria around the age of nine or ten. I knew I was seriously ill when my two older brothers, whose favorite pastime was to play pranks on me, hovered around me anxiously. My body had rapidly entered a dangerous stage with episodes of delirium and a strong possibility that the parasite had lodged in my brain. I can still remember lying in bed in a feverish haze, surrounded by my worried parents, as a solemn doctor with a stethoscope around his neck injected me with quinine. With the advice of Ayurvedic healers, nonstop cold compresses under my mother's watchful eye, and nourishing foods like khichri (a soupy rice and lentil stew) and clear soups, I recovered from malaria completely in due time.

the energy of food

Energy is the life force of food, from its inception as a fertile seed, which receives energy from soil and the environment, to the final stage of sowing and reaping. Nature is so fine, its pattern so intricate, that if we use food intelligently, it is like intimately knowing the symphony of the vast spectrum of nature. When a vegetable is first uprooted from the earth, it is brimming with the juice of life, but the longer it is uprooted, the less energy it holds. There are some exceptions, like dried foods and beans, which can be stored successfully under the right conditions. The vital energy in foods is what invigorates our organs and brings deep-rooted nourishment into our systems. Indians take the notion of local food and regionality to a new level. Farming communities are laid out over all regions of India, and most people eat what grows seasonally around their homes. The variations in soil, water, and air from one locality to another within a region are believed to produce subtle differences in the taste of grains, vegetables, and grazing animals. Tiny nuances in the way foods are grown, harvested, and prepared, which may seem irrelevant to an outsider, are of huge significance to Indians. The staple food of each locality still ties people to their land and community, and the villagers believe that eating locally grown foods fills them with the nature of their homes, which in turn gives them immunity and strength. I had never heard terms like *local* or *organic* in relation to food before I left India, and for a while I did not comprehend the meaning. Everything we ate growing up in India was local and organic simply because it was the only sustainable way that existed.

emotions of food

The quality of our breath, the life force within us, and the food we eat deeply influences the tissues of our body and thoughts of our mind. Through the physical processes of ingestion, digestion, assimilation, and elimination, they become the eternal juice for life. Just like memories of celebratory foods can get increasingly dazzling over time, nostalgia over my mother's cooking can reduce me to tears. A few years ago, I watched a woman eating a Sindhi churi laddu (see page 273) at the Bake Lab with tears rolling down her eyes because it transported her to her childhood in Karachi. What we eat is as important for our mental health as it is for our physical health. Food is our most vital link to cognitive remembrance, and how we receive it is just as important as how it was prepared. Are we receiving it with joy and gratitude or with careless nonchalance?

Physical and emotional touch and intent can change everything. Food carries energy, and if there is no love in the food, the best ingredients will not matter. At Pondicheri, with minimal hierarchy and titles, we have a wonderfully tight well-trained professional kitchen team who have worked together for years and share an easygoing comradery. Whether it's a packed night with guests lined out the door or a mellow evening, the energy of the kitchen is usually focused and disciplined yet relaxed. When I want to know the state of the mind of the cooks, I just have to taste the food. I know there is anger and trouble brewing in the team when the fundamental essence of the food starts to taste off. As the pandemic started, I could taste their anxiety. It could be something simple as a little too much water in the dal or under- or oversalting the rice.

According to Ayurveda, no food in careful moderation is intrinsically good or bad for us; it's our constitution and mental state that determine how we react to it. Food takes us through the complete cycle of being, from the original cosmic seed to the fragile sprout to the flourishing plant to our sustenance. However, the right attitude and emotions associated with the food are just as important as quality and provenance, if not more so. The wrong mental state can turn nourishment and the best of foods into poison. Unreconciled anger, fear, and grief can damage our body, slow down our digestion, and speed up our aging process much more than environmental toxins and foods that are notably harmful. Each thought is an impulse of subtle energy and consciousness that reverberates through the universe like a tiny drop into a cosmic pond, and it's up to us to choose thoughts that nourish our bodies. Our emotions have the power to transform food as we prepare it, cook it, and eat it. When we prepare a meal with love and joy, we are transferring that energy into the food for ourselves and our loved ones.

the elements

According to Ayurveda, there are elements—the building blocks of nature—that are always at work behind the scenes to keep life on Earth going. Every single being in the universe, including humans, animals, food, and matter, is composed of molecules or atoms of five basic elements: space, air, fire, water, and earth. These elements are constantly moving inside our body within our breath and, in turn, influence the energy centers in our body, called chakras. These chakras, essentially circular wheels or discs of energy, are always working, but if we can work with them by eating proper foods, taming our mind, exercise, relaxation and introspection, it can help us create a life of balance. It's an esoteric concept that resonated with me by slowing down and observing myself and nature around me to understand how food or emotions affected me. I had to feel what these elements meant in my own body to understand it. It's the configuration of these elements that sets us apart from each other and makes each of us a unique being. These elements, also responsible for action and energy, are an interplay of different vibrations, beginning with the most subtle element, space or ether, to the densest element, earth. They are the materialized form of universal energy, through which all life exists as a fluctuating continuum of frequencies.

All the elements and their attributes are present in every thing in nature, from a flower to a berry to a human, and it's the varying proportions that differentiate you and me from a rock, an apple, or another animal. The memory of earth is tucked in our hearts, the memory of water flows in our kidneys and our blood, fire is in our intestines, air is in our lungs, and the memory of space is stored in our brains. As humans, these elements form the basis of our tissues and organs and guide their functions. We mimic the universe in every single way—we can see that everything that is happening outside us is happening inside us if we just pause and notice. A cold, cloudy day can bring on emotions of grief but a warm, sunny day can elicit joy. When it's cold outside, we are also cold inside, we need more fire or heat, and we naturally crave warming foods like saag, a hearty dish made from pureed mustard greens or spinach. Alternatively, when it is hot outside, we naturally crave cooling salads or lassi, a yogurt drink. The predominance of each element changes continuously, and as intelligent human beings, we must adjust to create optimal environmental conditions for us and the world that surrounds us. It's the repeated disruption of these elements that creates the seed of disease, whether it is on the planet, or in a plant, an animal, or our bodies. (*The photo at left depicts, clockwise from the top, lettuce as a symbol of air, green juice as a symbol of ether, watermelon as a symbol of water, mushrooms as a symbol of earth, and chiles as a symbol of fire.*)

The first element that evolved is ether, or space, and it is the most subtle of the five elements. On a macro level, it serves as the sac that holds everything and is home for all objects in the universe. Within ether is the pure presence of spiritual energy that is the first expression of consciousness. It's an all-pervading, all-encompassing, omnipotent, omnipresent, and omniscient space, a vibration of all our vital systems together. The pull of space is subtle yet its power ever so strong. It's the place where we humans go to resonate within our observations seeking our spiritual core. This space is expansive, empty, clear, and immeasurable and has no resistance. You can call it soul or spirit. It's the part of us that does not die and lives past the body.

Foods that increase the ether element: fresh vegetable juices, sprouts, and algae. It also includes anesthetic drugs, psychedelic drugs like MDMA and ayahuasca, intoxicating drinks, and narcotic drugs.

From ether comes air, the attribute of motion or movement that accounts for oxygen and wind around our planet, for every breath we take, and for all human bodily urges. On a human level, it's the energy necessary to keep our limbs and organs moving and for carrying out all of our sensory and motor functions from the lungs to the heart. Its basic principle is the life force responsible for the flow of conscious intelligence from one cell to another, from plants to humans.

Foods that increase the air element: dried fruits, raw vegetables, brassicas, nightshades, and many beans, including chickpeas and black beans.

The third element that is created from friction in air is fire, the self-constructing element of earth that makes the universe visible. On a human level, it makes up our minds, intellect, vision, and imagination. It's the element that provides humans with a capacity to self-reflect and the power to continually renew ourselves, and leads us on a path of self-discovery and self-transformation. On a physical level, fire is the acids and enzymes in the body that help transform food into energy and regulate our digestion. All transformative processes, including disease, are governed by the element of fire. If our digestive fire is low, it makes us sluggish, tired, and low in energy. If it is too high, it makes us angry and irritable.

Foods that increase the fire element: spices like chiles, black pepper, cinnamon, cloves; ginger, garlic, and onions; and sour fruits like pineapple, lemon, and tamarind.

From fire comes water, the primal binding element of the planet. The oceans, seas, and all other bodies of water on the planet shelter life. Plants and animals cannot live without the lubricating flow of water, nor can our human bodies. It's the element of water that helps us taste and remember food. Water is necessary in our bodies to maintain our lymphatic system and electrolyte balance. Oxygen, minerals, and vital food particles are carried in our bloodstream through plasma, the basis of which is water.

Foods that increase the water element: milk and other dairy products; salt; juicy fruits like plums, watermelon, grapes, tomatoes, and coconut; and juicy vegetables like cucumbers and zucchini.

From water is the last element, earth, our physical body. On a macro level, it is the solid, dense, nurturing vital orb that provides life on this planet. It's the heavy, dull energy helping fill open spaces with dense foliage, flowers, fruits, and herbs. It's our bodies knowing naturally how to grow, the tree knowing exactly when to shed her leaves, or the plant knowing when to blossom into a flower, which has no separate awareness from the earth in which it is rooted. When we inflict damage on the earth element, we are weakening its natural impulses and resonance and drifting away from the core of what brought us here.

Foods that increase the earth element: seeds, nuts, meat, mushrooms, root vegetables, wheat, rice, and many other grains.

The Vedas created a cosmic map outlining a network linking this planet to the whole universe. The intelligence and movement of the elements in the cosmos is reflected in the functioning of our human bodies. Our field of energy is the same as that of the forest, the ocean, and the sun. As an example, the blood flowing through our veins corresponds to streams, rivers, and oceans. Our physical body is formed from the transmutation of these five elements into three operating principles or forces called doshas, which exist in all of us, from plants to animals to food. Dosha, literally meaning "that which has a fault," is an energy system that lives in the gap between body and mind and is in constant change. Every time there is a thought in our mind, a reaction in our body follows. The doshas embody our karmic and genetic codes, which are irrevocably linked to and affected by the cosmic codes of the galaxies, stars, and planets. All three doshas—Vata, Pitta, Kapha—correspond respectively to movement, metabolism, and absorption and exist in all of us in varying proportions. Despite being invisible, the doshas govern the physical processes in our body without being physical themselves. The most dominant dosha, Vata or wind, is formed from ether and air and governs all movement, the nervous system, and the life force. Pitta or fire is next; it is formed from water and fire and is responsible for enzymatic and hormonal activities in the body along with digestion, hunger, thirst, eyesight, and body temperature. The third dosha, formed from water and earth, is Kapha, which controls growth, stability, and structure of the body, lubricates the joints, provides moisture to the skin, and heals wounds.

All three doshas pervade the entire body, but Kapha rules the upper body, Pitta dominates the chest, and Vata the lower body and the nervous system. An excess of any one dosha creates a blockage in the various channels of the body. Nature needs all three of these doshas, which are contained in every cell, to build the human body as well as the universe. We can be witness to the forces of the elements inside and outside of us. We cannot hurt the external environment, the planet we live on or the air we breathe, without hurting ourselves, nor can we separate from one another. All progress and awareness begins at home, and our body is our first home.

the taste of food

Indian food is cherished globally because its novel and interesting flavors contrast with each other. Popular food pairings in the West combine ingredients that share or overlap flavors, like butter with rice, cream, or milk. When I think of food, I want opposing flavors, of sweet with salty, sour and spicy with hints of bitter and astringent to come together and perform a dance in my mouth. Spices are a big part of this, and even for breakfast, when I scramble eggs with cheese, instinctively I smear the bread with a pickle or a chutney to give the meal a zing. There is an ever-so-slight bitter element to every single thing I cook—it could be by adding a pinch of turmeric or popping a few fenugreek seeds. While bland food has its place during illnesses and recovery, the magical use of spices, herbs, and seasonings is what makes Indian food so appealing.

Food speaks to all of us—we just need to learn to listen. When the gates of cognition are wide open, the cosmic memory of the universe comes cascading in. Every food in nature has its innate markings, color, vibration, and taste, the essence of which has been refined over time. Nourished by the elements, every tree, plant, shrub, fruit, and seed possesses life-giving juice. Food is that which springs from the earth because of the nurturing rainwater, the invigorating fire of the sun, and the massaging breath of the wind. Each food bears the intrinsic nature of its species. The coconut, which grows high up in the trees, bears cool and milky fruit that is cosseted within its husk and shell. The ripened apricot knows just when to let go of the branch so we may feast on its succulent flesh. Vedic teachings tell us that food is much more than nutrition. In fact, by eating, we are churning the cosmic essences of the universe to recall our cognitive memories. We eat to remember all of time, from the beginning of our journey in the universe forward. Before a meal is even served, the juices of appetite are stimulated through our senses. This may start as far back as the field in which we saw golden grains rustling in the wind against a magenta sky with shafts of sunlight or when we were suffused with the aroma of mint as we pulled a few sprigs from a balcony garden. Closer to the time of eating, our tongues salivate to enliven the full spectrum of our taste and enjoyment.

The second a substance hits our mouth, a complex chain of reactions occurs, starting with an initial registration by our tongue, stimulation of brain cells that excite our appetite, the nutrition it provides, ending with the digestion of food. When we eat the right foods in the proper way, the intelligence of the body is in harmony with the external environment. It is an intelligence to be groomed, not the irresponsible throwing together of foods that appeal to our base senses or sight irrespective of nutrition or digestion. When we eat irresponsibly, we are doing an injustice to our body and the environment around us. The proper foreplay of eating arises from a clear understanding of our body, its physical and emotional needs, a regard for the universe and the bounty it provides, and how it connects to the environment at large. The delicious taste that ensues is one of the many graces of good taste. By tracing the continuum of bliss that food can afford us, the Vedic seers were able to define the properties and effects of food on the human system and the causes of disease. When food ceases to be medicine, medicine can become impotent.

Healthy cravings are a result of our cellular intelligence responding to our biologic needs, reflecting a body in balance. Unhealthy cravings are caused by an imbalance in our body due to increased or decreased elements. While we all have ups and downs in our life, understanding Ayurveda helps us use food to empower rather than sabotage our health. When food hits our tongue, its secretions and our taste buds help us categorize it into six tastes: sweet, sour, salty, pungent, bitter, and astringent. Through these, we can assimilate the very essence of the universe because they hold memories from the beginning of time. The six tastes are present in all food, yet with different permutations of each element. Every substance is made up of some combination of the five elements, which are present in all foods. When used in food in the appropriate doses, these six tastes can bring balance to our bodily systems and yield happiness and good health. (*The photo on page 31 depicts, clockwise from the top right, dandelion greens as a symbol of bitter, chile powder as a symbol of pungent, lime and lemon as a symbol of sour, Himalayan rock salt as a symbol of salty, ghee or jaggery as a symbol of sweet, and pomegranate as a symbol of astringent.*)

Sweet

Earth and water, enhancing the vital essences of life, are the primary elements of sweet foods. More than 60 percent of natural foods of creation are sweet. Sweet flavors are the most dominant of all tastes, and they comfort and nourish the body and relieve hunger. Used moderately, sweet is wholesome to the body, promoting the growth of plasma, blood, muscles, fat, bones, marrow, and reproductive fluids. The cuisines of Bengal and Gujarat are renowned for adding touches of sweetness, from jaggery to honey, at the end of cooking, but touches of sweetness appear in many regional foods of India. Maybe this is why traditional desserts, like mithai and laddus, are eaten in small portions. Proper use of sweets gives us strength and longevity and promotes healthy skin and a melodious voice. Sweet relieves thirst and burning sensations, enhances blood sugar, is nutritive to body tissues, and has a sustained cooling effect on the body. It provides stability and gives our bodies energy, vigor, and vitality. However, excessive use of sweet foods can cause colds, coughs, congestion, loss of appetite, sluggishness, and obesity. It also causes dehydration and thirst, which in turn blocks the water channels of our body. A person's healing capacity is diminished by excessive sweets, which creates a fertile environment for pathogenic bacteria, fungi, and other parasites to grow.

Psychology of sweet: Sweet tastes eaten in balance enhance love and compassion and promote joy, happiness, and bliss, but in excess, sweet will create attachment, greed, and possessiveness.

Examples of sweet foods: sugar, honey, jaggery, maple syrup, rice, milk, and wheat.

Sour

Increasing salivary secretions, sour taste is composed primarily of earth and fire elements. Sour foods refresh and stimulate our appetite, enhance the secretion of digestive juices, and add brightness to the taste of foods. Used in small quantities, sour heats and energizes the body, nourishes the heart, prevents flatulence, and is antispasmodic. When used inappropriately, sour foods can dry out our membranes and tissues and create congestion. Excess sour taste can make our teeth too sensitive, create excessive thirst by drying out our membranes, and cause heartburn, acid indigestion, and ulcers. It also lowers our pH, which can cause burning in our chest and stomach, leading to digestive disorders and diarrhea.

Psychology of sour: These tastes make our body sharp and alert, increasing comprehension and our attention span. In excess, they can induce judgment, criticism, jealousy, and hate.

Examples of sour foods: yogurt, vinegar, cheese, citrus fruits, unripe mango, amchur (dried mango powder), pickles, miso, grapes, and fermented foods.

Salty

Maintaining our electrolyte balance, salty foods are primarily composed of water and fire elements. Salty tastes cleanse bodily tissues and give fresh potential for retrieving wisdom from the universe. Given that our body cannot store salt, we need to consume it daily in order to regulate bodily functions in our fluids and muscles. Used in the right quantities, salty tastes stimulate our salivation; make our body limber; aid in digestion, absorption, and assimilation of nutrients; and help with elimination of waste. Salty tastes can reduce flatulence by removing gas from the colon. On the other hand, too much salt can cause hypertension by thickening and narrowing our arteries. It can induce water retention in our bodies, resulting in edema, swelling, and high blood pressure.

Psychology of salt: It enhances our spirit and gives us confidence, enthusiasm, and courage. An inquiring, probing mind is the result of salty tastes. Removing salt from our diets reduces our creative powers and makes us dull and depressed. On the other hand, too much salt can create addiction, possessiveness, and greed.

Examples of salty foods: table salt, rock salt, sea salt, seaweed, and tamari.

Pungent

Light, drying, and heating in nature, pungent foods are predominantly composed of fire and air. Small amounts of pungent foods will rekindle our digestive fire and improve digestion. They aid in circulation, break up clots in our blood, remove fat from our bodies and help eliminate waste. The pungent taste connects us to the vast memories of the universe's passion and stimulation. In excess, pungent foods can reduce fertility in both sexes; induce burning, choking, and fainting; and cause fatigue and thirst. Diarrhea, heartburn, and insomnia can also be caused by an excess of pungent foods.

Psychology of pungent: It brings clarity to our thoughts and helps our minds become sharp, focused, and attentive. Too many pungent foods can create anger, violent irritability, envy, and aggression.

Examples of pungent foods: chiles, black pepper, mustard, ginger, onion, asafetida, radishes, and garlic.

Bitter

Cooling and drying in nature, bitter foods are mostly composed of air and ether elements. And though bitter foods generally are not delicious on their own, used in small amounts, they are essential in increasing the flavor of other foods. Ideally we must have all six tastes in our mouth, and the most lacking in the American diet is bitter. The genius of butter chicken is in how bitter fenugreek tempers the creamy sauce. Bitter foods scrape fat and toxins from our body and help in killing germs. Bitter is anti-inflammatory, can work as a laxative, and helps cleanse our liver and pancreas. Bitter foods are antibacterial and antiviral, which is why most antibiotics are bitter. By itself, bitter is nauseating, and overconsumption can induce dizziness and dryness in our bodies. Overconsumption of bitter foods can reduce our bone marrow, leading to osteoporosis and sterility by reducing sperm.

Psychology of bitter: In moderation, bitter foods can promote celibacy and reduce our attachment to worldly objects. The yogis in the Himalayas are known to include aloe vera juice as part of an austere diet to promote spiritual liberation. Bitter increases self-awareness and introspection, which can sometimes lead to isolation and loneliness.

Examples of bitter foods: turmeric, bitter melon, fenugreek, endive, aloe vera, dandelion greens and roots, and coffee.

Astringent

Cooling, drying, and heavy in nature, astringent foods are derived from earth and air elements. Astringent tastes improve absorption of nutrients in our body. They help bind the stool and promote clotting by constricting our blood vessels. Extreme use of astringent foods can increase coagulation and clotting of the blood and constipation. This can lead to stomach disorders, cardiac spasms, stroke paralysis, and other neuromuscular disorders.

Psychology of astringent: Supportive and grounding, astringent foods can help our minds be organized, calm, and collected. Too much can make our minds and thoughts too scattered; give us a lack of focus; and create insomnia, anxiety, and fear.

Examples of astringent foods: pomegranate, teas made from roots and barks, black tea, chickpeas, green beans, yellow split peas, okra, turmeric, and most raw vegetables.

food combining

There are no wrong or right foods in Ayurveda. Nothing is forbidden, not even meat, but there is a time and place for everything. It takes into account that our resilient bodes will adapt to bad habits in the short run but will send us signals to change, which we must not ignore; and, to maintain ourselves at an optimum and stay in sync with nature, there are intricate rules to food combining. After years of attempting to understand them, I try to follow most but not all. The most important rule to follow is to eat foods that are alive with energy and nutrition. Most things that come in a can, bag, or box can have diminished energy, if any. For the most part, the only two canned foods I allow myself at home and at the restaurant are coconut milk and tomatoes in the winter. While Ayurveda mostly suggests we eat plant-based, natural, unprocessed foods, dairy from happy cows is acceptable. Meats, as long as they come from humane practices and organic sources, are acceptable to eat in small portions during cold spells or to decrease excessive air element in our bodies.

Freshly harvested seasonal vegetables and fruits that grow around us, without genetic modification and undue processing, have the most nutritional density. In summer, I try to eat light foods that cool my digestive fire, like lassi (a yogurt drink) and raw salads. In the winter, I ramp up spices like red chile powder and serrano chiles and enjoy eating spicy warming cooked foods like dal and bean and vegetable stews to keep my digestive fire going. Another important tenet of Ayurveda is to eat fruits on their own, not with other foods, with the inexplicable exception of mango. The only reasonable explanation I can come up for this is that every Indian, even the gods and the bards, loves mangoes so very much that when they wrote the Vedas, they left mangoes in to be eaten anytime with anything. Condiments like sweet fruit chutneys or pickles eaten in small quantities are okay.

As a general rule, avoid eating raw foods with cooked foods simply because they are energetically incompatible, resulting in an overload on our digestive capability, inhibiting necessary enzymes and increasing production of toxins. Despite knowing this, it does not always work out in my kitchen, as I love salads, particularly with warm seared vegetables. Leftovers have diminished energy; however, I get around that by taking food out of the refrigerator and letting it come to room temperature before I eat it and either eat it at room temperature or gently warmed. The best way to preserve the energy of leftovers is to freeze, not refrigerate, foods. Thaw them out slowly before using. Avoid cold foods, including cold water, as they are a shock to our system, and if you must consume them, do so in the summer when our digestive fire is at its peak.

savoring food

One of the kindest gifts we can give our bodies is nourishing food, eaten slowly and appreciatively at consistent times. The restaurant business has trained me in the unfortunate task of eating food at the speed of light, a skill I am not proud of. A piece of torn naan, an extra bit of salad left over on a station, the last bit scooped up from the pot become de facto meals eaten late into the night for many cooks who slog hours working a busy kitchen. After more than twenty years in the business, I still fall prey to these mistakes.

Allowing a few hours in between each meal is ideal. Taking a gentle walk after each meal will soothe our digestion. Ayurveda says to stop eating when we are still a little hungry to allow space and energy for proper digestion. It's like packing too many clothes in the washing machine, not allowing them space to move. In the Vedas, our hands and feet are referred to as organs of action with which we remember the five elements of nature. Our hands touch the wind, space, and fire; our feet tread water and earth. When we use our hands to eat, we can savor the food by harnessing our extraordinary potential for wholeness and feel in unison with the earth and universe. There is a reason why a fork is shaped like a hand and a spoon like our cupped palms.

Why Cook?

Cooking can be a delightful, sensual act when we use all our senses—sight, touch, smell, taste, and hearing. Think of it as an intricate engagement with flavors and ingredients while being alert to the possibility of change. The concept of flavor and taste in India refers back to the essence of an ingredient in its purest and finest part. Rather than thinking of spices and herbs as an enhancing additive, Indian tradition views flavor as an essential defining quality. Acknowledging that an entirely new flavor can emerge as a combination of ingredients, cooking is about creating flavor that is integral to a dish, not an adornment or afterthought. Indian cooking puts flavor at the center of cooking and eating, and the possibilities are endless.

When my mother fell ill when I was thirteen, I entered the kitchen, rolled up my sleeves to make my first awkwardly shaped roti, and have not looked back. I never stopped cooking, from throwing dinner parties for twenty or more people at the drop of a hat to fulfilling every food demand from my kids. Good cooking, like anything else, takes practice. Maybe it was the austere belief we shared that no food should be wasted, but I was fortunate enough to be married to a man who would eat anything I cooked. When I started cooking, many unabashedly bad ideas landed us with inedible dinners. He still ate, with gentle reminders to never try *that* again. I remember my first cheesecake that turned into a sorry soupy puddle on the coffee table as I was proudly cutting into it surrounded by guests. Over time and practice, trial and error, I taught myself the intricacies of simple home cooking, always looking for ways to improve and evolve. Even today, my happiest times are in the kitchen, concocting new combinations and ideas. It's my language, an expression of love, and how I shower affection on those around me.

About a decade ago, I started teaching cooking classes. I did notice that, despite knowing that food is going to end up inside our bodies, many people are hesitant to touch food. The part of cooking I enjoy the most is the visceral feel of raw ingredients and the delight in seeing them transform. Food is how we nourish the body, mind, and soul. How do we know that the food purchased in soulless shops and served up to us from restaurant kitchens is not filled with toxic energy of its cooks? How do we know corporate companies in the interest of big profit are not adding harmful untested chemicals to processed foods? While cooking can be an art form, cooking for oneself, being able to make a few basic meals at the very least, should be as important as knowing how to brush your teeth or dress yourself.

The Story of Spices

For thousands of years, India has been known as the land of spices. Aromatics have changed the course of history several times over, and it is because of them that travel, trade, and exploration became a way of life. Since the dawn of civilization, aromatic spices, from nutmeg to black pepper, have been centered around two regions in Asia: Kerala, on the southern tip of India, and the tiny Banda Islands off the Indonesian archipelago. For thousands of years, the Banda Islands were the only source of nutmeg. The trade was dominated by Arab traders, who would arrive in Kerala or Indonesia in dhows (traditional cargo sailboats), load aromatic spices, and travel by camel back to Egypt and then on to Venice by boat. The Arab traders kept the whereabouts of both these regions shrouded in secrecy, concocting fanciful stories about fire-spewing dragons guarding impenetrable jungles where the spices grew.

Legend has it that medieval Europe believed that the aroma of spices was a fragrant breath wafting from paradise over the human world. The vision of paradise, where pepper grew like a bamboo forest, as a real place somewhere in the East fascinated Western imagination. Medieval European civilizations were hooked on the flavors of pepper, nutmeg, and cinnamon. For millennia, spices were transported from India and nearby islands, at exorbitant prices, to Syria and Egypt, where they were promptly bought up by Venetian traders and shipped across the Mediterranean to Italy and other European countries. Wars were fought, kingdoms were destroyed, and new lands discovered all in pursuit of spices. The Egyptians revered spices; they used cinnamon and cassia for mummification, placing them in the tombs of the pharaohs to help with their onward journeys. The Romans saw spices as the ultimate luxury items and perfumed palaces and churches with them. Many Europeans believed that spices, because they came from such faraway exotic places, possessed magical powers.

Besides being used in food, spices were presented as gifts, treated like jewels, and collected like precious objects. Pepper frequently took the place of gold as a means of payment. At one time, a pound of ginger sold for the same amount as a whole sheep. In Venice, the higher the rank of a household, the greater its use of spices, and for festive occasions, the quantities were even greater. Food was no more than a vehicle for the use of spices, and Roman cookbooks from the fifteenth century incorporate such large amounts of spices in meat preparations that a present-day fiery vindaloo, the traditional pork stew from the coast of Goa, may seem mild in comparison.

Once habituated to the fragrant spices of India, Europe was ready to do anything to satisfy its craving, and an ensuing quest for a sea route to the source of this paradise became paramount. The hunger for spice was capable of mobilizing forces from Spain and Portugal, much as the present-day need for energy sources has mobilized forces of modern powers. A whole generation of adventurers and entrepreneurs sailed and lost their lives in search of the Spice Routes. Christopher Columbus and Vasco da Gama were merely the successful ones that made it to the history books. Despite unimaginably hazardous journeys, each hoped to capture for their country the command of an immensely lucrative spice trade, and each, almost incidentally, changed the whole world's concept of itself. Columbus's arrival in North America was more or less a byproduct of the quest for spices.

From the eleventh century through the seventeenth century, from the time of the Crusades to the period of Dutch and British East India companies, historians agree that foreign trade in and around India was essentially spice trade. When the Dutch invaded Portugal in the 1600s and ruled Indonesia for over two hundred years, they dominated the nutmeg trade in the five tiny Banda Islands. They conceded the smallest island, Run, to the British, which also grew nutmeg and mace in abundance. Not content in banishing their rivals to the smallest island and hankering after a nutmeg monopoly, the Dutch proposed a treaty giving the British another island in exchange for taking back Run. The name of that island? Manhattan, which the British accepted with a long face. After all, what spice could grow off the Hudson River? We all know what happened to Manhattan, and the British had their final victory lap as they smuggled nutmeg saplings and grew nutmeg in their colonies in the tropics, causing an eventual decline of the Banda Islands.

In many respects, spices played a catalytic role in the transition from the Middle Ages to modern times. After the discovery of sea routes to India, consumption first rose sharply but then tapered off. It was during the seventeenth century that the market for spices was saturated and new food products like coffee, tea, sugar, and chocolate emerged. While there are some remnants of spice usage in Italian and Dutch cooking, for the most part highly seasoned dishes no longer appealed to the Europeans and spices finally lost their primary power in world trade.

the magic of spices

Spices have grown wild in India, Indonesia, and other parts of Southeast Asia for over three thousand years. A spice comes from a plant's root, bark, stem, bud, leaves, flower, fruit, or seed. It is edible, aromatic, and dried. Spices come in a veritable rainbow of rich hues: brilliant red mace flowers, orange and yellow turmeric, brown cloves and cinnamon, green cardamom pods, black peppercorns and nigella seeds (kalonji), and white poppy seeds and peppercorns. Running through the bloodstreams of Indians for millennia, these jewels of the plant world are just as popular today in Indian cooking as they were thousands of years ago. Considered the umami of Indian cooking, spices are delicious and addictive. The variety, combinations, and use of spices are the major factors that distinguish and elevate Indian cuisine from any other. While cuisine from region to region of India may vary to a great degree, from a delicate fenugreek-flavored yogurt soup from Gujarat to a pungent Bengali mustard fish, all the way to a saffron-scented korma from Kashmir, what every regional Indian cuisine has in common is the use of a vast array of spices, though they are used in uniquely different ways. Sanskrit writings of over three thousand years ago describe many of the best-known spices, heralding their value as food preservatives and attaching significant importance to their medicinal properties. Over the centuries, the three functions of spices in cooking—medicinal, preservative, and seasoning—have become separated, and in present-day cooking, the concern with flavor has become the most important. However, what I want to share with you is the innate Indian intelligence and unique ability for spice combining that keeps an eye on health, digestion, and flavor. If you can learn to be even half as fearless as I am with spices, I have achieved my goal.

the pop

Native to India, the act of tempering spices in oil, which I call "the pop," also called "tadka," "chhonk," or "baghar" in Hindi, is one of the quickest yet most profoundly aromatic ways to enhance the flavor of certain spices. Not all spices can be popped. A pop is usually done with oil or ghee and whole spices such as mustard, cumin, or fenugreek seeds. Here is the simplest way to understand how a pop works. Heat up a given quantity of oil in a shallow frying pan over high heat, and when the oil begins to get a shiny surface and is just shy of smoking, gently drop the spices in. If the oil is at the right temperature, the spices will begin to make a popping and sizzling sound. Immediately turn off the heat and allow the sizzling to stop—it usually lasts no more than three to five seconds. Turning the heat off immediately when the seeds start popping is key; otherwise the spices will not only burn but they might fly around the kitchen, making a mess to clean up after. Cumin seeds transform when popped in hot oil. Aromatic ground spices such as cardamom and cinnamon are usually added at the end of the cooking process. Over gentle heat, they can be added whole or lightly crushed at the beginning to soften and impart lingering fragrance and flavor. Once you learn how and in what order to use spices, you can incorporate them into your daily cooking, whether you are cooking Indian food or any other cuisine.

sourcing and taking care of spices

The primary intent of colonial powers was to dominate the spice trade coming from the subcontinent of India. Corporate profits soared as spices were handled by more than half a dozen middlemen, with pennies going to farmers. Even today, it is not much different, however a small group of audacious online companies, like Burlap and Barrel, Diaspora Co., and Snuk Foods, whose goal is to disrupt the status quo by establishing direct farmer relations, offer quality fair-trade spices. We vote with our dollar and my recommendation would be to source spices from a company you can trust.

In addition, half of Americans live within fifty miles of a major city, most of which have large Asian or Indian populations. These cities have Indian grocery stores, and this is also where you will find good spices because of high sales volume. No Indian can live without spices, so try to find them in a store frequented by Indians. Except for amchur (dried mango powder), turmeric, and chile powder, try to buy spices whole when possible. If buying the spices in person, evaluate them visually for color and aroma. Green cardamom should be

Oil (or fat)

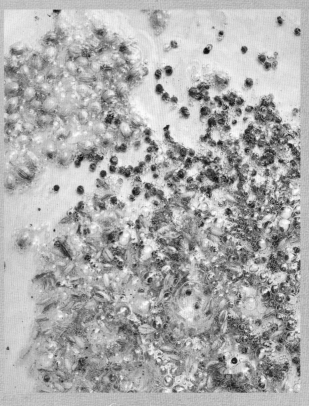

Whole spices

Kari leaves

Red chile

bright green with a sweet aroma; cumin seeds should be medium brown with a savory sharp scent, not gray or off-white. After you bring the spice home, again sniff it and evaluate the quality. The better the quality, the more intense the aroma. Store whole spices in airtight glass or metal jars in a dark space away from light, as storing spices in plastic will deteriorate their quality over time. Whole spices can keep for up to five years, if not more, when stored properly.

toasting spices

Toasting whole spices before grinding them into a powder enhances their flavor tremendously. You can toast spices in a dry skillet over medium heat in minutes—keep a close eye on the spices and make sure they don't burn or scorch. Alternatively, spread them on a baking sheet and bake them in a 300°F oven for 3 to 4 minutes. Let the spices cool before grinding. I have a small coffee-bean grinder specifically for grinding spices. A mortar and pestle work really well for a larger rough grind, and so does a small hammer. Place the spices in between a folded kitchen towel and gently tap with a hammer. When you grind them, do so in small portions and, again, store any leftover ground spices in a cool place away from light.

the order of spices

What I consider the big four spices—turmeric, mustard seeds, cumin seeds, and chiles—are usually added at the beginning of cooking. Turmeric can have an astringent raw taste if not cooked, so it is best added in small quantities at the beginning of cooking. Cumin seeds and mustard seeds are usually popped and soften and mellow out in flavor throughout the cooking process, but they can also be added as a burst at the end of cooking. If ground cumin is added, it goes in earlier in the cooking process. Chile powder is also usually added early in the cooking process—if it is added later, it is usually fried in oil. Aromatic spices, like cardamom, cinnamon, nutmeg, mace, and cloves, are usually added ground toward the end of cooking to preserve their aroma. In their whole form, they can be lightly crushed with a rolling pin, crushed in a mortar and pestle, or smashed with a light hammer to loosen their aromatic oils before frying in oil at the beginning of cooking. Crushing whole spices lightly and cooking them in long and slow simmering stews and curries releases the flavors in tiny bursts, when the mouth hits the chunks of softly cooked spices.

Turmeric

Turmeric is a modern rock-star spice. When the results of an extended study on the extensive anticancer, antioxidant, and anti-inflammatory properties of turmeric, or the chemical within called curcumin, emerged in 2003, I had a rush of anxious customers at my restaurant Indika asking for "curry" with turmeric. What the researchers did not miss was that it took a lifetime of eating turmeric to create those results, not an occasional pinch. Indians use turmeric in almost everything they cook, from snacks to breads to curries. In fact, the sacred thread, the marriage symbol that is tied around the bride's neck by the bridegroom during the wedding ceremony, is often dipped in turmeric paste.

Turmeric is a perennial tropical spice plant belonging to the ginger family and native to South India. Without peeling, the roots are cleaned, boiled, dried, and powdered to produce a nutty-tasting, aromatic powder. The leaves can be used for steaming breads or vegetables and they impart a distinctive aroma. Turmeric is primarily used as a coloring agent for most curries, vegetables, dals, meat, poultry, and fish dishes. Good-quality turmeric, aside from lending its characteristic yellow color, also gives out a wonderfully woody aroma. However, turmeric is one spice you want to taste as a back note, if at all—not a frontal flavor—in cooking. It is usually added at the beginning of cooking to mellow out the flavor. If added at the end, it works best to use just a pinch, as it can taste slightly bitter. If you can taste turmeric, you've added too much or added it too late.

In India, turmeric has been used for thousands of years as a remedy for stomach and liver ailments as well as topically for sores and cuts. The active compound of turmeric, curcumin, is known to possess anti-inflammatory, antiviral, and antiseptic properties. Preliminary research has shown that turmeric is also effective in preventing cancer, Alzheimer's disease, arthritis, and diabetes. (*See the photo of fresh and ground turmeric on page 46.*)

Daily uses for ground turmeric:

→ Add a pinch in scrambled eggs or omelets.

→ Add a pinch when marinating fish or shrimp to prevent them from sticking to the bottom of the pan. Note that the color of the fish will change to yellow.

→ Add to rice, quinoa, other grains, or pasta water at the beginning of cooking.

→ Add to pancake, crepe, dosa, or cake batter and cookie dough.

→ Add to braised vegetables or chicken or meat stews at the beginning of cooking.

→ Add a generous pinch to a glass of warm water mixed with honey, and sip when you have a cold or cough.

Daily uses for fresh turmeric root:

→ Add a slice of fresh turmeric root to a pitcher of drinking water—it will slowly infuse throughout the day.

→ Add grated fresh turmeric to a stew, soup, or curry at the beginning of cooking.

→ Make a fresh turmeric dressing. Combine ½ cup fresh lemon juice, a 2-inch piece of turmeric, a drizzle of honey, and a generous pinch of black pepper and salt in a blender and blend until smooth. Add a small piece of serrano chile for added heat. Stir with ½ cup of your preferred oil—light sesame oil and olive oil are both delicious. Store the dressing in the refrigerator and use with any salad.

Mustard Seeds

Mentioned in sacred texts from the Bible to the Koran, the tiny mustard seed, sourced from a brassica family with no connection to supermarket mustard greens, is packed with pungent flavor. There are three kinds of mustard seeds—yellow, brown, and black—and the flavor is released only when the seed comes in contact with cold water, setting off an enzyme called myrosinase, which unleashes the flavor. Best purchased whole, mustard seeds will keep for years if stored in an airtight container in a cool, dark place. Black mustard seeds are the variety most commonly used in India, and my favorite way to cook them is to pop them in hot oil (see page 40) at the beginning of cooking curries, stews, or pilafs. The two kinds of mustard seeds I keep at home are whole black mustard seeds and rai kuria, which are crushed black mustard seeds with the skins removed (hulled to reveal yellow seeds). I love their pristine yellow color, and they make a great addition to masalas or pickles.

Mustard seeds are used all over India, but the cuisines of Bengal and Bangladesh in particular are inextricably linked to mustard. Not only are freshly pounded mustard seeds added to most dishes, from soups and curries to vegetables, but also the whole spice is used to make masalas. Way before Romans brought mustard to France and Dijon mustard was created, Bengalis in Kolkata were making varieties of condiments called kasundi—a pickled, sometimes fermented, mustard sauce.

Mustard seeds are believed to be a diuretic, a stimulant, and an aid to help improve digestion, increase circulation, and ease muscular aches and pains.

Daily uses for mustard seeds:

→ Pop mustard seeds in any fat of your choice (such as ghee or olive oil) and add to quinoa or rice before or after cooking it.

- → Garnish creamy soups such as butternut squash or carrot soup with popped mustard seeds.

- → Mustard seeds complement vegetables in the brassica family, so before pan-searing cabbage, cauliflower, broccoli, or cabbage, pop mustard seeds in oil for added flavor.

- → Add popped mustard seeds to plain yogurt (see page 86) to make a simple raita or a creamy salad dressing.

- → Crush mustard seeds with a rolling pin and add to the brine in cucumber pickles.

- → Make Bengali mustard. Using a coffee grinder, grind ⅓ cup rai kuria (yellow hulled mustard seeds) to a smooth powder. Pour the juice of 1 orange over it and let the mustard soak for 10 to 15 minutes. In a food processor, mix the soaked rai kuria (with any remaining juice) with the flesh of 1 large or 2 small ripe mangoes, 1 teaspoon red chile powder, a pinch of ground turmeric, and 1 teaspoon sea salt and pulse until smooth. Heat 2 to 3 tablespoons mustard oil, pop a teaspoon or so of black mustard seeds, add a few kari leaves, and stir into the mustard mixture. It will keep in an airtight container in the refrigerator for up to 3 months.

Cumin

Unassuming in appearance with a nutty, peppery, almost odorous sweat scent that has earned it the nickname of "subway spice," the medieval cumin is an essential part of many cuisines around the world from Mexico to India, Africa, and the Middle East. Cumin, known as "jeera" in Hindi, is an essential part of most stews and curries in India. It is either used whole and popped in fat (see page 40) or toasted and ground and added during the cooking process. I love the savory, earthy flavor of cumin seeds for enhancing meat dishes and imparting a warm essence to seafood and vegetables. However, use cumin judiciously, as it can easily overpower other flavors. Its best to buy whole cumin seeds, as they can be stored for a long time. Toast the seeds in a small, dry frying pan over medium heat or in a 300°F oven for 3 to 4 minutes, until fragrant, let cool, and then grind them in a clean coffee grinder.

Black cumin, also called "kala jeera" or "shahi jeera" or "royal cumin," is darker and smaller than tan cumin but with a fruity, smoky, and complex aroma. Often found growing wild in Kashmir, black cumin tastes nutty, peppery, and reminiscent of caraway seeds. Kashmiris commonly use black cumin instead regular cumin, and you can too.

Studies in India have found that cumin, which possesses the unique compound cuminaldehyde, helps reduce blood sugar and prevent osteoporosis. Cumin's volatile and rich vitamins A and C content make it a potent antioxidant.

Daily uses for whole cumin seeds:

→ When making a salad dressing, pop a few cumin seeds in a little bit of oil (see page 40) and use this oil, seeds and all, to make the dressing.

→ Stir popped cumin seeds in to your favorite pilaf, dal, stew, or curry.

→ Add whole cumin seeds to vegetables before roasting them in the oven.

Daily uses for ground cumin:

→ Add toasted, ground cumin and a pinch of salt to plain yogurt (see page 86) for breakfast.

→ Add toasted, ground cumin to cheese dishes, like queso or a cheese dip, just toward the end.

→ Make cumin carrots. Preheat the oven to 350°F. Spread 8 to 10 thin carrots (if you can't find thin carrots, slice larger carrots in half lengthwise) over a flat baking pan, drizzle with a few tablespoons olive oil, and sprinkle with cumin seeds and salt. Cover tightly with foil and bake in the oven for 25 to 30 minutes, until tender and can be cut with a fork. Turn the oven heat off and let the carrots rest in the oven for another 15 to 20 minutes. Remove the foil, sprinkle the carrots with red chile powder, and serve with a squeeze of lemon juice or a dollop of plain yogurt.

Coriander Seeds

Coriander, the delicate seed of the assertive cilantro plant and one of most unique and versatile spices in any cook's arsenal, has been valued since ancient times for its startlingly floral, citrus, and slightly nutty flavor. Coriander grows in many parts of the world, from Morocco to Iran, parts of Europe, and, of course, India, where it is an essential spice. The varieties in India have higher concentrations of linalool, the volatile oil that contributes to its lemony aroma. When purchased whole, the seeds, which can vary from light brown to pink to a greenish yellow depending on where they were grown, will keep for years, as the essence of coriander seeds is released only when they are crushed or cooked. In customary Indian cooking, ground coriander is paired with cumin and added to the base of most curries. I prefer using it in its most unique form, lightly crushed or whole.

Packed with antioxidants, daily use of coriander seeds is considered a digestive tonic and is believed to be helpful in soothing irritable bowel syndrome and easing chronic constipation and most other stomach disorders. Coriander essential oil has been shown to reduce redness in inflamed skin due to psoriasis or eczema.

Daily uses for coriander seeds:

→ Pop the seeds in oil (see page 40) and add to dal or a lentil stew at the end of cooking.

→ Crush the seeds with a rolling pin and add to raw meatball mixtures or meat curries at the beginning of cooking.

→ Crush the seeds slightly with a rolling pin and add to biscuit or scone doughs.

→ Combine ½ teaspoon coriander seeds with ½ teaspoon cumin seeds, ½ teaspoon fennel seeds, and 2 cups hot water to make an infusion. Let steep for 10 to 15 minutes before drinking.

→ Make avocado masala. Peel, pit, and mash 2 large avocados. Heat a little olive oil in a small frying pan over high heat, pop 1 teaspoon lightly crushed coriander seeds, and add a few kari leaves. Add to the avocado mash along with about 2 tablespoons chopped fresh cilantro leaves and a pinch of salt.

Pepper

Arising from the fragrant berry of the *Piper nigrum* vine, the quintessential black peppercorn has a royal pedigree that launched a thousand ships, changing world history. It is arguably the most important spice in the spice-trading world and inspired Italian explorer Christopher Columbus to brave treacherous waters looking for India, the mystical land of pepper. As we know, he was off course by about eight thousand miles when he "discovered" North America. The fruit of this vine, native to the coast of Kerala, was considered more valuable than gold, helped build and diminish empires, caused long-drawn wars, and single-handedly helped carve out a trade route for spices. While "hot" food is often associated with India, red chiles entered the country only a few hundred years ago, but black pepper and its variants were used to provide heat in foods for millennia.

Black, white, and green peppercorns are the same berry, picked at different stages of ripeness and processed in different ways. Peppercorns lose their pungency and aroma quicker than any other spice does, so it's best to buy them whole and grind as needed. Instead of treating black pepper with a perfunctory sprinkle at the dinner table, for a deeper flavor that incorporates into the dish and is not just a surface flavor, try adding freshly ground pepper to stews, roasted vegetables, and pilafs just at the end of cooking.

The curative powers of the unique compound piperine help black pepper in jump-starting digestion and in working as a powerful stimulant and diuretic. One of my family's most effective home remedies to relieve a persistent cough is to rest a few whole black peppercorns on the back of the tongue for 10 to 15 minutes.

Daily uses for black pepper:

→ Add lightly crushed peppercorns to brewed coffee.

→ Add lightly crushed peppercorns to stews and curries at the beginning so they can soften up during the cooking process.

→ Add freshly crushed pepper to morning yogurts or smoothies.

→ Make black pepper roasted chicken. Separate 2 chicken breasts and marinate in a mixture of ½ cup plain yogurt (see page 86), 6 or 7 sliced garlic cloves, 1 teaspoon freshly ground black pepper, 1 teaspoon sea salt, and a generous drizzle of olive oil. Set the chicken on a baking pan and roast in a 400°F oven for 8 to 10 minutes, then turn the oven off to help prevent it from overcooking. (The chicken should be golden in color, and will continue cooking with residual heat.) Sprinkle on another 2 teaspoons black pepper, concentrating it toward the center of each breast and avoiding the sides. Leave the chicken in the oven for another 5 to 7 minutes until golden brown, to finish cooking.

Chiles

It's an interesting twist of fate that it was the Europeans, in particular the Portuguese, who introduced India to the glory of chiles only a few hundred years ago, and mostly to Indians along the southern coast. Within thirty years of Vasco da Gama arriving on May 20, 1498, in present-day Kerala, three varieties of chiles had been planted along the Malabar Coast. However, it was not until the 1700s that chiles reached the northern provinces of Punjab and Kashmir. Indians absorbed chiles into their cuisine with great enthusiasm, and India is now the world's largest consumer, producer, and exporter of chiles, most of them coming from the state of Andhra Pradesh.

The key to buying ground chile is to make sure it is pure chile powder, a bright shade of red in color, not the spice blend spelled *chili*, which often has garlic, oregano, and other seasonings mixed into it. The bright color is important, as it contributes to the finished dish, so don't buy a chile powder that is too dark in color. As chile is a warming spice that helps light our digestive fire, I tend to use it in my cooking much more in the winter than in the summer. Try the reshampatti, a Kashmiri chile; or Deggi Mirch (a branded chile powder from India); or a sharp paprika, a Hungarian chile; and if you prefer less spice, use a sweet paprika (the standard paprika you find in a grocery store) or a ground ancho chile (the dried Mexican poblano).

Daily uses for chiles:

→ Sprinkle red chile powder and salt on fresh fruits, like mango, papaya, or apple.

→ Add chile powder to chocolate cake batter or cookie dough.

→ Smoke whole dried chiles such as cascabel or pasilla over a hot flame for a few seconds and add to stews and curries for a smoky flavor.

→ Make chile oil. Heat 1 cup light sesame oil or peanut oil in a small pot over medium heat. As soon as the oil is shiny and hot, turn off the heat and immediately (carefully) add 1 tablespoon brightly colored chile powder, such as reshampatti or Deggi Mirch. Add 1 tablespoon minced garlic (see page 80), a few kari leaves, 1 tablespoon honey or sugar, the juice of 2 lemons, and ½ teaspoon sea salt. The oil will keep in a tightly sealed jar in the refrigerator for up to 1 month. Use it for finishing dishes with a hot note.

Nigella (Kalonji)

The prophet Muhammad has been credited with saying, "Black granules are the cure for everything except death," and it is fair to say that he was referring to nigella. Often scattered on top of breads in the Middle East as a form of blessing, the "blessed seed," aka kalonji seeds, are often mistaken for black sesame seeds for their similar appearance but have little else in common with sesame. They have a distinctive warm, smoky, and nutty flavor. While they have some use in Indian chutneys and for popping (see page 40) and adding to broths, for years we used them at my restaurants only to scatter on top of breads. One day while poring over an old book on spices, I learned that nigella was a popular medieval spice in Roman culture. Knowing the Romans ate a lot of meat, I raced home, toasted a few seeds, and ground them. I added them to a marinade for meat, and their nutty, smoky flavor deepened to a state nothing

short of miraculous. Ever since, we always include nigella in meat marinades, sometimes as a frontal note, other times as a background flavor.

Daily uses for nigella:

→ Pop the seeds and add to rice or quinoa pilaf.

→ Add ground nigella to ground meat to make hamburgers or to red meat marinades before grilling.

→ Sprinkle ground nigella on potatoes before roasting them.

→ Sprinkle whole nigella seeds on breads and rolls just before they go in the oven.

→ Add nigella to mushrooms while sautéing them.

→ Make nigella steak. Make a masala with 1 tablespoon ground nigella, 1 tablespoon amchur (dried mango powder), 1 teaspoon freshly ground black pepper, 1 tablespoon yogurt (see page 86), a pinch of ground cloves, and ½ teaspoon sea salt. Mix in a few tablespoons melted ghee or olive oil, rub the masala onto a 14-ounce aged rib eye and marinate for a few hours or overnight. Sear or grill the steak. This makes enough masala for two servings of steak. This masala can also be used as a marinade to preserve the meat. (*See photo on page 49.*)

Ajwain

Ajwain, aka carom or bishop's weed, is a tiny seed that comes from a plant resembling celery seed and caraway. It has a piercing peppery piquancy and so is used sparingly. It gives out an aroma of thyme when crushed lightly, but the flavor mellows with cooking. Ajwain seeds are used extensively in Ayurvedic practices for treating digestive ailments, fevers, and asthma.

Daily uses for ajwain:

→ Fold a small amount into bread or cracker doughs.

→ Add a pinch to fish and shrimp marinades to reduce the fishy flavor.

→ Add a pinch to lentils while cooking to reduce the bloating effect.

→ Combine 1 teaspoon ajwain seeds with a pinch of black salt and a pinch of asafetida and chew on the mix to ease bloating or gastric disorder, particularly after overeating.

→ Make ajwain tea. Place 1 teaspoon fennel seeds, 1 teaspoon ajwain seeds, and a handful of mint leaves in a mug. Pour in 2 cups boiling water, cover, and let the tea steep for 15 to 20 minutes. Strain and sip.

Fenugreek

Originally native to the Mediterranean region, fenugreek was a wild uncultivated plant that Romans and Greeks fed to horses and cattle with hay and seldom used for human consumption. Today it has practically disappeared from Greek cuisine and traces are hard to find. How it made its way to India is unknown, but we probably can attribute it to the prolific spice trade that went on for centuries and still exists today. An annual herb of a bean family, both the seed and the leaves of the plant are commonly used in Indian cooking. The fenugreek seed, rectangular and brownish yellow in color, is actually a bean like the mung bean, but because of its extreme aroma and bitter taste, it is treated as a spice. Used sparingly, it provides viscosity to lentil batters and is used in lentil and bean stews.

Dried fenugreek leaves are bitter in taste but have a captivating aroma and are used throughout India. They give chicken tikka masala sauce its characteristic flavor. Fresh fenugreek leaves, usually in season in cold-weather months, have a heady fragrance and are delicious in creamy or tomato-based fish or chicken stews, but because of their bitterness they need to be balanced with sweet flavors and/or creamy textures.

Fenugreek, seeds or leaves, are used as a digestive with a near-magical ability to lower blood sugar. It also helps prevent flatulence and premature graying of the hair. Nursing mothers are urged to consume fenugreek to promote milk production.

Daily uses for fenugreek:

→ Pop the seeds in oil (see page 40) and add to stews and soups at the beginning of cooking to impart an underlying bitter flavor.

→ Soak a few fenugreek seeds in water overnight, strain, and drink the water in the morning to soothe an upset stomach.

→ Soak 2 tablespoons ground fenugreek seeds in 1 cup yogurt (see page 86), apply to your hair and scalp, leave it in overnight, and rinse it out in the morning to reduce graying.

→ Make fenugreek mashed sweet potatoes. Combine 2 large peeled, diced sweet potatoes (roughly 1 pound each) and 1 cup water in a pot, season with sea salt and freshly ground black pepper, and bring to a boil. Lower the heat and simmer until cooked through. Drain off excess water if needed and mash in ¼ cup dried fenugreek leaves or 1 cup fresh fenugreek leaves, a few tablespoons thick yogurt or heavy cream, and a few tablespoons of butter or ghee. Serve warm. (*See photo opposite.*)

Saffron

The ancient Greeks used saffron to scent and purify their temples, and the ancient Romans bathed in saffron water. Cleopatra used it in a facial mask. There are over one hundred varieties of crocus flowers, but only one that contains the stigmas that become the spice saffron, the leafless blue crocus. Considered the caviar of spices, saffron is the carefully hand-harvested dried stigma of the *Crocus sativus* flower, native to Asia Minor and southern Europe. It is widely cultivated in India in the Kashmir Valley, where it is used in foods from the famous roghan josh (see page 212), a decadent lamb stew, to desserts and drinks. While Iranian saffron is known for its color (it contains a high degree of the chemical crocin that gives it its orange color), Kashmiri saffron is prized for its aroma and the flavors of additional active ingredients picrocronin and safranal. Iran is the largest producer of saffron, with Spain playing a minor part. It takes eighty thousand crocus flowers and a quarter million dried stigmas to produce one pound of saffron. No wonder saffron has a retail value of around $5,000 per pound. Saffron threads, reddish brown in color, have a sweetish taste, emit a captivating aroma, and add a beautiful orange-yellow color to food.

Saffron is incredible when used delicately in cold creamy dishes, like ice cream or custard, and it is extensively used in desserts, biryanis, and meat dishes in northern India. The flavor of saffron builds over time, so either soak it in water or milk the night before or cook it over low heat to maximize the flavor.

Saffron is an antiseptic, diuretic, and mild laxative. It is known to be strengthening to the body, and it can also help relieve dry coughs and liver and bladder ailments.

Daily uses for saffron:
- → Add a pinch of saffron to your morning yogurt (see page 86).
- → Add a pinch of saffron to rice pilaf, biryani, or mashed potatoes at the beginning of cooking.
- → Add a pinch of saffron to stews and curries.
- → Make a tea with a pinch of saffron and 5 crushed green cardamom pods and 5 black peppercorns.
- → Make saffron lassi. Combine 2 cups plain whole-milk yogurt, 1 cup water, a few tablespoons sugar, a pinch of sea salt, and a generous pinch of saffron. Whisk together and refrigerate for a few hours for the saffron to infuse into the yogurt. Pour into two glasses and sip up.

Asafetida

Legend has it that when crossing over the Hindu Kush Mountains, Alexander the Great's army brought asafetida to India, mistaking it for silphium, a once-rare spice used to tenderize tough meat. With a strong garlic-and-onion-like aroma, it is also called devil's dung and was used in the United States in 1918 to prevent the Spanish flu. Used as a spice, asafetida, also known as "hing" in Hindi, is a resin obtained from the gum of a perennial called ferula, native to the mountains of Central Asia, from Turkey, Iran, and Afghanistan all the way to Kashmir, India. The strong, "stinky," sulfurous aroma of asafetida can give the impression of onions, garlic, eggs, meat, and even black truffle. Used in minute portions and almost always fried in oil, it is used extensively in vegetarian Indian cooking, especially by the Jain community, whose religious beliefs prohibit the consumption of onions or garlic on the grounds that it would kill the plant. Add a pinch to hot oil just before cooking vegetables or starches. Asafetida aids in digestion and works as a laxative when used on a regular basis. It can also aid in reducing inflammation, enhancing memory, and regulating the menstrual cycle.

When I lived in Canada, where the cold winters did not provide a respite for airing clothes of strong odors, I refused to use asafetida. I didn't start cooking with it again until I moved to Texas. More than any other spice, asafetida gives Indian food the association of an aroma that is hard to eliminate from a house without good ventilation. Store it in a tightly sealed container to prevent the aroma from leaking out.

Daily uses for asafetida:

→ Add a pinch to oil before adding eggs to scramble them.

→ Fry a pinch in oil and add at the beginning of lentil or bean stews to reduce the effect of bloating.

→ Make asafetida yogurt. In a small frying pan, heat 2 tablespoons light sesame oil or another neutral oil with a generous pinch of asafetida and a generous pinch of red chile powder over medium heat. Add the oil to 2 to 3 cups plain yogurt (see page 86) and season with sea salt and 1 to 2 tablespoons sugar to balance the flavors. Garnish with chopped herbs and enjoy alongside meals or use it as a dipping sauce for breads or vegetables.

Fennel

Fennel is one of the few plants that can be used as a spice, herb, and vegetable. The green crescent-shaped seeds of the fennel plant have a mild, sweet anise scent and strong, spicy anise flavor. They may be used whole or ground and are best after being lightly toasted. The seeds are mainly used in pickles, pilafs, and seafood dishes. The smaller, thinner, greener seeds are called "royal fennel" or "Lucknowi fennel" and are far superior in flavor to plain fennel seeds; they are the only ones I recommend.

Fennel is an appetite suppressant, digestive aid, and nerve stabilizer, and fennel oil can be used as an antidote to insect bites and food poisoning.

Daily uses for fennel:

→ Crush the seeds and add to chai when brewing the water.

→ Pop fennel seeds in oil (see page 40) and add to pilaf or lentil stews at the end of cooking.

→ Add crushed fennel seeds at the end of braising okra.

→ Boil 1 cup water with 1 teaspoon fennel seeds, strain, and use for stomach indigestion in both children and adults.

→ Make a fennel digestive. A version of this is often served at the end of Indian meals to aid in digestion. Combine 1 cup fennel seeds with ½ cup white or black sesame seeds and ¼ cup coriander dal (the internal germ of the coriander seed, also called dhania ki dal), and a pinch of sea salt. Spread over a baking dish and toast in a preheated 300°F oven for 5 minutes. Cool and store in an airtight container. Chew on a teaspoon or two at the end of meals.

Cardamom

Known as the queen of spices (pepper being the king), green cardamom grows wild in the uplands of Kerala off the Malabar Coast. A sweet fragrant spice often called the vanilla of India, cardamom is used in almost every Indian dessert. Cardamom pods grow from tall plants on hillsides from rhizomes close to the ground, which makes harvesting challenging. Maturing every six to seven weeks and framed by a beautiful white flower, cardamom stems grow on alternate pods throughout the year. Working on a cardamom plantation requires eight hours of squatting on the haunches, a job usually done by women in Kerala. Green cardamom pods have an earthy sweet aroma, while the seeds inside are distinctly lemony with a menthol-like coolness. Green cardamom is best used whole or lightly crushed. Green cardamom seeds, which can be bought separately, can be ground into a powder.

Daily uses for green cardamom:

→ Steep 4 or 5 green cardamom pods in 2 cups boiling water for 15 to 20 minutes to make a tea.

→ Simmer green cardamom pods, black peppercorns, and crushed ginger in water for 5 to 10 minutes along with assam tea leaves and milk to make masala chai. Strain before drinking.

→ Add whole cardamom pods to a pot of rice or quinoa at the start of cooking.

→ Make cardamom tea. Pour 2 cups boiling water over a few cardamom pods, some freshly sliced turmeric root, and a fresh sprig of oregano or rosemary. Cover and let the tea steep for 15 to 20 minutes before pouring.

Black cardamom is a plant in the same family as green cardamom, which grows in northern India, close to Sikkim. It is a large, blackish, knubby-looking spice with a dark, smoky aroma. It is used extensively in Punjabi and Kashmiri cuisine and is an essential component of garam masala (see page 69). According to Punjabi tradition, when a newborn arrives, water steeped in black cardamom is given to the breastfeeding mother to help flush out toxins that cause digestive problems. It can be used whole to infuse meat stews and lentils.

Daily uses for black cardamom:

→ Add ground black cardamom husks and seeds to barbecue sauce or meat marinades for a delicious smoky flavor.

→ Infuse whole pods in meat or bean stews; remove the pods before serving.

→ Add ground black cardamom to mincemeat or lamb kebab marinade.

→ Make black cardamom roasted broccoli. Cut a large broccoli head into smaller florets, cut the stems into smaller chunks, and marinate with 1 tablespoon ground black cardamom, 1 teaspoon ground ginger, a few tablespoons olive oil, and sea salt to taste. Roast in a preheated 350°F oven for 10 to 12 minutes, until the broccoli is cooked and turns a darker green. Squeeze lemon juice over the top and serve.

Cinnamon

True sweet cinnamon is grown mostly in Sri Lanka. The cinnamon that is grown in most of Asia, including India, is cassia, a flat bark with a slightly milder flavor than sweet cinnamon and a spicy undertone that marries well with both sweet and savory dishes. While true cinnamon is used in the West to flavor sweets and breads, in India it is a component of garam masala (see page 69), biryanis, and pilafs. I use it extensively in cooking, but my favorite way to use whole cinnamon is to make various infusions.

Cinnamon is a proven blood purifier, aphrodisiac, and painkiller. It can help cure skin rashes and stop bleeding, vomiting, and loose bowels.

Daily uses for cinnamon:

→ Add a stick of cinnamon to iced tea while brewing it.

→ Add a stick of cinnamon to rice or quinoa pilafs before cooking.

→ Add a pinch of ground cinnamon to a stew or curry at the end of cooking to retain its aroma.

→ Make a cinnamon infusion. Place 1 stick of cinnamon in a mug, pour boiling water over it, steep for 15 to 20 minutes, and sip. Cinnamon water has an incredible sweetness. Repeat a few times, until the cinnamon loses its flavor.

→ Make cinnamon tea. Pour 3 to 4 cups boiling water over a large stick of cinnamon, a few sprigs of oregano, and lightly crushed black peppercorns. Let the tea infuse for 20 minutes before drinking.

Cloves

At the height of the spice wars in 1605, the Dutch wrestled control of the Moluccas, or Spice Islands (present-day Indonesia) from the Portuguese, breaking their sixty-year monopoly of the clove trade. The Dutch then proceeded to uproot and burn the entire clove forest, restricting growth of cloves to only a remote area, closely guarding the source and sending the price skyrocketing. Anyone caught trying to steal clove seedlings was put to death. Nearly two hundred years later, a Frenchman by the name of Pierre Poivre smuggled flowering clove buds to the French West Indies and cultivated the plants there. Eventually the spice spread to other countries for cultivation, from South America to North Africa. Cloves are used all over the world and are a key ingredient in Chinese five-spice powder, garam masala (see page 69), and Middle Eastern spice blends.

The clove tree grows to majestic proportions with flowers forming pretty clusters at the tip of every twig. The cloves sit on these clusters and are carefully picked and harvested with great skill. Their name comes from their shape, which comes from the Latin *clavus*, or nail. Cloves have a warm, pungent aroma from their key component, eugenol. They are an astringent, stimulating, and rejuvenating spice and an aid to digestion. Cloves are also used for relief from toothaches and sore gums.

When tempered with cooking and in small amounts, cloves add warmth, depth, and sweetness, but their flavor may be unpleasantly bitter and overpowering if used in large amounts. Cloves can be used to flavor pilafs, meat curries, and certain desserts.

Daily uses for cloves:

→ Lightly crush 2 or 3 cloves by using either a mortar and pestle or a rolling pin and a cutting board and add to brewed chai or iced tea at the start of brewing.

→ Lightly crush a few cloves and add to a simple pasta dish or stew.

→ Make clove rice pilaf. Rinse 1 cup white basmati rice a few times and let soak for a few hours. Drain and combine with 2 cups water, 8 to 10 chopped or crushed cloves, sea salt to taste, and a few tablespoons olive oil or ghee in a large pot and bring to a boil over high heat. Lower the heat, cover, and simmer for 10 minutes. Turn the heat off and let the rice rest for 10 to 15 minutes. Fluff and serve.

Nutmeg and Mace

Native to the Banda Islands of Indonesia, nutmeg and mace come from the same plant. The history of the Banda Islands is not a pleasant one: the Dutch ruthlessly outmaneuvered the British, massacred a large proportion of the natives, and established a monopoly on the nutmeg trade. They guarded their prize so carefully that nutmegs had to be sterilized with lime before being exported so they were incapable of reproducing. The British, however, had smuggled a few plants to some of its colonies, including Grenada, Sri Lanka, and the West Indies. With a sweet, delicate flavor less assertive than the nutmeg but highly aromatic, mace is the red mesh that encloses the hard nutlike seed that holds the nutmeg. Nutmeg has to be treated carefully, as it has a chemical, myristicin, that can prove hallucinogenic if used in excess.

Daily uses for nutmeg and mace:

→ Pour boiling water over a mace flower, steep for 15 minutes, then sip. Repeat and use until the flavor of the mace has disappeared.

→ Add ground mace to chicken or meat stews at the end of cooking.

→ Add ground mace to rice puddings or custards at the beginning of cooking.

→ Use freshly grated nutmeg in meat kebab marinades.

→ Make mace cream. Combine 2 cups heavy cream with 1 teaspoon ground mace, ½ cup sugar, and a pinch of sea salt and whip by hand with a whisk or using a stand mixer until stiff. Refrigerate until ready to serve with dessert, pastries, or whenever you would use whipped cream.

Amchur

Most people would not think of mango as a spice, but when green mango is peeled, sun-dried, and ground, it turns into a light-brown sour spice called amchur, with a distinctive sour tang and a slight sweet aftertaste. Amchur is an essential spice in chaats as a sour finish. It is best used as a finishing or sprinkling spice and can be used in place of lemon or lime. Since it does not possess any heat or pungency, amchur was the first spice I had my children try as babies; I'd stir it into mashed potatoes or rice. Amchur works as a mild laxative and helps with digestion.

Daily uses for amchur:

→ Sprinkle amchur generously on warm buttered popcorn.

→ Sprinkle amchur on roasted potatoes just when they come out of the oven.

→ Sprinkle amchur on roasted chicken after it is almost fully cooked.

→ Add amchur to tough cuts of meat before cooking; it works as a meat tenderizer.

→ Make amchur fish. Marinate a fillet of fish (any type) with sea salt, pepper, minced garlic (see page 80), and ghee (see page 77) or olive oil. Sear the fish on the stove top or roast in the oven and generously sprinkle with amchur just before serving.

Salt

Even though salt is a necessary mineral we need to consume every day, it has been my observation that what separates a good cook from those who want to be good cooks is the ability to salt food properly. Salt amplifies sour flavors, balances bitterness and sweetness, and rounds off the pungency of spices to add the right flavor to foods. Without salt, no flavors taste right. The key to using salt is to add it wisely. High doses of salt are added to processed foods, but with home cooking, salt is best added mostly at the beginning of cooking to allow it to penetrate into the food. The only way to really learn how to salt is to cook and taste. Salt doesn't only make food salty; it amplifies other flavors so you can taste the heat or the pungency of spices better. Whether using sea salt, kosher salt, or a flaky salt (aka finishing salt), try to find minimally processed salts with no additives. At the restaurants, we use kosher salt, but at home I use four different salts: sea salt for daily cooking, pink Himalayan chunks of rock salt for adding to stews and beans at the beginning of cooking so it dissolves, flaky sea salt for finishing grilled vegetables or meats, and black salt when I want to be transported to India's street cooking.

Black salt is not a true sodium salt but a sulfur compound or deposit that has a pleasant, tangy taste and smoky aroma. The sulfur in it mimics the notorious smell of eggs or boiled onions, but this taste recedes 20 to 30 minutes after using the salt. The salt is mined from underground deposits in central India, Pakistan, and Afghanistan. It is brownish black in its natural form, but when ground it takes on a pinkish tone. Black salt is typically sprinkled over appetizers, snacks, and starters and is a popular component of street foods in India.

Daily uses for black salt:

→ Sprinkle it on freshly cut fruit or salads.

→ Add it to warm popcorn with ghee (see page 77) and turmeric.

→ Add it to chutneys toward the end of cooking.

→ Make a cabbage salad. Thinly slice half a head of purple or napa cabbage, combine with 2 tablespoons raisins and 2 tablespoons sesame seeds, and sprinkle with 1 teaspoon black salt, 1 sliced serrano chile, and the juice of 1 lemon. Let the salad rest for 30 to 45 minutes for the flavors to meld, then stir, add chopped fresh herbs like mint or cilantro, and serve. The salad will keep in the refrigerator for 2 to 3 days.

masalas

Masalas, the secret weapon of Indian kitchens to be deployed as needed, are quite simply a blend of spices and seasonings. One can be as simple as freshly grated coconut with sesame seeds, ginger, and sliced green chiles tucked away in the refrigerator to toss into a dal or a curry, or a blend of warm aromatic spices such as cardamom, cinnamon, and black pepper crushed in a mortar or pestle and used to make an instant chai masala. An Italian pesto can be a masala, and so can the Turkish blend of spices ras el hanout, as can the Spanish sofrito with peppers, onions, garlic, and olive oil. Fresh herbs, like cilantro and mint, can be pounded with ginger, serrano chiles, and olive oil to make green masala lathered on morning toast with fried eggs or smeared on a beautiful wild salmon fillet just before it goes in the oven. All four of the following masalas will keep for up to 3 months in an airtight container away from light.

chai masala

MAKES ¼ CUP

4 large cinnamon sticks

2 tablespoons green cardamom pods

1 teaspoon black peppercorns

1 teaspoon whole cloves

3 or 4 mace flowers

While chai masala will add a heady fragrance to your chai, it has so many other uses for cooking. Since it is left in chunks, it is best added at the start of cooking to infuse the flavors. Add 1 teaspoon to hot oil or ghee just before cooking a stew or curry for a fragrant finish. Or add a generous tablespoon or two to the water when making meat or vegetable stock. You can also make a tisane with it by just adding 1 teaspoon to a cup along with sliced ginger and a sprig of mint and pouring hot water over it.

Preheat the oven to 300°F.

Combine all the spices in a small bowl. Spread them on a small baking sheet and toast in the oven for 3 to 4 minutes, until fragrant. Let cool and pulse in a coffee grinder until the spices are lightly crushed, not entirely ground.

coffee masala

MAKES ¼ CUP

4 cinnamon sticks

2 tablespoons black peppercorns

2 tablespoons green cardamom pods

2 star anise pods

½ teaspoon whole cloves

Add coffee masala to ground coffee before brewing, but don't limit it to coffee. Rub it on a piece of chicken or steak before grilling or roasting or add to meat stews at the end of cooking for a fragrant finish.

Preheat the oven to 300°F.

Combine all the spices in a small bowl. Spread them on a baking sheet and toast in the oven for 3 to 4 minutes, until fragrant. Let cool and grind in a coffee grinder to a powder.

curry masala

MAKES 3½ CUPS

1 cup toasted ground cumin

½ cup dried ground turmeric

½ cup toasted crushed coriander seeds

½ cup freshly ground black pepper

½ cup red chile powder (add more if you like your food hot)

½ cup crushed fenugreek leaves

2 tablespoons toasted ground fennel seeds

Try to make small batches of this and use it up within 4 to 6 months or the flavors will dissipate. Use this in combination with garam masala (see facing page), which is best added at the end of cooking.

Combine all the spices in an airtight container and store in a dark cool place.

garam masala

MAKES 1 CUP

¼ cup green cardamom pods

6 large cinnamon sticks

5 star anise pods

5 black cardamom pods

1 teaspoon whole cloves

4 whole mace flowers

1 whole nutmeg

Garam masala, which literally translates to "warm spice blend" (meaning heating for the body) is the one masala that most Indian kitchens have tucked away in a cabinet. The recipes and proportions can vary wildly, but they will all possess a large amount of aromatic spices. Some will contain coriander and cumin. I prefer to leave it to aromatic spices, like the ones here, which adds a delicious heady finish to foods.

Preheat the oven to 300°F.

Combine all the spices in a small bowl. Spread them on a baking sheet and toast in the oven for 3 to 4 minutes, until fragrant. Let cool and grind in a coffee grinder to a powder.

Spice Chart

ajwain

PROPERTY heating
TASTE pungent
WHEN TO ADD at start
 of cooking
PAIRING bread doughs,
 seafood, brassicas

amchur

PROPERTY heating
TASTE astringent
WHEN TO ADD at end of
 cooking, as a sprinkling
 spice
PAIRING topping on
 roasted meats,
 vegetables, popcorn

asafetida

PROPERTY heating
TASTE pungent
WHEN TO ADD fry in oil
 at start of cooking
PAIRING lentils, beans,
 brassicas

black cardamom

PROPERTY heating
TASTE pungent, sweet
WHEN TO ADD whole or
 ground at start of
 cooking
PAIRING barbecue rubs,
 meat kebabs, dals,
 infuse in alcohols

black cumin

PROPERTY heating
TASTE bitter, pungent
WHEN TO ADD whole,
 crushed, or ground at
 any time of cooking
 process
PAIRING cheese, tomatoes,
 creamy sauces

black pepper

PROPERTY heating
TASTE pungent
WHEN TO ADD whole,
 crushed, or ground at
 any time of cooking
 process
PAIRING creamy sauces,
 like yogurt, coconut,
 or cream

cardamom

PROPERTY heating
TASTE pungent, sweet
WHEN TO ADD whole at
 start of cooking, ground
 at end
PAIRING meat curries,
 rice pilafs, desserts,
 infuse in alcohols

chile

PROPERTY heating
TASTE pungent
WHEN TO ADD at any time
 of cooking process
PAIRING use powder or
 whole to add fieriness
 to all foods

cinnamon

PROPERTY heating
TASTE pungent, sweet
WHEN TO ADD whole at
 start of cooking,
 ground at end
PAIRING meat curries,
 rice pilafs, sweets,
 and desserts

clove

PROPERTY heating
TASTE pungent
WHEN TO ADD whole at
 start, ground at end
 of cooking
PAIRING crushed in rice
 pilafs, curries, breads,
 masalas

coriander

PROPERTY cooling
TASTE bitter, pungent
WHEN TO ADD crushed and ground at start of cooking
PAIRING curries, meatballs, bread doughs

cumin

PROPERTY heating
TASTE bitter, pungent
WHEN TO ADD whole, crushed, or ground at any time of cooking process
PAIRING all vegetables, curries, meats, bread doughs

fennel

PROPERTY cooling
TASTE sweet, bitter
WHEN TO ADD whole, crushed, or ground at any time of cooking process
PAIRING bread doughs, seafood, okra, raw at end of meal

fenugreek leaf

PROPERTY heating
TASTE sweet, pungent
WHEN TO ADD toward end of cooking
PAIRING potatoes, fish, creamy tomato stews

fenugreek seed

PROPERTY heating
TASTE bitter, astringent, pungent
WHEN TO ADD only at start of cooking
PAIRING crushed in stews, dals, braises

kalonji

PROPERTY heating
TASTE bitter, pungent
WHEN TO ADD whole, crushed, or ground at any time of cooking process
PAIRING barbecue rubs, meat kebabs, mushrooms

mace

PROPERTY heating
TASTE sweet
WHEN TO ADD whole at start of cooking, ground at end
PAIRING desserts, creamy curries, infuse in alcohols

mustard

PROPERTY heating
TASTE pungent
WHEN TO ADD whole at start of cooking, ground during cooking
PAIRING curries, pickles, rice pilafs, potatoes

nutmeg

PROPERTY heating
TASTE pungent, sweet
WHEN TO ADD whole at start of cooking, ground at end
PAIRING desserts, creamy curries, infuse in alcohols

saffron

PROPERTY cooling
TASTE sweet, pungent
WHEN TO ADD only at start of cooking
PAIRING meats, stews, clear soups, desserts

star anise

PROPERTY heating
TASTE pungent
WHEN TO ADD whole at start of cooking, ground at end
PAIRING desserts, creamy curries, infuse in alcohols

turmeric

PROPERTY heating
TASTE pungent, astringent
WHEN TO ADD only at start of cooking
PAIRING curries, grains, pulses

pantry staples and other essentials

Aromatic Essences

The nose is the gateway to the brain, and every scent we inhale registers with our minds and emotions. A sense of smell is one of the most ancient roots of our emotional life, and, as a result, scent has a unique capacity to evoke emotions and transport us to earlier times. Ayurveda is equally concerned with what we breathe and how we breathe, and regular pranayama—detailed breathing practices—can help our olfactory senses sharpen deeply. Just like when I smell vetiver (also known as "khus" in India), an essence similar to lemongrass, I am transported to summers in Gujarat, when on hot days we would suck on khus shaved ice or drink khus sherbets. The smell of sandalwood incense makes me instantly feel like I am back in an old temple in India. Medieval apothecaries that line narrow streets in New Delhi markets harken back to the days when rosewater and sandalwood essences were used to dab onto the edges of nostrils, throats, and behind the ears as perfume. My mother would dab jasmine essence on her handkerchiefs and rub her face with almond oil and rose water at the end of every day. And rose petals were cooked down to create an extract called gulkand and combined with coconut, fennel, and many other seasonings in the after-dinner digestive made out of betel nut leaves known as pan.

Vetiver (khus) and rose water, usually sold in small glass jars as an extract, are used in desserts and on rare occasions as a finishing essence in rich nut-filled curries. Kewra water (also known as keora or kewda), a flowery sweet aromatic essence extracted from the pandanus or the male flower of the fragrant screw pine, is also used in desserts and sometimes in savory foods.

Coconut

Grown near the coasts of Kerala, Goa, and Tamil Nadu, coconuts have been used in India for thousands of years. On visits to India, I scour the streets for vendors selling green unripened coconuts, usually sprawled on sidewalks in giant piles and opened with a quick slide of a knife. The best part is after

I drink the juice, the vendor cuts the coconut open, scrapes the insides, and hands me the piéce de résistance—the soft snowy pulp. Brown coconuts are simply the ripened version of the tender green ones. While buying frozen or dried coconut is convenient, once you venture into cracking into a coconut and taste the fresh meat, there's no looking back.

To open a coconut, using the edge of a knife, first poke a hole into one or two of the three "eyes," or soft spots, in the coconut and drain the juice into a glass. If residue from the hard shell falls into the juice, strain it through a tea strainer. Holding the coconut in one hand and a hammer in the other, hit it softly on all sides for about a minute, then place the coconut on a steel counter or floor and hit it hard to crack it open into two or three large pieces. While sipping the delicious coconut juice, pry the white portion off the shell into chunks using an oyster knife or paring knife. The white flesh will have a thin brown outer shell, but this is perfectly edible, and the chunks can be grated by hand or in a food processor. To make coconut milk, combine the flesh of one coconut with 2 cups water and blend until smooth. The silkiest and sweetest coconut milk is made from the pulp of green coconuts, if you are lucky enough to get your hands on some. Organic canned coconut milk free of additives or preservatives is an easy alternative.

fats

The flavor in spices is carried through fats, and most chefs use liberal amounts of fat in their cooking. My mother would often say, and I have found it to be true, that when the perfect amount of fat is used in a curry, you'll know the curry is ready when the fat separates and bubbles to the top to create a shiny layer. Fat is not only a cooking medium; it also contributes to and carries flavor, from the unctuous depth of ghee to the sweetness of coconut oil and the herby slight bitterness of olive oil. Slow lazy breakfasts with whipped butter on warm toast or dipping rotis or parathas in melted ghee is one of our family's weekend pleasures. Adding roasted garlic and freshly crushed black pepper to ghee or olive oil transports us to heaven.

Melt

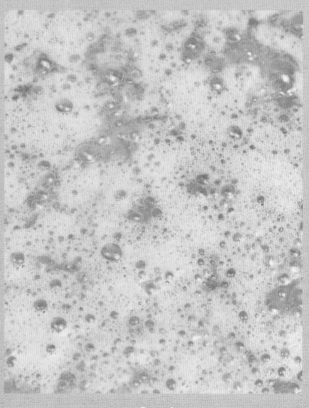

Boil

Simmer

Strain

homemade ghee

Ghee, the golden unctuous elixir of medieval Indian cooking, has been used for more than six thousand years and is considered the most healing of all substances. It is simply unsalted butter that is cooked until the milk solids separate into a caramelized mass and out emerges a golden clarified butter. Many hundreds of years ago in India, ghee would be stored in wells, and when soldiers returned home from war, the ghee was used to heal wounds. My grandparents ate their entire meals cooked in ghee and lived to their eighties. The smell of warm melted ghee is always nostalgic for me—it brings me back to the mornings when my mother would make a crisp aloo paratha and douse it with ghee before handing it to me for breakfast. As with most things, the quality of butter you use will greatly impact the quality of your ghee. Buy the best organic unsalted butter you can find. Ghee keeps at room temperature for up to 1 year and is known to develop a depth of flavor as time passes.

Melt the butter in a heavy-bottom saucepan over medium heat. Be careful: as the butter heats up, it might splatter and splash around. Continue cooking over medium heat, and as soon as it comes to a boil, lower to the lowest heat setting and cook for 45 minutes to 1 hour. The milk solids will first begin to separate out and rise to the top, concentrate, and subsequently sink to the bottom and turn a deep caramel color. They probably will get stuck to the bottom (see note) and a clear golden liquid with a nutty, complex aroma and taste will appear. Turn the heat off and let the ghee rest for 15 to 20 minutes, then strain it through a metal strainer, removing the milk solids. The milk solids can be reused in sautéed vegetables or added to a dal or a flour mixture. If the milk solids appear to have burnt slightly, the ghee will still be fine, albeit a touch darker. To this day, I overcook ghee so often that I now call it brown butter ghee and simply move on.

Variations

Saffron Ghee: Add a generous pinch of saffron while boiling the butter and add another pinch after it's strained.

Spice-Infused Ghee: Depending on how strong you want it, add your choice of 1 tablespoon or more lightly crushed cloves, cardamom, cinnamon, or nutmeg (or any other fragrant whole spices) to the ghee while boiling and remove while straining.

MAKES 1½ CUPS GHEE

1 pound unsalted butter

A note about cleaning: The milk solids will probably stick to the bottom of your pan, and after you have scraped off what can be reused, here is a trick to clean the pot. Let the pan rest for 5 to 10 minutes, then wash it using soap and a sponge. The milk scum will come right off. Alternatively, add water to the pot and cook rice or lentils in it. The milk solids will dissolve, adding delicious flavor to the food, and cleanup will be easy!

olive oil

High-quality olive oil is my daily-use cooking oil. The olive tree is one of the oldest cultivated trees, before even written language was invented. Native to Asia, olive trees spread from Iran, Syria, and Palestine to the rest of the Mediterranean basin six thousand years ago. First extracted into olive oil in Greece, this green liquid gold was brought to the Iberian Peninsula by the Phoenicians and Greeks. With a legend of mythical proportions, olive oil was often used as currency and commanded high prices in medieval times. At one time, it was the oil used to fuel churches' oil lamps and altars. Following the advice of Hippocrates, medieval pharmacists prescribed olive oil for numerous ailments, from skin disorders to kidney stones, and as an antidote against certain poisons.

Though I never used olive oil in India, when I saw how well its slightly bitter, peppery flavor complements spices and Indian cooking in general, I immediately embraced it and have been using it for decades. The primary fat in olive oil is oleic acid, a monosaturated fat that is filled with antioxidant and anti-inflammatory properties. The health benefits of olive oil reduce with high-temperature cooking, so I usually use a little olive oil in the first stages of cooking and drizzle a finishing olive oil at the end.

A few years ago, my son, Virag, returned from a study-abroad program in Spain excitedly carrying home a bottle harvested days before. It was an exquisite green color with the light fruity fragrance of fresh-cut grass and a slight peppery bitterness that tingled my throat. Olive oil deteriorates as it keeps, and after tasting fresh olive oil, I never looked at it the same way again. A large proportion of commercial grocery-store olive oil is rampant with rancidity, fustiness, and mustiness, so I recommend testing brands with small bottles before moving on to bigger quantities. However, once you taste good fresh olive oil, there is no turning back. Greeks use more olive oil than any other nationality, particularly those from the island of Crete. My obsession with good olive oil has only grown as I have made friends with small importers of Greek or Italian origin who bring in freshly harvested naturally extracted olive oils and have taught me how to taste and smell olive oil by swishing it in my mouth followed by a quick gulp to tell the different varietals apart. For everyday cooking, I use a single-origin olive oil from Crete, and I use a variety of Tuscan extra-virgin olive oils for drizzling on top of foods.

coconut oil

Coconut oil is a sweet oil that imparts a delicious yet unusual coconut flavor to foods. I use coconut oil occasionally in cooking and baking and also for massaging into my skin and hair. Not only does it strengthen and nourish the scalp and skin, when warm, our skin and scalp absorb it slightly better than most other fats. Given how easily coconuts grow on the Malabar Coast of Goa and Kerala, coconut oil is particularly popular with cuisines from those regions.

other oils

Mustard oil, cold pressed from brown or black mustard seeds, is very common in India, particularly in Bengali cooking. Both the oil and the seeds have some of the properties of wasabi with a hotness that warms the nose and head. While medical studies are inconclusive, due to a high percentage of irritants like erucic acid and isothiocyanates, the sale of edible mustard oil was banned in Western markets for years and was sold under the guise of "massage oil." These days, however, it is freely available at Indian grocers in America. When using it, however, remember to heat it to a high smoke point to denature the irritants.

Light (untoasted) sesame oil, called "gingelly oil" in India, is a neutral-flavored oil that can be used in place of coconut oil. Peanut oil and rice bran oil both have a high smoke point and are ideal for deep-frying. Walnut and pistachio oils make great finishing oils.

flours

Roti flour, which is simply finely ground whole-wheat flour, is the staple flour of most kitchens in India. The main difference between roti flour and supermarket whole-wheat flour is that the latter is coarsely ground. The finer the grind of the roti flour, the softer the roti. White all-purpose flour, called maida, is seldom used in everyday cooking. Chickpea flour, ground-up chickpeas, on the other hand, is another staple of an Indian kitchen. Used in making batters for fritters such as pakoras, sweets such as mithai (small nuggets of fudgelike candies), or as a roux for a sauce or curry, it is infinitely useful. I have used it as an egg replacement (1 egg = 1 teaspoon) in plant-based baking and have sneaked a generous pinch into bread and cake recipes to add complexity and depth of flavor. To minimize my use of refined white flour, I also turn to rice flour. It has a milder flavor than chickpea flour and can also be used in conjunction with chickpea flour for batters, stuffings, and pancakes.

minced garlic

MAKES ABOUT 1 CUP

2 cups peeled garlic cloves

Approximately ¼ cup olive oil

In India, garlic is considered sweet, pungent, and warming and is as much a medicine as it is a flavoring ingredient. It has been known to remove plaque from arteries and purify and increase blood flow. It can be used as an antiseptic, sedative, and disinfectant. Some Indians believe that a small garlic clove swallowed each morning gives vitality and virility and rejuvenates the intestines.

In the bowl of a food processor, pulse the garlic until finely minced. Store in an airtight container with a thin layer of the oil on top for up to 1 month in the refrigerator. As long as there is a layer of oil over the minced garlic, it will keep without spoiling or losing flavor.

ginger puree

MAKES ABOUT 1½ CUPS

1 pound ginger

About 1 cup water

Ginger is ground zero for most of my cooking; I use it in most preparations from savories to sweets. When buying ginger, seek out pieces with translucent and tender skin. If the only ginger available has thick brown skin, pick pieces with as few nubs and bruises as possible. Do not peel ginger—in India it is commonly believed that ginger's maximum flavor lies just beneath the skin. Considered warming, cleansing, and stimulating, ginger has been regarded as medicine in Ayurveda and Chinese medicine for over five thousand years. Ginger is one of the most highly recommended aids for digestion, muscular pain, and constipation. Ginger juice mixed with honey is good for treating congestion and facilitates breathing by opening up wind passages.

Cut the ginger into ½- to 1-inch pieces—if any of the skin appears tough, slice it off and discard it, but otherwise leave the peel on. Pour the water into the bowl of a blender, then add the chopped ginger. Blend in short intervals, turning the mixture around with a spatula to get at all of it, until pureed. Store in an airtight container in the refrigerator, where it will keep for up to 2 weeks. Use the puree with the liquid unless specified otherwise.

herbs

Herbs add a marvelous fragrant finish to most dishes, contain a variety of anti-oxidants and phytochemicals, and are visually stunning. A few years ago, one of my coworkers, Mary Cuclis, started a massive herb garden in her backyard, and for years after, I would be regaled with abundant herb bouquets including curling fragrant oregano vines, rosemary stalks, gorgeous nasturtium blossoms, thick clumps of zesty cilantro, heady basil, lemon balm, and more. I started bringing the herbs home, and at first I felt I had to use the oregano in Italian recipes or rosemary in recipes from the Mediterranean, but soon I was playing with adding fistfuls of oregano to a simple fish curry, lemon balm to my morning chai, and rosemary chopped up in roti doughs. It fostered a love for herbs like no other, and now we consume a voracious amount. At home, I will happily garnish a curry or stew with whatever I have on hand—basil, oregano, lemon balm, or rosemary. Inspired by Mary's green thumb, we now have massive pots of herbs at the restaurant and at my home to supplement for when our suppliers are running low.

The one herb I cannot live without—well, cannot cook without—is kari leaf (also referred to as curry leaf). There is no connection between a kari leaf and a curry: sometimes leaves go in a curry recipe, and sometimes they don't. I've intentionally chosen this spelling of *kari leaf* to make the distinction that kari leaves and curries are not intrinsically connected. When I left India, this plant native to my home country with an aroma reminiscent of lemon and pine was the flavor I missed the most. Before visits back to India, I would ask my mother to sun-dry kari leaves and I would return clutching the precious flavor I loved so much. I have used rosemary, which has a similar pinelike flavor, in place of kari leaves in an absolute bind. Now at the restaurant, along with many customers who have taken cooking classes with me, we grow these plants here in Texas. Kari plants grow slowly but do well in most climates. They can grow into bushes or large trees over time. Once they take root, they are sturdy and can fill your garden with their distinctive aroma. While they are used in a variety of ways all over India, I typically use them in stews, braises, and soupy lentil broths.

caramelized onion puree

MAKES ABOUT 2 CUPS

½ cup olive oil, plus more for the top layer

6 or 7 large white onions (roughly 5 pounds total), cut in half and roughly sliced or chopped

Everybody has a different definition of wealth. My mother estimated hers by counting her diamond earrings and gold necklaces. My idea of wealth is having a well-stocked refrigerator with hard-to-make basics, like caramelized onion puree, minced garlic (see page 80), ginger puree (see page 80), and ghee (see page 77). If spices are the soul of Indian cooking, onions are the heart, especially in northern Indian–style cooking. How you cut them, cook them, for how long, the color of the caramelization—all of this has an immense impact on the end result. Cooking onions may be the most time-consuming part, but once you learn to make your own caramelized onions, there is no turning back. You can use them for many other things, such as an addition to stews, pasta sauces, or masalas. Before I was in the restaurant business, I would make caramelized onions every couple of months and keep them in little plastic bags in the freezer so I would always have them on hand.

Heat the oil in a large frying pan or wok over high heat and add the onions. Cook, stirring, every 3 to 4 minutes, until they begin to show a light brown color. They will sweat and begin to reduce in volume. Lower the heat to low and continue to simmer, stirring occasionally, until they are dark golden brown and considerably reduced in volume. If they appear to stick to the bottom of the pan, add a few tablespoons of water to deglaze the pan. This entire process will take 1 to 2 hours. Set the onions aside for 5 to 10 minutes to cool slightly.

While still warm, pulse the caramelized onions in a food processor until smooth. Store the onion puree in a tight-fitting container with a thin layer of oil on top or distribute into small plastic bags or ice-cube trays and freeze until you're ready to use them. The puree can be frozen for up to 6 months.

Sweat

Sauté

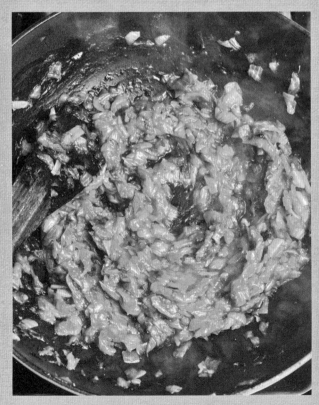

Caramelize

Store

83

homemade paneer

MAKES 1½ POUNDS

1 gallon whole milk, preferably organic A2 milk

2 teaspoons sea salt

1 teaspoon freshly ground black pepper

1 teaspoon lightly crushed cumin seeds

¼ cup distilled vinegar or fresh lemon juice

2 to 3 tablespoons olive oil

Paneer is the only cheese India can lay claim to—it is simply an unripened farmer-style cheese, except that it has no rennet, only vinegar or lemon juice. It has a pure clean flavor that blends well with herbs or spices. The higher quality the milk, the better the taste of the paneer. A2 milk has the A2 b-casein enzyme that is easier to digest than the A1 b-casein. In India, it is believed that all cows in medieval times were A2 cows.

In a heavy-bottom stockpot, combine the milk, salt, pepper, and cumin seeds and bring to a boil over medium-high heat, stirring frequently. Make sure not to scald the milk, or the paneer will take on a smoky flavor.

Just when the foam begins to rise, pour in the vinegar, lower the heat to medium-low, and simmer for 5 to 6 minutes. The milk should form big curds, which should rise to the top, separating from the whey, the clear liquid in which the curds are floating. As soon as the liquid is clear, turn the heat off and let the paneer rest in the liquid for 20 to 30 minutes.

Over the sink, pour as much of the liquid into a cheesecloth- or a kitchen towel–lined colander as you can without disturbing the curds. Using a slotted spoon, gently lift the curds out of the pot and place on the cheesecloth. With the back of the slotted spoon, press the curds gently to squeeze and discard most of the whey. The round shape of the colander will shape the paneer into a wheel. Fold the cheesecloth over the paneer to cover it completely and let it drain in the sink for 2 hours with light pressure from a bowl or pot filled with water placed on top. Too much pressure will result in a dense block of paneer. Refrigerate the wrapped wheel for at least 24 hours for the cheese to firm up.

When you're ready to finish the paneer, preheat the oven to 325°F.

Oil a baking sheet, gently unwrap the wheel directly onto the baking sheet, and drizzle the remaining oil onto the wheel. Bake for 15 to 20 minutes, until the paneer top has a nice golden brown color. Remove and let it cool. Wrap tightly in plastic wrap and store in the refrigerator for up to 2 weeks or the freezer for up to 4 months.

sweeteners

Given that I own a bake shop, people often laugh when I tell them that I do not have a sweet tooth. While I seldom crave cakes or cookies, I do like to add an element of sweetness to all my meals, which may be the reason I rarely have sweet cravings after. Whether it's a few pomegranate seeds or kishmish, a slender green raisin common in India (originating in Afghanistan) tossed on a salad, something sweet is always part of the meal. Roasted butternut squash tops a savory saag, and at some point in cooking dal or a vegetable curry, a sweet element goes in. It could be a touch of jaggery, minimally processed date or palm sugar, or a final drizzle of local honey or maple syrup on savory roasted vegetables. Or we will have a sweet chutney on the side to balance the food. Spending years in Canada helped me appreciate maple syrup, and I use it liberally in drinks and salad dressings. Again, this is my subconscious desire to stay in tune with the six tastes of Ayurveda, knowing that they bring deep satisfaction to food.

For baking and other such needs, natural (and unbleached) cane sugar remains a pantry staple.

Jaggery

Made from unrefined concentrated cane juice, date palm, or palm sap, jaggery is similar to piloncillo from Mexico. Usually sold in light to dark brown chunks or blocks, jaggery is sweeter than cane sugar and much easier to digest, so when swapping it in, use less.

Honey

Honey is considered one of the most perfect foods in Ayurveda. However, it must be eaten judiciously and never be cooked, as cooking denatures its properties and renders it toxic. After I make my morning chai, I stir in honey for sweetness. It's wonderful in salad dressings or to drizzle on top of a salad.

tomatoes

When good, fresh local tomatoes are not in season, I lean toward canned tomatoes. There are many brands of good canned tomatoes with minimal or no additives, yet my preference is Mutti, a recent import from Italy (a brand I have no affiliation with, whatsoever). I have found their finely chopped tomatoes, tomato puree, and tomato paste to be the best on the market, and all the recipes in this book were developed using Mutti products.

homemade yogurt

MAKES 4 CUPS

4 cups whole milk, preferably organic A2 milk

2 to 3 tablespoons full-fat fresh yogurt with live cultures

Yogurt is widely used in India for many different purposes. It was seldom available commercially during my childhood years, and even today, most families make plain yogurt each night for the next day's use, using a bit of yogurt as culture for the next batch. There are homes in India that have been using the same culture for decades, and the flavor improves over time. Yogurt is usually eaten unsweetened and plain, on the side of a meal to cool off the spices and, more important, to balance flavor, or as a raita—a salad of vegetables and spices tossed with yogurt. Yogurt is also used to make lassis, added to marinades, and used as a creamy component in curries.

In a small saucepan, heat the milk to a boil over medium heat, frequently stirring using a metal or wooden spoon to prevent the milk from sticking to the bottom. As soon as it reaches approximately 155°F (use an instant-read thermometer to test it), turn the heat off. It should be warm but not hot to the touch. Add the fresh yogurt and whisk the entire mixture until the yogurt has properly blended in with the milk. Transfer to a serving bowl or container. Place the container in a warm place (in a turned-off oven with the pilot light or viewing light on works best) undisturbed for 10 to 14 hours or overnight. The yogurt should be set. If not, leave it in the oven for another 6 to 8 hours. Refrigerate until ready to use. Save a little bit of the yogurt to make the next batch of yogurt and so on and so on.

The Dairy Dilemma

In the Vedic tradition, each animal is considered sacred, as it holds the complex memory of life on Earth. The shamanic cultures also identify themselves by the name essences of animals. Each animal possesses its rhythm of grace, movement, and self-nourishing instinct. The appearances and movements of animals clarified their deepest search for spiritual unity with the Earth.

The cow is considered the manifest keeper of the memory of the Earth's spiritual essences, and "protecting the cow" is an ancient Vedic term inferring protection of the scriptures and nurturing of the land. If the cow became extinct, we would not be able to maintain the memory necessary for human survival on Earth. Given the way we treat cows, it is no coincidence that every symptom the cow suffers in her captivity is mirrored in the present condition of the human species.

The cow's essential nature is nurturing, solid, stoic, and giving, like a mother. Cow's milk is considered a pure perfect food, but only if the cow is treated with reverence, love, and respect. In the agribusiness of American cattle farming, cows wallow in freezing mud in their own excrement, exist in darkness and death with no mobility, and are pumped with thousands of chemicals and antibiotics. The system victimizes the animals and the farmers, pollutes the land and our environment, and, in the end, does us humans untold harm. Ayurveda believes that the energy of the animal is inherited by humans when we consume it; in this case the mental agony of the cow is transferred to the consumer and manifests as fear, isolation, and melancholy.

However, with a surging demand for ethically sourced meats and dairy, there is a resurgence of small organic dairies producing milk and milk products in a humane way, and while their products are significantly pricier, it is a small price we as consumers are paying for our health and the health of our planet.

what is curry?

The word *curry* has had its share of controversy over the years. In 1974, celebrated Indian cookbook writer Madhur Jaffrey wrote that the word "curry" was as degrading to India's great cuisine as "chop suey" was to China's. In 2003, she went on to publish a book, *The Curry Bible*: an indication of how much currency the word had gained. Food bloggers have tried to start a trend to cancel the word, claiming that it is an offensive blanket term to describe any Southeast Asian dish with gravy or stew. While at first, I also rebelled against the use of the word, twenty years in the restaurant business and I have come to accept it. The word is here to stay.

The truth is that curry is neither a spice nor a spice mix. It's just a sauce with spices in it. The British borrowed the term *curry* from the Portuguese, who described *caril* or *caree* as any broth or gravy that Indians made with butter, nuts, vegetables, and a multitude of spices. In an attempt to capture the overwhelming variety of "broths," the English classified curries as Bombay, Ceylon, or Madras. This broad categorization missed the subtle variations and nuances of each preparation across the many kitchens of India. To the British, curry was not just a term that described an unfamiliar Indian approach to food, but a dish in its own right created for the British in India. Outside of restaurants, the word *curry* is practically nonexistent among Indians. There are specific names for broths, braises, and stews, which cannot be simplified as just a curry. Curry powder, a commercially prepared mix of spices (mostly turmeric, cumin, and coriander), is a Western notion dating to the eighteenth century. It was first prepared and sold by Indian merchants to members of the British Colonial government and army returning to Britain. No self-respecting Indian cook uses curry powder, or none that I know. If you have any in your pantry, throw it out unless it is fresh and well-sourced. Or better still, make your own fresh curry powder (see Masalas, page 67). Indians may use upward of ten spices in one dish, but they are all added individually and at different times in the preparation. They may be used whole, ground, toasted, crushed, or just popped in oil (see page 40) to release flavor.

Curry has traveled the globe. From Africa to the Caribbean to Fiji and other Pacific islands, curries are common fare. Japanese train stations and shopping malls have stands selling curry and rice and here in the United States, the popularity of curries just keeps rising.

Curry Chart

This is a basic guide to making a homemade curry. Use this chart
to learn how to build layers of flavor and create your own curries.
First, decide on your main ingredient and how much time you have:
vegetables make for a quick-cooking dish, while bone-in meats
take longer to cook. There are endless variations, and this chart
is simply meant to be a starting point to create your own curries.

---

1. Heat the Fat

PICK ONE
Ghee (see page 77), olive oil, coconut oil, sesame oil, mustard oil

2. Pop the Spices (see page 40)

PICK ONE OR A COMBINATION OF THE FOLLOWING
Cumin seeds, mustard seeds, coriander seeds, fennel seeds, fenugreek seeds

3. Add Whole or Lightly Crushed Spices

PICK ONE OR A COMBINATION OF THE FOLLOWING (OPTIONAL)
Green cardamom, black peppercorns, coriander seeds, cloves

4. Add the Kari Leaves (optional)

5. Sauté the Alliums

ADD ONE OF THE FOLLOWING AND COOK UNTIL TRANSLUCENT OR SOFTENED
Minced onions or leeks

OR ADD
Caramelized Onion Puree (page 82)

OPTIONAL
Asafetida can be used to replace or intensify the onion and garlic flavor

AFTER THE ONIONS ARE NEARLY COOKED, ADD
Minced Garlic (page 80)

6. Add Ground Spices

ADD THE DESIRED GROUND SPICES

Turmeric, ground cumin, ground coriander, red chile powder

7. Choose Main Ingredient(s)

ADD ONE OF THE FOLLOWING RIGHT AWAY

Vegetables, such as carrots, squash, potatoes, eggplant

Fish fillets, chunks, or steaks

Dark-meat chicken pieces (bone-in or boneless)

Meat chunks (bone-in or boneless)

8. Stir in an Acid

ONCE THE MAIN FILLING IS NEARLY COOKED, ADD

Chopped or pureed tomatoes (canned or fresh) and/or plain whole-milk yogurt (see page 86)

9. Add Creaminess and Thickness (optional)

PICK ONE OR A COMBINATION

Coconut milk, heavy cream, toasted ground nuts

10. Mix in Aromatic Spices

PICK ONE OR A COMBINATION OF THE FOLLOWING

Garam Masala (page 69), ground cardamom, cinnamon, cloves, mace

11. Add Quick-Cooking Green Vegetables (optional)

COOK JUST UNTIL WILTED

Peas, spinach, kale, watercress, collard greens

12. Turn the Heat Off

13. Finish with Bright Flavor

PICK ONE

Lime juice, lemon juice, a sprinkle of amchur (dried mango powder)

14. Fold in or Garnish with Aromatic Herbs

ADD ONE OR A COMBINATION OF THE FOLLOWING

Cilantro, basil, mint, thyme, sage, parsley

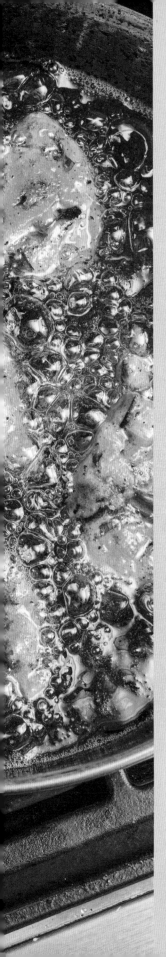

Recipes

Never a recipe book in sight, I watched my mother cook foods from our ancestral land of Sindh for decades. All her cooking, and that of my cousins and aunts, was done by memory and intuitive, simple know-how. Small changes were observed, whispered, and passed down generation to generation. Masters at improvisation, they adjusted based on seasonality and availability. My mother was a tinkerer—she never stopped trying out new ideas, from incorporating Gujarati vegetables into Sindhi preparations to mastering Parsi and South Indian foods. I was not much different. I barely owned any recipe books, even when I opened my first restaurant, Indika, back in 2001. I took the time to teach all my cooks the nuances of each dish, and it was a few years before I started putting methods down on paper.

We all possess an intuition; we just need to tap into it. The concept of flavor and taste in India can be broken down to the essence of an ingredient in its purest and finest part. Spices and herbs aren't just an enhancing additive but an essential defining quality with entirely new flavors emerging as a combination of ingredients. Cooking is about creating flavor that is integral to a dish, not an adornment or afterthought. Indians put flavor at the center of cooking and eating, and the possibilities are endless.

However, good cooking, like most other things, comes with good preparation. Having lived in over half a dozen houses in my adult life, the kitchen has always been the heart of the home where I begin and end my day. And an organized, clean, uncluttered kitchen with the right tools is where good cooking starts. Waking up to a pile of dirty dishes in the sink is never a good way to start the day. A cluttered counter with unnecessary gizmos just gets in the way. Whether using European Dutch ovens or triple-steel stockpots or saucepans, the pot you cook in makes all the difference, and it is worth investing in a few good ones.

Regarding recipes, don't take them too seriously. Recipes are like stories, a viewpoint, an expression of one person's or family's idea of how a dish should be prepared. There is never just one way, and this is what makes food so exciting. All of us have the freedom to create a meal exactly the way we like it, not how a recipe tells us. Good cooking, like most things, takes time and practice. This is where our intuition comes in. The more we use it, the better we get at it. I had to make a lot of meals, some bad, to become a skilled cook. I still don't use recipes when I cook, but I urge you to take these recipes, try them, change them, and use them for ideas and as guides to make them your own.

A few notes: Taste as you go for best results. Each detail of how you cook affects a recipe. The timing of cooking is affected by the stove you use. A large gas stove will be fast. Electric or induction may take longer for recipes to reach their doneness. A smaller stove will yield slower results. Is your oven calibrated? This will affect baking time. The brand of sea salt and canned tomatoes you choose will affect the taste, as will the sweetness and seasonality of the produce you use and so on. The size of the pan will matter—wide and shallow will absorb fast, and deep and narrow not so much. Are you using a heavy-bottom saucepan or pot? You get the point. The only way to cook is with your senses. Touch. See. Hear. Smell. Taste. And enjoy!

Pancakes and Eggs

India is the land of pancakes and crepes, but not in the way most people in the West might imagine. With neither chocolate chips nor sweet syrups to accompany them, these pancakes are fermented glories made with interesting combinations of coconut, rice, millet, and/or lentils. They may be sweet or savory, and the sheer breadth of varieties that can be made with the various batters, be it dosa, chilla, or malpua, could stand up to any crepe on the streets of Paris.

Chilla, a savory pancake made from chickpea or millet flour that's ready in minutes, is one of my favorite breakfasts. Buried deep in the belly of Crawford Market in the city of Mumbai, a few vendors make a living flipping chillas from bubbly batters with spices, herbs, or cheese on large skillets over coal-burning stoves on their carts. This batter can also be fermented, but I prefer the instant one with eggs. It can be topped with mushrooms, avocado, and eggs and becomes a great vehicle for vegetable or meat leftovers.

At the top of the pancake pile is the dosa: the quintessential fermented crepe of southern India. Dosas are stuffed with potatoes or other spiced vegetables and sometimes meats. Uthappam is a thicker and fluffier variety of dosa, more like a savory Western pancake with toppings. Both dosa and uthappam are made from the same batter, which is a basic 3:1 ratio of rice to lentils that are soaked, ground, and fermented. Dosa batter is easier to make than any basic sourdough bread recipe and is naturally gluten-free and easier to digest. My biggest dream for this book is that it inspires home cooks across the world to discover the delights of these ethereal spongy crepes and pancakes, with dosa batter regularly fermenting away on kitchen counters and dosas becoming their newest family staple.

dosas

For years, the idea of making dosas at home intimidated me. On many occasions, I would stare mesmerized at the rapid rhythm of street vendors in Chennai or New Delhi expertly spreading bubbly fermented dosa batter in a circular or oval shape on massive flat skillets and rapidly handing dosas out to hungry customers. I made a few unsuccessful attempts at home and have one distinct memory of over-fermented batter spilling all over my kitchen counter and floor overnight. Relegating it to restaurant food, I stayed away from learning how to make dosas for years. On our opening team at Pondicheri was a young woman, Mary Cuclis, who had traveled to India and urged me to try. I resisted again. One day she pulled out a handwritten recipe given to her by a hotel cook in India. Within months we had dosas on the Pondicheri menu, and I have never looked back.

Making dosas at home is a whole different matter. At the restaurant, dosas are made on large flat griddles, but home-style dosas are made on smaller frying pans or cast-iron skillets. Dosas made at home will seldom be as big, thin, or dramatic as restaurant dosas, but the smaller pancake-size dosas are just as good, maybe even better. Despite owning restaurants, I always have dosa batter in my home refrigerator so there's always a delicious meal minutes away. Dosas are a canvas for all sorts of toppings and fillings, from eggs to mashed potatoes to sautéed spiced greens or caramelized bananas—the sky is the limit.

These crispy beauties of South India can go from wispy and paper thin resembling a deeply flavorful potato chip to a thick pillowy pancake, technically called an uthappam or uttapam, that showcases the savory, tangy taste of fermentation. While dosas are historically made with a short-grain white rice and urad dal, a white lentil, many other combinations are possible. In a pinch, I have made dosas with sushi rice, brown rice, parboiled rice, arborio rice, basmati rice, or jasmine rice. It's a shame to waste basmati on dosas because the specialty of the aged rice is in the length of the grain, which gets blended up into dosa batter. For the lentils, in addition to white urad dal (the shelled and split form of whole black urad dal), any mung lentils, split or whole, will also work. Please note that this recipe calls for a larger amount of fenugreek seeds than traditional dosa recipes, because I have found that the increased fenugreek, which is also a bean, adds to the viscosity of the batter, which in turn makes for a lighter and fluffier dosa.

recipe continues

Making dosas for the first time is bound to be a challenge, mainly in mastering the spread of the batter, but don't despair. Oddly shaped dosas might appear to be mistakes but will make delicious snacks as you go. The more you make dosas, the better you will get at creating your best versions. I suggest making thicker pancakelike dosas first before moving onto thinner ones; or, like me, you might stick to making thick dosas, which are simply wonderful in their own right. I usually cook dosas in ghee or coconut oil; however, olive oil and light sesame oil also work really well.

MAKES 2 QUARTS (8 CUPS) DOSA BATTER

3 cups white rice

1 cup white urad dal

1 tablespoon fenugreek seeds

1 tablespoon sea salt

Coconut oil or ghee (see page 77) for cooking

Put the rice, dal, and fenugreek seeds in a large glass or metal bowl or container and rinse in cold tap water two or three times by covering with water and pouring it off the sides. Cover with cold tap water by 6 to 8 inches. Soak the mixture, uncovered, at room temperature for at least 4 hours or overnight. Don't leave it out for longer than that, or the lentils will start to ferment before they have been ground. After soaking, the rice and lentils will double in size.

Drain the mixture by holding a hand over it and pouring almost all the water into the sink. Transfer half of the mixture to a powerful blender. Add ½ cup water and the salt and, starting on low speed and gradually moving to a higher speed, blend until the batter is grainy, pourable yet smooth, and resembles thick pancake batter. Depending on the power of the blender, this could take several minutes. Repeat with the rest of the batter, adding as much water as needed. (At this point, if by mistake you have added too much water and the dosa batter is too runny, add a few tablespoons rice flour or millet flour to bring the batter to the right consistency before you set it aside for fermentation.)

Note: Fermentation is the process of converting carbohydrates to alcohol or organic acids with the help of microorganisms. *Lactobacillus* bacteria along with other microorganisms already present in lentils and rice and in the air will bring about the fermentation that contributes to the leavening or rising of the batter. This is the same bacteria that converts milk to yogurt, and it is the act of fermentation that gives dosa batter its characteristic taste, aroma, and ease of digestibility. The tiny fenugreek seeds contribute to the flavor, help maintain carbon dioxide, which makes the batter viscous by absorbing excess moisture, and make pancakes airy and fluffy.

Transfer the batter to a large container roughly double its size to ensure there is enough room and surface area for the batter to rise during fermentation. I have used everything from plastic food storage containers to a glass pitcher to a large metal stockpot for fermentation. Cover with the lid ajar to allow atmospheric oxygen to come through. Let the batter sit at room temperature for 8 to 24 hours (the colder the weather, the longer the fermentation will take). At home, I usually put the batter on the kitchen counter right next to the stove with a plate underneath it. On particularly cold days, you can put the batter in a turned-off oven with the oven light on. The light will provide just enough warmth to jump-start fermentation. However, be cautious during warm weather, as the batter might rise above the top of the container and spill over.

Depending on the ambient temperature, in a few hours a fermented aroma will emanate. This is an indication that the microorganisms are active and the batter is on its way to being ready.

The batter is ready when, at the very least, it has puffed up slightly, possibly risen by a few inches, and bubbles have formed all over, including the surface. If the batter appears to have separated and has liquid on top, don't worry—it will still ferment. Once the batter is ready, whisk it well,

recipe continues

Rinse, soak, and grind

Ferment

Pour

Season

and if not using it immediately, cover and refrigerate for up to 2 weeks. It may separate in the refrigerator but will come together when you whisk it and bring it to room temperature before cooking. The batter develops flavor with time and, in my opinion, it is best between 24 and 48 hours.

Heat a flat metal frying pan over high heat. Once the pan is hot, brush it with very little oil, then quickly wipe the hot surface with a paper towel to remove excess grease. The pan needs to be seasoned but not greasy or the dosa batter will slide around when you try to spread it. Pour ¼ cup batter in the middle of the pan. Using the bottom of a ladle or metal measuring cup, using very light pressure, quickly spread the batter outward in a circular motion. You are looking to create a round pancake anywhere between 6 to 8 inches in diameter or larger. Drizzle a little oil on top and around the dosa. A dosa is technically cooked only on one side, so let it brown on the bottom and crisp up at the edges and on top. This will take roughly 2 minutes. If yours is thicker, more like a pancake, it will need to be flipped over with a metal spatula. If you were unable to spread it smoothly and the dosa has thin or thick pockets, flip it over with your metal spatula to cook the other side. Carefully loosen all sides of the dosa, add your desired stuffing or topping, and serve either faceup or folded over.

When making the next dosa, the pan will not need to be greased again. Dedicate the first few dosas to edible experimentation—lopsided misshapen thick or thin dosas make great snacks. If you need to cook them on both sides, they will still taste good, so taste your way through.

herb masala dosa

MAKES 6 TO 8 DOSAS

2 cups dosa batter (see page 100)

½ cup minced white onions

1 cup minced mixed fresh herbs (any and all herbs will work, such as cilantro, mint, basil, and sage)

1 serrano chile, minced

1 teaspoon coriander seeds, crushed

1 teaspoon sea salt

2 tablespoons coconut oil or olive oil

Plain yogurt or Peanut Chutney (page 226) for serving

Combine the dosa batter with the onions, herbs, chile, coriander seeds, and salt. Drop 3- to 4-inch mounds of batter onto a preheated greased flat skillet (see above) and spread them slightly. Cook on both sides (see above) and serve with plain yogurt or chutney.

Variations

Egg Dosa: There are so many ways to make an egg dosa, from stuffing it with sliced boiled eggs or egg salad or simply throwing a fried egg on top of a dosa. I urge you to find your own perfect egg dosa, but here are a few ideas. (*See the recipe photo on page 98.*)

Crack an egg directly on top of dosa batter just after adding the batter to the pan. Gently spread it over the surface and let it cook along with the dosa. Dot with lightly crushed whole spices such as cumin, coriander, fennel, or mustard seeds. Serve sprinkled with sea salt and topped with herbs or microgreens.

Beat an egg with a pinch each of turmeric, sea salt, and black pepper; spread it onto a half-cooked dosa; and let it cook with the dosa. You could also add

recipe continues

chopped herbs and minced serrano chile to the beaten egg before pouring it over the dosa.

Scramble an egg with your choice of seasoning and place it on one half of a dosa as a filling, sprinkle with cheese, and fold the other half over.

Grilled Cheese Dosa: Make an 8-inch dosa and spread grated cheese over the entire surface while it is cooking. Flip it in half and the cheese will melt as the dosa finishes cooking.

Make a dozen 3- to 4-inch-diameter dosas. Spread a few tablespoons of any melting cheese over half of the dosas, press the remaining dosas on top, and cook them again on a skillet until the cheese is melted.

Make two 8-inch dosas. In the meantime, combine 1 cup grated melting cheese with 1 minced serrano chile, ½ cup minced green or red onion, ½ cup diced tomato, and a pinch of sea salt. When the second dosa is almost finished cooking, spread this mixture over the top and press the other dosa on top. If possible, cover the whole dosa with a dome-shaped lid or an inverted large, heatproof bowl to create steam, which will help melt the cheese. Using one or two large spatulas, flip the whole dosa over and cook the other side. Remove, cut into wedges, and serve. This is my personal favorite and makes a great appetizer.

Green Dosa: Heat 2 to 3 tablespoons oil in a large frying pan over high heat and pop some mustard seeds (see page 40). Immediately add 2 to 3 cups chopped greens (spinach, kale, dandelion greens, mustard greens, collard greens, or watercress). Cook the greens just until wilted. Use this mixture to stuff one dosa, then smear with Peanut Chutney (page 226).

Beet Shiitake Dosa: Combine 2 cups dosa batter with 1 medium grated raw red beet, a pinch of sea salt, ½ teaspoon red chile powder, and ½ teaspoon freshly ground black pepper. Let it rest for 30 minutes to 1 hour for the color to infuse into the batter. Cook a dosa with sliced shiitake mushrooms and scallions to cover the top of the dosa. Season the mushrooms with salt and pepper. Flip to sear the mushrooms for about 1 minute, until softened and browned.

Dosa Pizza: Make an 8-inch dosa pancake (uthappam) using dosa batter; once you have flipped it over in the pan, spread ½ cup Roasted Cherry Tomato Chutney (page 227) over it and top with 1 cup melting cheese, such as gruyère or raclette. Cover the top of the pan with a dome-shaped lid or an inverted large, heatproof bowl so the cheese melts. Top with chopped fresh herbs such as basil, oregano, or cilantro and serve immediately.

Dosa Waffles: Pour dosa batter directly into a greased waffle maker to make a dosa waffle. Or for a more luxurious waffle, whisk 1 cup dosa batter with 3 large eggs, 2 tablespoons oil or melted butter, and ½ teaspoon sea salt. Pour into a waffle maker and cook until browned all over. Makes 2 large lacy waffles.

Masala Dosa: Stuff a thin dosa with South Indian Potato Mash (page 168) and serve Dal Soup (page 177) and Coconut Chutney (page 228) on the side. This combination is the traditional way dosas are served and is a hearty dose of carbohydrate, so plan on a nap afterward.

Cream Banana Dosa: Make a large thin dosa, and halfway through the cooking process, sprinkle 2 tablespoons sugar over the surface of the dosa. Let it cook and caramelize slightly, then place a sliced banana on top. Sprinkle a pinch of red chile powder on top and pour 2 to 3 tablespoons heavy cream on top. Fold over and eat immediately. This can be enjoyed for breakfast or dessert.

coconut pancakes

Malpua, a traditional pancake made with barley or wheat flour, sugar, cardamom, and cream, is what inspired the coconut pancakes we serve at Pondicheri for breakfast. Often served in temples as celestial offerings, malpua dates back to Vedic times and has gone through many iterations over the centuries. It is usually very sweet, dense, and rich, but this version is light and fluffy, drizzled with jaggery caramel and perfect for those who love sweet (but not too sweet) breakfasts. For a more decadent version, add a drizzle of plain heavy cream or sweetened whipped cream, or add blueberries or chocolate chips to the batter. The batter will keep in the refrigerator for 2 to 3 days and can be frozen for up to 3 months. Defrost in the refrigerator for 48 hours before using. (*See the recipe photo, far left, on page 96.*)

To make the jaggery caramel: Heat the sugar in a dry pan over high heat and cook without stirring until it turns brown in color, 3 to 4 minutes. Turn the heat down to low and carefully add the jaggery, cinnamon, cardamom, black pepper, salt, and heavy cream. The sugar will be very hot, so stand back to avoid getting burnt from splattering sugar. Bring to a simmer and let simmer until smooth, another 3 to 4 minutes. If there are lumps in the caramel, use a whisk to break them up. If small lumps persist, strain the caramel. The caramel will keep in the refrigerator for at least 1 month (sugar works as a preservative).

To make the pancakes: In a large bowl, combine the eggs, coconut milk, kewra water, ghee, grated coconut, and ginger puree and whisk until smooth. In a separate bowl, whisk the rice flour, almond flour, sugar, cardamom, salt, baking powder, and baking soda until evenly combined. Pour in the wet mixture and fold until evenly mixed.

Heat a large skillet over high heat until hot. Brush with a little ghee, then drop 2 tablespoons batter onto the skillet and top with some almonds. Repeat with as much batter as will fit on the pan and cook for 1 to 2 minutes, until the pancakes are lightly browned on the bottom, then flip to finish cooking. Repeat until you've used up all the batter.

MAKES 16 TO 18
SMALL PANCAKES

JAGGERY CARAMEL

½ cup cane sugar

½ cup jaggery

½ teaspoon ground cinnamon

½ teaspoon ground cardamom

½ teaspoon freshly ground black pepper

½ teaspoon sea salt

½ cup heavy cream

PANCAKES

3 large eggs

One 14-ounce can coconut milk

1 teaspoon kewra water (see page 72)

¼ cup melted ghee (see page 77), plus more for cooking

1 cup grated fresh coconut

1 tablespoon Ginger Puree (page 80)

1½ cups rice flour

1 cup almond flour

½ cup cane sugar

1 teaspoon ground green cardamom seeds

1 teaspoon sea salt

1½ tablespoons baking powder

½ teaspoon baking soda

¼ cup toasted sliced skin-on almonds

avocado mushroom chilla

Chillas are a great start to the day and can be made within minutes. They are typically made with chickpea flour, but any kind of lentil flour, millet flour, or other whole-grain flour works. They can be enjoyed for breakfast plain, stuffed with a favorite melting cheese, or topped with sliced tomatoes, plain yogurt, and fresh herbs or microgreens. Sometimes I stuff them with a smidgen of feta cheese and a lot of sautéed greens for dinner. Chillas are also great as a first course or appetizer when made as fat little pancakes and topped with cheese and chutneys.

Maitake or shiitake mushrooms hold up to the assertive taste of the chickpea best, but feel free to substitute any mushroom you have on hand. Alternatively, use sliced onions, zucchini, carrots, or any other vegetable that can cook quickly with the chilla. Chilla batter will keep in an airtight container in the refrigerator for up to 3 days.

Combine the chickpea flour, coriander seeds, turmeric, black pepper, and salt and whisk to combine. Add the milk, eggs, and oil and whisk until smooth. The consistency should be thinner than pancake batter. If it appears too thick, add a tablespoon or two of water.

Heat a seasoned, preferably nonstick, skillet over medium heat until hot and add 1 tablespoon oil. Pour about ¼ cup of the mixture into the skillet and spread, either by tilting the pan or with the back of a ladle, into a 6-inch circle. Immediately scatter a few of the sliced mushrooms and green onions on the chilla. Cook for a minute or two, then gently loosen the edges, flip the pancake over, and cook for another minute or two, until golden brown on the second side. Transfer to a plate and repeat to cook the remaining pancakes.

To top each pancake: Add a few slices of avocado and radish, a sprinkle of salt, a few crumbles of feta, and a drizzle of honey and herbs.

MAKES 6 CHILLAS

1 cup chickpea flour

1 teaspoon coriander seeds, lightly crushed

¼ teaspoon ground turmeric

1 teaspoon freshly ground black pepper

½ teaspoon sea salt

¾ cup whole milk

2 large eggs

¼ cup olive oil, plus more for cooking

2 cups thinly sliced mushrooms, such as maitake or shiitake

2 green onions, white and green parts, minced

TOPPINGS

2 avocados, peeled, pitted, and thinly sliced

1 radish, thinly sliced

Sea salt, for sprinkling

1 cup crumbled feta cheese

2 tablespoons honey

Fresh herbs sprigs (such as cilantro, mint, or basil)

parsi eggs

SERVES 4

¼ cup olive oil

1 teaspoon black mustard seeds

2 cups diced baby potatoes
(½-inch pieces)

½ teaspoon ground turmeric

2 teaspoons sea salt

1 tablespoon Minced Garlic
(page 80)

1 teaspoon toasted ground cumin

1 teaspoon freshly ground
black pepper

1 serrano chile, minced

2 cups canned crushed tomatoes

4 green onions, white and green
parts, minced

⅔ cup fresh or frozen green peas

4 large eggs

Chopped fresh cilantro for garnish

While I grew up eating eggs, they were and continue to be strictly forbidden in most vegetarian households of India. In some homes, orthodox matriarchs may give in to the demand of one family member; however, the egg preparation will be relegated to electric stoves out in the balcony or backyard, so as not to contaminate the main kitchen with what's considered nonvegetarian food. Most bakeries in India offer varieties of eggless cakes. These days, as the influence of the West grows, the adventurous younger generation will venture out to eat eggs in street carts, away from the probing eyes of elders. Scrambled into a bhurji (a soft scramble with vegetables and spices) with onions, tomatoes, peppers, and herbs; soft-boiled and drizzled with chutney; or flipped into an omelet, eggs are usually served with pan-seared bread.

At home, my family ate omelets and scrambles, but the simple masala egg toast was my favorite. The Parsi community is well known for their love of eggs, and this recipe is an adaptation of one of their basic egg-and-potato breakfast treats. I love making these eggs with tiny halved baby potatoes. (*See the recipe photo, top right, on page 96.*)

In a large pan, heat the oil over high heat until shimmering. Pop the mustard seeds (see page 40), then immediately add the potatoes, turmeric, and salt. Cook, stirring frequently, for 2 to 3 minutes, then turn the heat down to medium, cover the pan, and cook until the potatoes are soft, 5 to 7 minutes. Add the garlic, cumin, black pepper, chile, and tomatoes; bring to a simmer; cover; and simmer for 4 to 5 minutes. Add the green onions and peas and cook for 2 to 3 minutes. Crack the eggs directly on top of the potatoes. The whites will slide down in between the potatoes and set in place. Cover and continue cooking until the whites are cooked through and the yolks remain soft, or cooked to your liking. Garnish with cilantro and serve.

masala egg toast

At one point during my teen years, my parents employed a cook by the name of Masoor. His cooking was simple yet masterful, and I learned many a trick by just watching him wield his magic with spices and marinating foods using his sensibilities with no recipes or books in sight. His was the only cooking my mother would not hover over. He understood our family and knew how to cook for each one of us. This was no easy task, as my two older brothers had their daily demands. There were mornings when Masoor would expertly put out five different dishes on the breakfast table: my father's favorite poppy-seed halwa, a creamy rich pudding; my mother's hot and crispy paratha, a flaky layered flatbread, with a spicy pickle; my perennially hungry two older brothers' enormous omelets; and my masala egg toast. This recipe serves four but can easily be made for just one. (*See the recipe photo, center, on page 96.*)

In a large frying pan, heat the ghee over high heat until melted. Add the slices of bread and toast on one side until crispy and browned. Flip the bread over and crack 1 egg directly on top of each slice. While the egg is still raw, sprinkle the toasts with the cheese, ajwain seeds, and salt. Add the red onion, tomato, and serrano chile and cook for 2 to 3 minutes, until the eggs are set. If you want the yolk to harden, cover the pan with a lid or an inverted large, heatproof bowl as they cook. Garnish with the cilantro and serve.

SERVES 4

2 tablespoons ghee (see page 77)

4 slices soft bread, such as brioche or challah

4 large eggs

1 cup grated melting cheese, such as Gruyère or raclette

½ teaspoon ajwain seeds

½ teaspoon sea salt

¼ cup minced red onion

½ cup diced tomato

1 serrano chile, minced

2 to 3 tablespoons chopped fresh cilantro leaves and stems

Street Foods

Street foods of India are unmatched in the world, from the savory hashlike uppma in the south to sprouted mung salads and pani poori in Mumbai. Chaat is the quintessential street food. Chaats are the heartbeat of many a busy street or park corner where a vendor puts down their basket or cart of wares and locals gather for a quick bite. Most locals will tell you which corner to go to for the best street foods. It's these street vendors from whom I reserve my deepest admiration. In the middle of a torrid downpour clutching a flimsy umbrella, I recall standing by a roasted-peanut vendor who stubbornly refused to give me the sand-spiced peanuts until they were perfectly crisped with the delicate skin just sliding off. When he did hand them over, it was with a triumphant smile. They were perfection.

Chaat, originating in northern India, is any savory snacky inventive combination of fresh vegetables with drizzles of yogurt and aromatic herb-infused sweet, spicy, and savory chutneys, topped with crunchy titbits. Take a bite, and all at once your mouth is hit with an explosion of flavors from the creamy tartness of yogurt to the silky smoothness of tamarind chutney to the crunch of sev, a crispy chickpea noodle, or straw or fried potatoes topped with aromatic herbs.

I once read in a travel book that chatting is India's favorite pastime, and as an Indian, I could not agree more. Sitting on the stoop; sipping chai or a lassi with a neighbor, friend, or relative; munching on a samosa or a kebab dipped in chutney is a common sight in India. Picking up samosas from the corner street vendor, and walking into a friend's or relative's house unannounced can be a regular affair in many neighborhoods. Sometimes business deals, courtships, and marriage proposals are handled over plates of chaat and pots of chai!

If you have never tasted pani poori, the queen of chaats, I suggest finding the nearest Indian chaat house to try it. Or at the very least, try our rendition of it (see page 117). *Pani poori* literally translates into "water puff," the poori being a hollow, walnut-size fried wheat puff. In the hands of an expert street vendor in Mumbai or Delhi, the poori is held in the palm of the hand and deftly punctured with the thumb, resulting in a hole the size of a quarter in the middle of the poori. This is then filled with varying combinations of chickpeas, sprouted mung beans, diced potato, and a smattering of sweet tamarind chutney. The stuffed poori is then momentarily dipped, by hand, into a huge terra-cotta vessel—swathed in brightly colored orange or red cotton fabric to keep it cool—containing mint and cumin tamarind water. This entire process, from start to finish, takes about 30 seconds, and the poori is set on the customer's tiny paper or leaf plate as they stand in a line each waiting their turn. The whole poori is popped in the mouth, which at once is flooded with lip-smacking, tingling tastes. The explosion of contrasting elements—sweet, spicy, earthy, crunchy, sour, fresh—is unforgettable.

chaats

Chaat literally means "to lick," as in finger-licking food. When I was growing up, what we considered chaat was the equivalent of junk food, even though everything was freshly made and nothing came from a box or a bag. During college, my parents would frown upon my chaat obsession, as I would spend an entire month's allowance on street snacks, like samosa chaat, bhel poori, or pani poori, in just a week and then beg my mother to make these foods at home. They are delicious and the food I craved most after I emigrated from India to Canada. Despite enduring the long journey to India and sometimes arriving in the dead of the night, I would demand that my parents stop at any pani poori stand open on our way home!

Making chaat can be as simple or as elaborate as you desire, but turning chaats into a quick salad by incorporating fresh greens like chopped or torn sturdy romaine, mint leaves, or endive is a delicious way to go. Chaat is always an anything-goes improvisation based on seasonality and availability, so get creative and make your own unique combinations. Once you start, you will come up with so many ways to enjoy each one of the components. Following, I've outlined what I consider the basic elements of chaat, every part building on the others to create an explosion of flavors and a party in your mouth. To make your own chaat, take one component from most of the categories, combine, and enjoy.

Sweet

A touch of sweetness is essential to chaat—something as simple as diced ripe mango or pomegranate seeds. Tamarind Chutney (page 114) is the most common addition to chaat but by no means essential. In a pinch, I have used diced pineapple, roasted apples, grated fresh coconut, sliced papaya, mango, guava, or grilled peaches as delicious chaat salad components.

Spicy

If the components are prepared with the right spices, no added spice is needed. Chaat masala—a mixture of black salt, cumin, chile powder, and other spices—is usually sprinkled on a chaat just before serving to give the dish a final zing, but it is not essential. And chile powder, black pepper, serrano chile, and even smoked chiles can become delicious components of a chaat salad.

Earthy

Lentils, potatoes, tomatoes, and even roasted or pan-seared eggplant are all good bases. Dahi wada, a common street chaat in New Delhi, is simply a cold lentil fritter (made from urad dal), soaked in yogurt, drizzled with tamarind chutney, and topped with herbs. Lentil dumplings are usually fried and delicious simply dusted in chaat spices and/or drizzled with chutneys. Alternatively, chickpeas can be cooked into a stew or sautéed with spices. Sprouted mung lentils can be another delicious element.

Crunchy

The crunch in a chaat can be as simple as potato chips. More traditionally it can come in the form of papdi, which is samosa dough fried into strips or rounds. Store-bought semolina pooris, roasted corn, fried or roasted potatoes, tortilla chips, toasted pita triangles, or sev would work. Sev is a crunchy spiced chickpea noodle available in different thicknesses at Indian grocery stores and online.

Sour

Yogurt tinged with cumin and black salt is the most common sauce on chaats, but a squeeze of lemon or lime juice or a sprinkle of amchur (dried mango powder) or fresh pomegranate seeds will also do the trick.

Fresh

While not traditional to chaats in India, sturdy greens like romaine and endive leaves can be a wonderful addition. Sliced avocado and heirloom tomatoes make a great foil for chaat. Cold roasted chicken pairs beautifully with endive or romaine. Grilled sweet shrimp are a match with cucumbers. Herbs such as basil, cilantro, and mint leaves make for an aromatic finish to most chaats.

The three mother sauces of chaat are tamarind chutney, cumin yogurt, and cilantro chutney, but even just two out of the three can make up a delicious chaat. For the first time, my suggestion would be to make all three sauces and enjoy different chaats over the course of a week. Together these three sauces form the holy trinity that dress a chaat to perfection, but feel free to take it into your hands and improvise.

tamarind chutney

MAKES 3 TO 4 CUPS

One 7-ounce block dried tamarind pulp with seeds

3 cups boiling water

1 cup grated or chopped jaggery, or 1¾ cups cane sugar

1 tablespoon ground ginger

2 teaspoons ground cumin

1 teaspoon red chile powder

1 teaspoon sea salt

1 teaspoon black salt

10 to 12 fresh figs, stemmed and chopped (optional)

Tamarind chutney, a dark, rich, slightly spicy sauce, can be sweetened with sugar, jaggery, or dried fruits like figs, dates, or apricots. I am not a fan of tamarind concentrates and prefer using a block of dried whole tamarind; however, be cautioned that even a packaged block of tamarind with a label claiming it's seedless typically comes with seeds and pulp that will have to be carefully discarded (I describe how to do this in the recipe). This is the most time-consuming of the three sauces but well worth the time, and it keeps in an airtight container in the refrigerator for a month or longer. This chutney also works great as a final drizzle to brighten up grilled vegetables, tofu, and barbecued meats. *(See recipe photo, top left, opposite.)*

Place the tamarind block in a small saucepan and pour the boiling water over it. Set aside for a couple of hours to cool. Using your fingers, break up the tamarind as much as you can. Bring to a boil over high heat. As the water heats, the tamarind block should mix into the water. Cover the pot, decrease the heat to low, and simmer for 20 to 30 minutes. Stir in the jaggery, ginger, cumin, chile powder, sea salt, and black salt. Add another cup or so of water if the mixture starts to get too thick and tar-like. Cover the pot again and simmer for another 15 to 20 minutes, until the jaggery has dissolved. Add the figs and turn off the heat.

Within 5 to 10 minutes of the chutney coming off the stove, using the back of a ladle or a spatula, push it through a large-hole strainer. This requires some effort, as it is easy to leave much of the chutney in the strainer rather than the bowl holding the finished chutney (make sure to not lose the pulp that gathers below the strainer). The chutney should have a pourable consistency (if not, add water) and can be stored in an airtight container in the refrigerator for up to 1 month.

recipe continues

cumin yogurt

MAKES 2 CUPS

2 cups plain whole-milk yogurt
(see page 86)

1 teaspoon toasted ground cumin

1 teaspoon cane sugar

½ teaspoon black salt

When choosing yogurt, it's best to pick a thick Greek yogurt with 4 to 5% milk fat. If using homemade yogurt, which tends to have more liquid, strain the yogurt through a fine-mesh strainer or cheesecloth for a couple of hours to extract the whey. The resulting cumin yogurt should be thick and creamy but with a pourable consistency. Coconut yogurt can be used as a dairy-free option; however, it may need the juice of a lime or lemon to add tanginess. (*See the recipe photo, far right, on page 115.*)

In a small bowl, combine the yogurt, cumin, sugar, and black salt and stir to mix. Cover and store in the refrigerator for up to 2 weeks.

cilantro chutney

MAKES 2 CUPS

2 bunches cilantro

1 small apple (any variety),
cored and sliced

1 serrano chile

½ cup roasted peanuts

1 cup plain thick Greek-style yogurt,
preferably whole-milk

Juice of 1 lemon

1 teaspoon sea salt, or as needed

In my family, we use cilantro chutney as a sandwich spread, a dipping sauce (add more yogurt if you like it creamier), and a marinade. One of my kids' favorite after-school snacks was cheese toast or carrots and cucumbers dipped in cilantro chutney. The chutney is at its brightest in flavor about two hours after it's made, and while it may keep refrigerated in an airtight container for up to 1 week, it's best consumed within 2 to 3 days. For a nut-free version, replace the peanuts with pumpkin seeds or sesame seeds. Because of its cooling properties for the constitution, cilantro is best eaten in the summer. The stems of cilantro have flavor and fiber, so use all but the bottom stringy 1 to 2 inches. (*See the recipe photo, bottom left, on page 115.*)

Rinse the bunches of cilantro under a stream of cold running water, then cut off and discard the bottom 1 to 2 inches of stems. Shake the cilantro bunches to remove excess water and set aside to dry.

Combine the apple, chile, peanuts, yogurt, lemon juice, and salt in a blender. Blend, starting at low speed and slowly increasing the speed to high, until completely smooth. Add the cilantro leaves with stems, ½ bunch at a time, and blend until the mixture is mostly smooth with just a little graininess. Taste and add more salt if needed. Cover and refrigerate until ready to serve.

pomegranate pani poori

At the end of their college terms, I begged my kids to go spend a summer in India to connect with their roots. They would immerse themselves into daily life in India. Consequently, my daughter, Ajna, spent an entire summer in New Delhi. She stayed as a paying guest in a railroad apartment in a hostel smack in the middle of an old part of Delhi. Every day, Ajna would walk by several pani poori vendors on her way back from the nonprofit where she was volunteering, and despite the dire warning from our extended family to not eat any street foods for sanitary reasons, she made pani poori part of her daily repertoire. By the end of the summer, she had a favorite vendor—he knew exactly how she liked her pani, with lots of sweet tamarind chutney. She developed a stomach of steel and a deep appreciation for the culture of India that summer.

Making traditional pani poori water is a labor-intensive overnight process using tamarind and fresh herbs. I find this version using pomegranate juice far simpler and just as satisfying in flavor. The puffs are easily purchased from an Indian grocer. (*See the recipe photo on page 110.*)

To make the pomegranate water: In a medium saucepan, combine the pomegranate juice, mint, sugar, ginger juice, cumin, red chile powder, and black salt and bring to a boil over high heat. Lower the heat and simmer for 2 to 3 minutes, then turn the heat off. All you are looking for is for the sugar to dissolve and the flavors to infuse. Let the water rest for 1 hour. Discard the mint, add the lemon juice, and refrigerate the pomegranate water. This water is best served chilled and will keep for up to 1 month in the refrigerator.

To make the filling: Place the potato in a stockpot and cover with water. Bring to a boil, cover, and simmer for 15 minutes or longer, depending on the size of the potato, until tender. Mash the potato or leave in chunks. Let cool and refrigerate until ready to use.

In a medium bowl, combine the black channa, potato, mint, cilantro, pomegranate seeds, red chile powder, and black salt and stir to mix. Refrigerate until ready to serve.

Puncture a poori with your fingers to make an opening. Place roughly 1 teaspoon of filling inside the poori, pour in enough pomegranate water to fill the poori, and immediately put it inside your mouth. Do not bite into it: commit and pop the whole thing into your mouth. Repeat and enjoy.

MAKES 30 POORIS

POMEGRANATE WATER

3 cups pomegranate juice (I like POM brand)

Generous handful of fresh mint leaves

⅓ cup cane sugar

¼ cup ginger juice (see Note)

1 teaspoon toasted ground cumin

1 teaspoon red chile powder

1 teaspoon black salt

Juice of 2 lemons

FILLING

1 cup chopped potato (from about 1 large russet potato)

½ cup black channa (see page 133)

¼ cup chopped fresh mint leaves

¼ cup chopped fresh cilantro leaves

2 tablespoons fresh pomegranate seeds

1 teaspoon red chile powder

1 teaspoon black salt

30 store-bought pani poori puffs

Note: To make ginger juice, squeeze out the water from Ginger Puree (page 80).

potato cakes

**MAKES 10 TO 12 CAKES
(5 TO 6 APPETIZER SERVINGS)**

⅓ cup plain Greek-style yogurt
(4 to 5% milkfat)

2 green onions, white and green
parts, minced

¼ cup currants or raisins

2 teaspoons fennel seeds, crushed

1 serrano chile, minced

1½ teaspoons sea salt

1 pound (5 to 6 medium) red
or golden potatoes, boiled for
15 minutes or until tender and
chilled overnight

1 tablespoon Ginger Puree (page 80)

1 tablespoon dried fenugreek leaves

1 teaspoon freshly ground
black pepper

1 tablespoon cornstarch, plus more
as needed

2 to 3 cups frying oil (such as rice
bran, sunflower, or peanut oil)

Called "aloo tikkis" in India and often found crisping on the edges of massive skillets at roadside restaurants, these potato cakes can be stuffed with a variety of devastatingly delicious mixtures. They make a great appetizer or a side dish. Some memorable combinations I have tasted include cardamom-scented ground meat, spiced cashews and raisins, lentil herb purees, and eggs (pictured opposite). Here we make a rendition stuffed with yogurt spiced with fennel seeds and currants. To minimize the moisture and for crispy results, it is best to boil the potatoes the day before and use them cold. Red or golden potatoes work better than russets, which tend to have more moisture. To turn these potato cakes into a chaat, simply drizzle them with Cilantro Chutney (page 116) and Tamarind Chutney (page 114) and top with minced cucumber and mango. (*See also the recipe photo, bottom right, on page 115.*)

To make the filling, in a large bowl, combine the yogurt, green onions, currants, fennel seeds, chile, and ½ teaspoons of the salt and stir to mix. Set aside.

Without peeling the potatoes, grate them into a large bowl. If any skin goes into the bowl, leave it there; discard whatever comes off on the grater. Add the ginger puree, fenugreek, black pepper, cornstarch, and remaining 1 teaspoon of salt and mix to incorporate. Make a tiny cake and test-fry to check for firmness and flavor. If the cake falls apart, add about 1 teaspoon cornstarch and test-fry another one.

Press and spread ¼ cup of the potato mixture into the palm of your hand and stuff 1 teaspoon of the yogurt filling in the middle. Close the sides and seal the potato cake into an even round, making sure no part of the filling is peeking out, then set aside on a plate. Repeat with the rest of the cakes. At this point, the potato cakes can be covered and refrigerated for up to 1 day.

Choose a woklike pan or pot and fill it halfway with the frying oil. Heat the oil to 350°F over high heat, then lower the heat and bring it down to 300°F.

Deep-fry the cakes using a slotted metal spatula or spoon for 2 to 3 minutes on each side, until browned and crisp all over. Drain on paper towels and serve warm.

Variation

Egg Koftas: Bring a small stockpot of water with 12 eggs to a boil over high heat. Boil vigorously for 1 minute, then turn the heat off. Let the eggs rest in the hot water for 30 to 45 minutes, then peel them. Coat each egg in 2 tablespoons of the potato cake mixture, packing the egg tightly. Deep-fry for 3 to 4 minutes, then drain on paper towels, slice in half, and serve.

kashmiri kebabs

MAKES 20 SMALL KEBABS

1 pound ground meat, such as beef or lamb

½ cup finely minced red onion, plus 1 large red onion, cut in half and then into thick slices

Generous pinch of saffron

1 teaspoon Kashmiri chile powder

1 teaspoon ground black cardamom seeds

1 teaspoon ground green cardamom seeds

1 tablespoon Minced Garlic (page 80)

1 tablespoon Ginger Puree (page 80), squeezed dry using the back of a spoon

1 serrano chile, minced

1 cup chopped fresh cilantro leaves and stems

2 tablespoons plain whole-milk yogurt (see page 86) or sour cream

2 tablespoons chopped toasted cashews

2 tablespoons currants or raisins

2 teaspoons sea salt

Juice of 1 lemon

Kashmir has always been a utopia for artists, dreamers, and poets. During the seventeenth century, when he first set his eyes on the enthralling landscape of Kashmir, Jahangir, who went on to become one of India's emperors, exclaimed, "If there is a heaven on Earth, it is here, it is here!" Kashmir, a region of unsurpassed beauty surrounded by the snow-covered peaks of the Himalaya mountains, is the northern-most territory of India. Every season brings new vistas, from the heady fragrance of a million flowers growing on trees, shrubs, and creepers during the summer to the pristine white snowy mountaintops in the winter. With a largely Muslim population, Kashmir boasts some of the most deliciously nuanced meat dishes in the country, from kebabs to curries. Cooking chunks of marinated whole or ground meats over an open-flame spit fire has been around for thousands of years. As a matter of fact, it was even part of Aryan Vedic sacrifice. The modern-day kebab, even though it may have originated in the Middle East, has a long history in India. Even today, in neighborhoods with larger Muslim populations, street vendors will grill kebabs on small coal-burning grills. These kebabs can also be turned into burgers, sliders, or meatballs. The black and green cardamom seeds add a smoky sweet flavor to the kebabs.

When choosing meat, pick one with 10 to 15 percent fat or the kebabs may turn out dry.

In a large bowl, using your hands, combine the meat with the minced onion, saffron, chile powder, black cardamom, green cardamom, minced garlic, ginger puree, chile, cilantro, yogurt, cashews, currants, and salt until thoroughly mixed. Cover the bowl and let the meat rest in the refrigerator for at least 2 hours or up to overnight.

Preheat the oven to 400°F.

Spread the sliced onion on the bottom of a baking pan. Shape the meat into 2-inch patties and place them on the pan on top of and around the onion. Bake for 10 to 12 minutes—when clear juices are flowing, the kebabs are cooked through. Alternatively, cook the kebabs on an outdoor grill for 4 to 5 minutes on each side. Let the kebabs rest for 5 to 10 minutes before serving with a squeeze of lemon juice.

Combine

Roll

Fold

Fry

samosas

The samosa originated in the Middle East and made its way to the subcontinent following the central Asian invasions of India. Derived from the Persian word *sanbosag*, at the time *samosa*, *samusa*, or *sambosa* referred to a family of pastries from dumplings to pies native to Africa, Asia, and China. What finally emerged in the sixteenth century was a triangular-shaped pastry filled with ground meats, nuts, and dried fruit that went on to define one of the most popular street foods in India. These days samosas can be stuffed with anything from potato masala to corn to keema (spiced ground meat). To make a samosa chaat, simply drizzle samosas with Tamarind Chutney (page 114) and Cilantro Chutney (page 116).

Over the years, we have done versions filled with sweet potato, vegetable mixes, and goat meat at our restaurants. While they are usually best just out of the fryer, baked samosas are a whole lot less messy and just as delicious. The samosas filled with crabmeat delicately enhanced with ajwain were, hands down, the most popular appetizer at Indika from Day One.

To make the dough: In a large bowl, combine the all-purpose flour, semolina flour, salt, black pepper, and ajwain seeds with your fingers. Pour the yogurt and beaten egg yolk into the flour mixture and mix thoroughly. Add the ghee and 3 to 4 tablespoons water, mix thoroughly, and knead lightly until the dough is soft and pliable. Shape it into a log and wrap in plastic.

Preheat the oven to 425°F and line a baking sheet with parchment paper.

Divide the filling into eight equal portions. Cut the dough into four sections. Roll each section into a ball. On a floured surface, roll each ball out into a roughly ⅛-inch-thin disc 8 to 9 inches in diameter. Repeat with the other three balls. Cut each round in half and dab or brush the entire ½-inch perimeter of the semicircle with water. Place a portion of filling in the center of the half circle. Fold one point of the half circle diagonally over the center of the filling to meet the rounded side and seal in place. Fold the other point over the mound and seal in place. This should result in a roughly triangular pastry with three points. Place the samosa on the prepared baking sheet. Repeat with the rest of the pieces of dough and filling. Brush the egg white lightly over the dough.

Bake the samosas for 15 to 20 minutes, until golden. Alternatvely, deep-fry the samosas in a wok or a saucepan filled with frying oil heated to 325°F.

recipe continues

MAKES 8 SAMOSAS

SAMOSA DOUGH

1½ cups all-purpose flour, plus more for dusting

2 tablespoons semolina flour

1 teaspoon sea salt

1 teaspoon freshly ground black pepper

1 teaspoon ajwain seeds

2 tablespoons plain whole-milk yogurt (see Note on page 86)

1 egg yolk, beaten (see Note)

⅓ cup ghee (see page 77)

2 cups samosa filling (see pages 124 to 125)

1 egg white, beaten (see Note)

Rice bran, sunflower, or peanut oil for frying (optional)

Note: To make the dough plant-based, replace the yogurt and egg with coconut yogurt and replace the ghee with olive oil. This version is best fried but can be also baked; instead of the egg white, brush them generously with oil before baking.

STREET FOODS

123

crabmeat filling

MAKES ENOUGH FOR
8 LARGE SAMOSAS

8 ounces jumbo lump crabmeat

½ cup chopped fresh cilantro
leaves and stems

1 tablespoon sour cream or
plain Greek-style yogurt

½ teaspoon ajwain seeds

1 small serrano chile, minced

½ teaspoon sea salt

1 tablespoon ghee (see page 77)

1 teaspoon black mustard seeds

1 teaspoon Minced Garlic (page 80)

8 to 10 kari leaves, minced

Gently pick through the crabmeat to remove any shell or cartilage. Place it in a medium bowl and mix with the cilantro, sour cream, ajwain seeds, chile, and salt. Set aside.

In a small frying pan, heat the ghee over high heat. Pop the mustard seeds (see page 40), then add the minced garlic and kari leaves. Cook for 2 to 3 seconds, then fold into the crab mixture. Cover and refrigerate for up to 1 day, until you are ready to make samosas.

grilled corn filling

MAKES ENOUGH FOR
8 LARGE SAMOSAS

1½ cups grilled fresh corn kernels
(from 2 small ears of corn)

2 to 3 tablespoons chopped
toasted cashews

1 serrano chile, minced

1 tablespoon chickpea flour

1 tablespoon Ginger Puree (page 80)

1 tablespoon dried fenugreek leaves

1 teaspoon sea salt

2 tablespoons olive oil

1 teaspoon cumin seeds

Pinch of asafetida

10 to 12 chopped kari leaves

Cilantro Chutney (page 116) or
Roasted Cherry Tomato Chutney
(page 227) for serving

In a medium bowl, combine the corn, cashews, chile, chickpea flour, ginger puree, fenugreek leaves, and salt and stir to mix. Set aside.

In a small frying pan, heat the oil over high heat. Pop the cumin seeds (see page 40), then add the asafetida and kari leaves. Cook for 2 to 3 seconds, then fold into the corn mixture. Refrigerate the filling for up to 3 days, until you are ready to make samosas. Serve with cilantro or tomato chutney.

potato herb filling

Cut the potatoes into ½-inch cubes or gently mash them. Place them in a medium bowl and add the green onions, red chile powder, fenugreek leaves, ginger puree, herbs, and salt and stir to mix. Set aside.

In a small frying pan, heat the oil over high heat. Pop the cumin seeds (see page 40), add the kari leaves, and then fold them into the potato mixture. Refrigerate the filling for up to 3 days, until you are ready to make samosas. Serve with tamarind chutney.

MAKES ENOUGH FOR
8 LARGE SAMOSAS

1½ cups roasted or boiled skin-on whole potatoes

2 green onions, white and green parts, minced

1 teaspoon red chile powder

2 tablespoons dried fenugreek leaves

2 tablespoons Ginger Puree (page 80)

1 cup chopped fresh herbs (such as cilantro, basil, oregano, or mint, stems and leaves)

1 teaspoon sea salt

2 tablespoons olive oil

1 teaspoon cumin seeds

15 to 20 kari leaves, chopped

Tamarind Chutney (page 114) for serving

bombay benedict

This version is a clear departure from the classic eggs Benedict, with an explosion of flavors from a tangy bhaji from the streets of Mumbai that may inspire you to abandon its original form. Pav bhaji is a spiced vegetable hash—bhaji served with toasted buns (pav) is one of the most iconic streets foods of Mumbai. It has its origins during the 1860s American Civil War era and is a true mashing of cultures. A huge demand for cotton from India at the time meant textile mill workers were spending late nights and long hours fulfilling orders. Bombay Cotton Exchange traders also had to work late into the night receiving orders via telegrams from the United States. Unable to go home at a decent hour, they needed more substantial meals. Ingenious street vendors would collect leftover breads and rolls from Jesuit churches, mash up an assortment of unsold leftover vegetables, and turn it into a curry of sorts. They would top it with a dollop of butter and herbs and serve it with pan-seared bread.

The bhaji is highly spiced, so do temper to your taste by adding less spice if desired, and it has an ungodly amount of butter. Just like most street foods of India, it is improvised based on season, so feel free to use whatever's growing, like carrots, sweet potato, squash, cauliflower, or brussels sprouts, but be sure to pick one or two that are starchy. Enjoy it with toasted bread or pan-seared dinner rolls. Amul is a lightly processed cheese from India—it is available in Indian grocery stores. You can replace it with an aged cheese, like raclette or Pecorino.

For the pickled mayonnaise, try to find a brand of pickle that is made by an Indian company—Neerav, Deep, Pathak, and Laxmi are all good brands.

To make the Bhaji: In a medium frying pan, heat the ghee over high heat. Pop the crushed coriander, cumin, and fennel seeds (see page 40). Immediately add the onion, vegetables, garlic, turmeric, and salt and cook just until the vegetables take on some color. Lower the heat, cover and cook for 5 to 7 minutes, until the vegetables take on some color, then add 2 cups water and bring the mixture to a boil. Decrease the heat and simmer for another 15 to 20 minutes, until the vegetables are cooked through and soft. If they aren't, using the back of a spoon, mash them up to create a thick yet chunky mixture.

recipe continues

BHAJI

½ cup ghee (see page 77)

1 teaspoon lightly crushed coriander seeds

1 teaspoon lightly crushed cumin seeds

1 teaspoon lightly crushed fennel seeds

1 cup minced white onion

4 cups diced (½-inch) vegetables (see headnote)

10 to 12 garlic cloves, sliced

1 teaspoon ground turmeric

1½ teaspoons sea salt

1 to 2 tablespoons red chile powder

½ teaspoon ground cinnamon

¼ teaspoon ground cloves

½ teaspoon ground black cardamom

2 cups diced fresh tomatoes, or ½ cup canned crushed tomatoes

2 tablespoons Ginger Puree (page 80)

½ cup fresh or frozen green peas

½ bunch cilantro leaves and tender stems, chopped

3 tablespoons grated Amul cheese or a sharp aged cheese

2 to 3 tablespoons melted butter or ghee (see page 77)

1¼ teaspoons sea salt

3 tablespoons distilled vinegar

4 large eggs

½ cup Pickled Mayonnaise (see note)

½ cup heavy cream

Ghee (see page 77) for spreading

4 thick slices brioche or challah bread

Add the red chile powder, cinnamon, cloves, cardamom, tomatoes, and ginger puree to the frying pan and simmer for another 3 to 4 minutes, or until fragrant. Add the peas and cook for another minute or two, or until they are cooked through but still bright green, then turn the heat off. Stir in the cilantro, cheese, and butter. Set aside.

In a medium saucepan, combine 4 cups water with 1 teaspoon of the salt and the vinegar and place over high heat. Crack each egg into small bowls. As soon as the water comes to a boil, drop the eggs in one at a time. Cover and cook for 2 to 3 minutes, until the whites have firmed up but the yolk is still soft, then gently remove the eggs with a slotted spoon and set aside on a plate or in a bowl.

In a small saucepan, combine the pickled mayonnaise with the heavy cream and the remaining ¼ teaspoon salt and heat over medium-low heat. Do not let it boil or bubble.

Heat a large frying pan over high heat. Spread ghee on both sides of the brioche and pan-sear until crisp and browned on both sides. Spoon ½ cup bhaji on each toast. Top with a poached egg and drizzle the pickled mayo sauce over it. Serve immediately.

Variation

Plant-Based Pav Bhaji: Skip the eggs and mayo and replace the ghee with coconut oil and use olive oil for the finishing touch. Leave out the cheese or replace it with chopped toasted almonds or cashews.

Note: For a shortcut, pickled mayonnaise stir together ½ cup store-bought mayonnaise with 1 teaspoon minced Indian pickle (mango, lemon, or mixed). In the bowl of a food processor or with a hand mixer, combine one whole egg and one egg yolk with the juice of one lemon and 1 tablespoon Indian pickle. Mix until smooth, then add 1 cup sesame, avocado, or peanut oil in a slow steady stream until the whole mixture congeals into a light-colored mass. Stir in 2 tablespoons thick Greek-style yogurt. This makes 1½ cups of mayonnaise and it will keep for 5 days in the refrigerator.

uppma

The first time I tasted the creamy deliciousness of Southern corn grits on a nondescript suburban American hotel breakfast buffet, my mind flashed with visions of how a pop of mustard seeds, a crackle of fried kari leaf, and a drizzle of jaggery and lemon would have added flavorful touches to my breakfast. Grits were introduced by Native Americans in the sixteenth century using stone-ground corn or hominy and are now a staple in many parts of the country. Grain or vegetable mashes are common in many ancient cultures, from the African fufu made with plantain and cassava flours to uppma, an aromatic toasted semolina vegetable hash from southern India.

Uppma can be made from corn or rice grits, semolina, or polenta and is a great vehicle for leftover vegetables. If using heritage grits that are larger, they may need more water and more cooking time. Regardless of what you use as a base, uppma should be soft, cooked through, and not gritty or crunchy. For the pop, use any split, not whole, lentils you have on hand. Split peas, or mung, masoor, or urad dal will work fine. For a plant-based and just as delicious version, use coconut oil as the cooking fat and replace the yogurt with water. (*See the recipe photo, bottom left, on page 198.*)

In a large saucepan, heat the oil over high heat. Add the lentils and pop the mustard seeds (see page 40) with them. The lentils will darken slightly. Immediately add the kari leaves and asafetida, followed by the diced vegetables and chile. Cook, stirring frequently, for 5 to 7 minutes, until the vegetables have wilted and have a slight char or color. Add the turmeric, salt, ginger puree, yogurt, and 2½ cups water. Bring the mixture to a boil, then lower the heat and simmer for 4 to 5 minutes, until the vegetables are cooked through.

Slowly, in a steady stream, add the grits to the saucepan, stirring constantly to prevent lumps. Cover and let simmer until almost all the liquid has been absorbed, 4 to 5 minutes. Stir in the peanuts, then let the uppma rest for 10 to 15 minutes to thicken and firm up. Garnish with lemon juice, fresh herbs, and a drizzle of ghee, if desired, then serve.

SERVES 4

¼ cup peanut oil or light sesame oil

2 teaspoons raw split lentils (see headnote)

1 teaspoon black mustard seeds

10 to 12 kari leaves

Pinch of asafetida

2 cups diced (½-inch) vegetables (such as squash, bell peppers, or cauliflower) or whole peas

1 serrano chile, minced

½ teaspoon ground turmeric

1½ teaspoons sea salt

2 tablespoons Ginger Puree (page 80)

½ cup plain whole-milk yogurt (see page 86)

1 cup corn grits or rice grits

½ cup roasted peanuts, chopped

Juice of ½ lemon

Handful of fresh herbs (such as cilantro or mint)

2 to 3 tablespoons ghee (see page 77; optional)

sindhi pakoras

SERVES 4 TO 6

2 to 3 cups frying oil (peanut, sunflower, or rice bran)

2 cups diced (½-inch) or grated starchy vegetables (such as potato, carrot, or turnip)

½ cup minced or sliced white onion

2 cups chopped greens (such as spinach or kale)

1 cup loosely packed chopped fresh herbs (such as cilantro, mint, basil, or parsley)

2 cups chickpea flour

2 tablespoons Ginger Puree (see page 80)

½ cup plain whole-milk yogurt (see page 86) or water

1 teaspoon ground turmeric

1 teaspoon red chile powder

1 teaspoon ajwain seeds

1 teaspoon freshly ground black pepper

1 teaspoon lightly crushed coriander seeds

2 teaspoons sea salt

Scant pinch of baking soda

Chutney or Cumin Yogurt (page 116) for serving

Pakora, the original fritter of India, is made with spiced chickpea flour and vegetables and goes by other names such as pikora, bhajiya, and bhaji. While there are street vendors selling pakoras, they are quick and easy to make, so they are also commonly made at home. You can use any vegetables, from kale to corn to potatoes or zucchini. Sindhi pakoras are rustic fritters made with finely chopped seasonal vegetables and are fried twice for extra crispiness. They can be made ahead of time and fried the second time just before serving.

Choose a woklike pan or pot and fill it halfway with the frying oil. Warm the oil over high heat to 350°F as tested on a candy thermometer, then lower the heat to bring the oil down to 300°F until the pakoras are ready to be fried.

Combine the starchy vegetables, onion, greens, and herbs in a large bowl. Add the chickpea flour, ginger puree, yogurt, turmeric, red chile powder, ajwain seeds, black pepper, coriander seeds, salt, baking soda, and ½ to 1 cup water, and, with your fingers, mix until evenly distributed and the mixture is thick and batterlike.

Test the frying oil by dropping in a little batter; if it immediately rises and sizzles in the oil, it is hot enough. Drop 1 tablespoon of the batter into the oil. Repeat, frying six to eight pakoras at a time (no more, so the oil maintains its temperature), until all sides are golden brown in color. At this point, they just need to set; they don't need to cook all the way, as they will be fried again. Using tongs or a slotted metal spoon, remove and drain the pakoras on paper towels. Repeat with the remaining batter. At this point, the pakoras can be set aside until ready to serve.

Break each pakora in half with your fingers. Fry the pakoras again in small batches until crisp and then serve with your favorite chutney or cumin yogurt.

Combine

Batter

First fry

Second fry

black channa salad

Often called kala channa, black chickpeas are the smaller, darker, and more intensely flavored cousins of the larger tan ones. They are firmer in texture and not as easy to puree as tan chickpeas. However, they make a great addition to a soup, salad, pilaf, or stir-fry and are high in fiber, protein, and iron. If you can't find these at your local Indian grocer, you can find them online. California heirloom-bean company Rancho Gordo grows a variety they call desi channa. I would suggest doubling the recipe and keeping half the chickpeas aside to make Corn Mint Chaat Salad (page 134) or Chicken Chaat Salad (page 134) or to create your own chaat combinations. (*See bottom left of facing photo.*)

Put the channa in a medium bowl and cover with cold tap water by 6 to 8 inches. Soak the mixture overnight. The next day, discard the soaking water and put the channa in a medium saucepan. Add 4 cups fresh water and bring to a boil over high heat. Pour out the first water to remove the foam and impurities—if necessary, use a large strainer or colander. Add another 4 cups water, bring to a simmer, then decrease the heat to low, cover, and simmer for 1 to 1½ hours, adding more water if needed (until the channa are tender or squishy when you press into them). There should always be enough water to submerge the channa. Turn the heat off and let the channa rest in the liquid for 20 to 30 minutes, then drain.

Heat the oil in a large frying pan over high heat and pop the cumin seeds (see page 40). Immediately add the asafetida, followed by the channa, black pepper, and black salt. Continue cooking until the masala evenly coats the channa. Take the pan off the heat, then stir in the amchur. Let the channa cool for 15 to 20 minutes. Toss with or serve alongside the cucumbers, cubed mango, and cilantro and finish with a drizzle of lemon juice.

SERVES 4

1 cup dried black channa

3 tablespoons olive oil

1 teaspoon cumin seeds

Pinch of asafetida (optional)

1 teaspoon freshly ground black pepper

1 teaspoon black salt

2 tablespoons amchur (dried mango powder)

4 to 5 Persian cucumbers, cubed

1 large mango, cubed

1 bunch cilantro, leaves and stems chopped (bottom 3 inches of stems discarded)

Juice of 1 lemon

corn mint chaat salad

SERVES 4

4 ears corn, shucked

½ teaspoon black salt

½ teaspoon red chile powder

Juice of 1 lemon

1 bunch baby romaine leaves or hearts

½ cup black channa (see headnote, page 133)

1 cup loosely packed fresh mint leaves

1 cup sev (or potato chips or tortilla chips)

1½ cups Cumin Yogurt (page 116)

1 cup Cilantro Chutney (page 116)

½ cup Tamarind Chutney (page 114)

Corn was not a common vegetable when I was growing up in India, so we seldom cooked it at home. My favorite memory of eating corn was on street corners, when vendors would roast cobs on tiny stoves, fan them with thick dried leaves, and rub them with chile powder, salt, and lemon juice. The best time to make this chaat is smack in the middle of summer when sweet corn starts showing up at farmers' markets. Here is a take on corn mint chaat that is relatively easy to execute at home. (*See the recipe photo, top, on page 132.*)

Grill the corn directly over a medium flame on your stove top, rotating every few minutes until most of the kernels have an even char. Alternatively, roast the corn in a preheated 350°F for 20 to 30 minutes, turning a few times. Using a knife, cut the kernels off the cobs into a medium bowl and toss with the black salt, red chile powder, and lemon juice.

Spread the romaine leaves over a serving plate or individual plates. Top with the black channa, grilled corn, and mint leaves and then alternate the sev with drizzles of cumin yogurt, cilantro chutney, and tamarind chutney. Enjoy immediately.

chicken chaat salad

SERVES 4

Leaves from 1 head romaine lettuce or 2 heads Belgian or curly endive

2 black pepper roasted chicken breasts (see page 50), chilled and sliced into strips

1 cup papdi

1 cup black channa (see headnote, page 133)

1 ripe but firm mango, peeled and cut into long, thin strips

1 cup Cumin Yogurt (page 116)

½ cup Cilantro Chutney (page 116)

½ cup Tamarind Chutney (page 114)

Pinch of red chile powder

Pinch of ground cumin

Back in 2001, we opened Indika with this salad, and it was an instant success. To satisfy my chaat cravings, I ate it for lunch for three weeks straight. The sweet, spicy, tangy flavors paired with greens made it a satisfying, substantial salad. We served it at Pondicheri in New York City; our landlord would come in for it regularly and declared it the best chicken salad in the city. Feel free to replace the papdi with potato chips or tortilla chips or leave it out entirely. For a vegetarian version, replace the chicken with avocado. (*See the recipe photo, far right, on page 132.*)

On a shallow bowl or platter, layer the romaine leaves with the chicken, papdi, black channa, and mango, alternately drizzling with the cumin yogurt, cilantro chutney, and tamarind chutney. Finish with the red chile powder and cumin and enjoy immediately.

cauliflower manchurian

I could not have a chapter on street foods without mentioning the influence of the Chinese community in India. Centuries ago, a few thousand Chinese immigrants migrated to Kolkata, which now boasts a large and possibly the only Chinatown in India. Over time, a new cuisine emerged in Kolkata using Chinese seasoning and cooking techniques combined with fragrant Indian spices. It offered denizens a larger variety of dishes, particularly for vegetarians. Today, Chinese Indian cuisine is an integral part of the food scene all over India, from restaurants to street vendors, and the relationship gives locals and diners a reminder of the rich history between two ancient cuisines. Manchuria is a region of northwest China, and cauliflower Manchurian, a mash-up devised by creative cooks, is as addictive as it is delicious. Be prepared to fall in love with the Manchurian masala—it's good on almost everything. It was one of the mainstays of my parenting days: not only is it one of my guilty pleasures, but I could also get my kids to eat all kinds of vegetables paired with it. The Maggi hot and sweet ketchup brand is a fixture in my refrigerator; use it in place of regular ketchup. You will find it online and in Indian grocery stores.

To roast the cauliflower: Preheat the oven to 400°F. Cut the cauliflower into florets, place in a large bowl, and toss with the salt, black pepper, ground ginger, and sesame oil. Spread on a baking sheet and roast for 15 to 20 minutes, until the florets hold their shape and are not soft or cooked through when you test one with a knife.

To make the Manchurian masala: In a small saucepan, combine the orange juice, soy sauce, sambal oelek, mirin, ketchup, and garam masala; stir to combine; and bring to a boil over medium heat. Lower the heat and whisk in the cornstarch slurry. Simmer for a minute or two, until thickened, then turn the heat off.

To fry: In a wok or a shallow stockpan, heat the frying oil to 350°F.

In a small bowl, combine the chickpea flour, rice flour, cornstarch, turmeric, and salt. Stir in ½ to 1 cup water to make a smooth batter; add more water if needed. Dip the cooked cauliflower florets in the batter, then drop them into the hot oil. Cook until crispy and browned on all sides, 3 to 4 minutes total. Drain on paper towels and repeat with the rest of the florets. Pour the Manchurian masala over the florets, stir to combine, and serve immediately.

SERVES 4

ROASTED CAULIFLOWER

1 small head cauliflower

1 teaspoon sea salt

1 teaspoon freshly ground black pepper

1 tablespoon ground ginger

¼ cup light sesame oil or peanut oil

MANCHURIAN MASALA

½ cup fresh orange juice with pulp

¼ cup soy sauce or tamari

¼ cup sambal oelek (Indonesian chile sauce)

½ cup mirin or rice vinegar

½ cup hot and sweet ketchup (or regular ketchup)

½ teaspoon garam masala (see page 69)

2 tablespoons cornstarch dissolved in ¼ cup water to form a slurry

FOR FRYING

2 cups frying oil (sunflower, peanut, or rice bran oil)

½ cup chickpea flour

½ cup rice flour

½ cup cornstarch

1 teaspoon ground turmeric

1 teaspoon sea salt

masala popcorn

SERVES 4

½ cup popcorn kernels

3 tablespoons mustard oil

1 teaspoon sea salt

½ teaspoon ground turmeric

1 tablespoon confectioners' sugar

½ teaspoon red chile powder

1 tablespoon amchur
(dried mango powder)

2 to 3 tablespoons melted butter
or ghee (see page 77) for finishing

Popcorn is just as popular in movie theaters in India as it is in other parts of the world—the only difference being that it is coated in a masala. The masala may be as simple as turmeric, red chile powder, and salt, or for more interest, amchur and a touch of sweet. Popcorn is not only a great canvas for spices, but it also reflects the flavor of the fat beautifully. For a nutty sweet finish, instead of mustard oil, try using coconut oil to pop the kernels. For an entirely plant-based version, use coconut oil or olive oil as a finishing oil.

Combine the popcorn kernels, mustard oil, salt, and turmeric in a deep pot or Dutch oven with a tight-fitting lid over medium heat. Stir the kernels constantly until the first one pops. Immediately cover and cook. Once the popping sound begins, lower the heat, and once the sound of popping has subsided, turn the heat off. This whole process will take less than 5 minutes. Immediately stir in the sugar, red chile powder, amchur, and melted butter and serve.

Vegetables

"If the diet is pure, the mind will be pure. If the mind is pure, the intellect will be pure," said an ancient Vedic seer. Purity of mind and spirit is a cardinal Indian virtue, ranking in importance with self-control, detachment, and nonviolence. For many millions of Indians, the purity of mind and body demands a diet of rigid vegetarianism. What's beautiful about vegetarians in India is they are not trying to make a meatless meal look or taste like meat. For vegetarians, the meal should be manifestly and triumphantly vegetarian: hearty, appetizing, nutritionally well-balanced, and satisfying with a flair of its own. The reverence for life, fundamental to the whole concept of vegetarianism, applies to all aspects of life. This is why you'll find pigeons or monkeys on rooftops, squirrels in trees, and cows on the streets coexisting with humans.

Salads may seem ordinary to most people, but I had never laid eyes on lettuce until I arrived in North America. While vegetables and legumes were the mainstay of our meals in India, if there was anything raw on our dinner table, it was chopped cabbage or onions with a squeeze of lime. My first experience with a salad was a memorable one: cold and crisp lettuce lightly coated in an olive oil–lemon vinaigrette, topped with crumbled goat cheese and crunchy nuts. Over the years, I have infused salad dressings with every imaginable spice pop, and I've added minced mango chutney, lime pickle, garlic pickle, and such to dressings to brighten their flavors. The one thing I aim to have made in my refrigerator is salad dressing. I know if there is dressing made, I am more likely to eat a salad than if not. The simplest dressing for me is equal parts olive oil with popped cumin seeds, lemon juice, salt, and pepper.

SERVES 4

2 cups cherries (any variety), pitted and cut into half

1 cup Roasted Cherry Tomato Chutney (page 227)

Juice of 1 lemon

½ teaspoon sea salt

1 small head radicchio leaves, torn

1 cup loosely packed fresh mint leaves

¼ cup toasted whole cashews

This salad is best made at the height of the short cherry season, when the fruit is filled with ripe sweet flavor and pairs beautifully with tart cherry tomatoes. The radicchio adds a refreshing yet slightly bitter element to the salad.

In a large bowl, toss the cherries with the cherry tomato chutney, lemon juice, and salt. Just before serving, gently toss with the radicchio, mint leaves, and cashews.

pondicheri salad

SERVES 6

PICKLED CARROTS

1 pound (6 or 7 medium) carrots, sliced into thin wheels

2 tablespoons mustard oil

1 teaspoon crushed cumin seeds

½ teaspoon red chile powder

1 teaspoon sea salt

Juice of 2 lemons

JAGGERY DRESSING

2 tablespoons store-bought spicy lime or mango pickle

2 tablespoons jaggery

2 tablespoons Ginger Puree (page 80)

¼ cup fresh lemon juice

¼ cup extra-virgin olive oil

½ teaspoon black salt

10 cups local heirloom greens (see headnote)

1 cup sprouted mung beans (see page 174)

¼ cup toasted pumpkin seeds

¼ cup toasted sunflower seeds

¼ cup currants

This classic namesake is a nourishing yet light salad that has been on the menu for the entire life of the restaurant. We have regular customers who eat a version of it every single day. The addition of pickled carrots and sprouted mung makes it substantial enough to turn into a meal on its own. Additional toppings may include sliced avocado, grilled mushrooms, roasted chicken, and shrimp. It's best to pick a variety of seasonal greens, like arugula, baby lettuces, dandelion, endive, and carrot greens, all of which complement the lip-smacking delicious jaggery dressing with its dash of black salt. The mustard oil in the pickled carrots can be easily substituted with olive oil; just add 1 teaspoon ground mustard seeds to the pickle masala. (*See the recipe photo, bottom left, on page 138.*)

To make the pickled carrots: Put the carrots in a medium bowl. In a small frying pan, heat the mustard oil over high heat and pop the cumin seeds (see page 40). Turn the heat off and add the red chile powder, salt, and lemon juice. Pour over the carrots and let them marinate for a few minutes. The pickled carrots will keep, covered, in the refrigerator for up to 1 week.

To make the dressing: Mince the pickle (including both the masala mixture and fruit) into almost a puree. Place in a bowl and add the jaggery, ginger puree, lemon juice, olive oil, and black salt. Cover and refrigerate until ready to use. The dressing will keep in the refrigerator for up to 1 month.

In a serving bowl, toss the greens with the pickled carrots (leaving the juice behind), sprouted mung beans, pumpkin seeds, sunflower seeds, and currants. Toss with ½ cup of the dressing and serve.

mango tomato avocado salad

This salad is a celebration of early summer where I live. Surrounding farms start putting out beautiful juicy heirloom tomatoes on farm-stand tables and markets. The Ataulfo mangoes from Mexico start to come in droves. A few summers ago, when I spent a length of time with an olive oil aficionado and began to understand how to taste and appreciate good olive oil, this salad emerged as a favorite. I ate it at least a few times a week all summer long. When the tomatoes were gone, I replaced them with radishes. *(See the recipe photo, top, on page 138.)*

Slice the tomatoes into half, then cut them into angular wedges. Peel the mangoes, cut them in half, and then cut them into angular wedges. Repeat with the avocado. Spread all three on a large serving plate or four individual plates. Sprinkle with the salt.

Heat the plain olive oil in a small frying pan and pop the mustard seeds (see page 40), then add the kari leaves and cook for a couple of seconds. Immediately add the chile and turn the heat off. Drizzle this oil over the salad. Squeeze the juice from the lemon over the salad and drizzle with extra-virgin olive oil. Garnish with fresh herbs and serve immediately.

SERVES 4

2 medium ripe heirloom tomatoes

2 large mangoes

1 large avocado

Generous pinch of sea salt

1 tablespoon olive oil

½ teaspoon black mustard seeds

10 to 12 whole kari leaves

½ to 1 small serrano chile, minced

1 lemon

Extra-virgin olive oil for serving

Fresh herbs (such as cilantro, basil, or mint) for garnish

brussels blueberry salad

Native to the Mediterranean and part of the brassica family of plants, brussels sprouts gained huge popularity in Belgium, thereby earning their name. These tiny cabbages, in many ways, may be the perfect vegetable. They are filled with precious phytochemicals and chlorophyll, the light-absorbing miracle molecule that contributes to healthy, glowing skin. They provide detoxifying enzymes for our bloodstreams, reduce oxidative stress, and stimulate our immune systems to reduce the risk of cancer. Brussels sprouts are high in fiber, antioxidants, vitamins, and minerals, but most important, they taste wonderful. They are simple to prepare, whether raw, roasted, or seared, but the key is not to overcook them. Like most plants in the brassica family, they are best tempered with gas-preventing spices like ajwain and ginger. A few blueberries add a touch of sweetness to round out the flavor of this dish. *(See the recipe photo, bottom left, opposite.)*

Trim the brussels sprouts and cut them into halves or quarters depending on their size.

Heat the oil in a large frying pan over high heat and pop the mustard seeds (see page 40). Add the kari leaves and asafetida and cook for a couple seconds, then immediately add the brussels sprouts, salt, and black pepper. Cook for 3 to 4 minutes, stirring constantly so they get partially cooked and slightly seared but stay bright green and crunchy. Add the chile, ajwain seeds, ginger puree, blueberries, pumpkin seeds, and lemon juice and turn the heat off. Stir to combine and let the salad rest for 30 to 45 minutes. Serve at room temperature.

SERVES 4

1 pound brussels sprouts

¼ cup olive oil

1 teaspoon black mustard seeds

10 to 12 kari leaves

Pinch of asafetida

1 teaspoon sea salt

1 teaspoon freshly ground black pepper

1 serrano chile, minced

1 teaspoon ajwain seeds

1 tablespoon Ginger Puree (page 80)

½ cup fresh blueberries

½ cup toasted pumpkin seeds

Juice of 1 lemon

jain cabbage salad

SERVES 4

3 tablespoons light sesame oil

1 teaspoon black mustard seeds

Pinch of asafetida

8 to 10 kari leaves, chopped

1 small head purple cabbage

1 serrano chile, sliced

Juice of 1 lemon

2 tablespoons chopped fresh mint leaves

1 cup chopped roasted peanuts

1 teaspoon sea salt

Jain cuisine is one of the most austere in the world. Originating between the fifth and seventh centuries BCE, the motto of Jainism is that every single living being has a soul and the purpose of souls is to help one another. Meat is condemned by the Jains because it heightens passions and encourages the virile, animal side of human nature, and vegetarianism is followed because of its light, nutritious, and easily digestible nature. This diet enables the body to channel energy, that would have otherwise been used to digest meat, into the improvement of the mind. Jains practice ahimsa (nonviolence), and that translates to the orthodox Jains not eating anything that grows below soil, like a carrot, because uprooting it would kill the plant. More liberal Jains will drink milk only from happy cows producing excess milk. I grew up in Gujarat with a large population of Jains and would watch them in fascinated awe as they carefully walked around with socks only, no shoes. This was to not harm even an invisible bug or a fly, and they'd carry a broom ahead of them to gently sweep aside something they could not step over. This cabbage salad can be served warm, room temperature, or cold. (*See the recipe photo, far right, on page 144.*)

Heat the oil in a large frying pan over high heat. Pop the mustard seeds (see page 40), then add the asafetida and kari leaves and cook for a couple of seconds. Immediately add the cabbage and chile. Cook until the cabbage is just wilted, 2 to 3 minutes. Turn the heat off and transfer the cabbage to a bowl. Stir in the lemon juice, mint leaves, peanuts, and salt and serve.

simple braised okra

Many years ago, a Bengali friend prepared okra for me that has remained a singular memory. She seasoned it with crushed fennel seeds, a touch of chile powder, and salt. I adapted that idea, called it Braised Okra, and placed it on my menu at Indika. It went on to become one of our most popular side dishes. A year later, when it returned to the menu in the summer, I renamed it Okra Braised with Fennel. There was an uproar from our customers, and the same folks who had been enjoying it obsessively now refused to order it, claiming they did not like fennel. It took some convincing on the part of my service team to explain to them that it was the same preparation. This is as simple as a dish gets—the only things to be aware of is that okra takes in a lot of oil, practically drinks it, and you want to avoid overcooking it so it retains its bright green color. When buying okra, do the snap test: Snap the bottom tips, and if they snap in two, the okra is fresh and young. If the tips bend, the okra will not be tender. (*See the recipe photo, top left, on page 144.*)

Halve the okra lengthwise into diagonal rounds, leaving the tops intact.

Heat the oil in a heavy-bottom saucepan over high heat and pop the fennel seeds (see page 40). Immediately add the okra and salt and cook for 2 to 3 minutes, or until it turns bright green, then lower the heat to medium. Do not stir the okra too often, or it will turn slimy, and do not cook it for too long. If the okra appears dry, add another tablespoon or two of oil. As soon as the okra has turned a slightly brighter green, turn the heat off. Stir in the red chile powder and amchur and serve.

SERVES 4

1 pound tender okra

¼ cup olive oil, plus more as needed

1 teaspoon fennel seeds

1 teaspoon sea salt

½ teaspoon red chile powder

1 teaspoon amchur
(dried mango powder)

cactus curry

In his brilliant book *In Light of India*, Nobel Prize–winning author Octavio Paz, who for many years was the Mexican ambassador to India, talks about the undeniable similarity between mole and a curry, the combination of sweet and spicy, the reddish color full of sumptuous reflections and its accompaniment to a meat or vegetable. Mole, which comes from *muli*, meaning "sauce" in Nahuatl, is a rich sauce made from chiles, nuts, and spices.

Nopal cactus, also known as prickly pear cactus, is native to the southwest United States and Mexico. You can find it in Mexican grocery stores. The Mayo Clinic extols the virtues of nopales and comes short of calling them a superfood. They are antiviral and anti-inflammatory, very high in fiber, and used to treat diabetes. They have a light, tart flavor and a mucilaginous texture, which can be reduced by washing away the surface residue after boiling them. The acid in the tomato masala makes the sliminess around the nopales diminish considerably and the chickpea roux gives the curry a delicious base. This mole-like curry is wonderful with simple boiled white rice or rice tossed with seasonal greens.

Trim the prickly parts of the cactus by scraping them off with a knife. Cut the paddles into 2-inch cubes and place in a large saucepan. Add the turmeric, 1 teaspoon of the salt, and roughly 4 cups of water and bring to a boil over high heat. Lower the heat, cover, and simmer for 20 minutes, then turn the heat off. The cactus should be limp with a dark greenish color. Let the pot of water and cactus rest for 20 to 30 minutes, then drain. Rinse the cactus under running water to remove most of the slime on the surface.

Meanwhile, heat the ghee in a large Dutch oven or stockpot over high heat and pop the cumin seeds and cardamom pods (see page 40), then add the kari leaves and cook for a couple of seconds. Add the sweet potato. Decrease the heat to medium-high and cook for 4 to 5 minutes, or until it has darkened a little bit in color, stirring frequently, then stir in the crushed tomatoes, cashews, caramelized onion puree, chickpea flour, red chile powder, garlic, cactus, and remaining 1 teaspoon salt. Cover, decrease the heat to low, and cook for another 5 to 7 minutes, or until the mixture has darkened a little bit. Increase the heat to high, add 2 cups water, and bring the mixture to a boil. Decrease the heat to low again, cover, and simmer for 10 to 15 minutes, until the sweet potato is soft yet holds its shape. Stir in the garam masala, drizzle with extra-virgin olive oil, if desired, garnish with herbs, and serve.

SERVES 4

4 or 5 whole nopal cactus paddles

Pinch of ground turmeric

2 teaspoons sea salt

¼ cup ghee (see page 77)

1 teaspoon cumin seeds

6 to 8 green cardamom pods

10 to 15 kari leaves, chopped

1 small sweet potato, cut into 1-inch cubes

One 14-ounce can crushed tomatoes

½ cup whole raw cashews

¼ cup Caramelized Onion Puree (page 82)

2 tablespoons chickpea flour

1 tablespoon red chile powder

1 teaspoon Minced Garlic (page 80)

1 teaspoon garam masala (see page 69)

Extra virgin olive oil for finishing (optional)

Chopped fresh herbs (such as cilantro, mint, or basil) for garnish

jackfruit masala

One 2-pound whole jackfruit (or a section of a larger jackfruit—to yield 8 cups jackfruit pulp)

½ cup ghee (see page 77)

1 tablespoon black peppercorns, lightly crushed

1 tablespoon cumin seeds, lightly crushed

1 tablespoon coriander seeds, lightly crushed

1 teaspoon green cardamom seeds, lightly crushed

4 cups minced yellow or white onions

40 to 50 kari leaves

15 to 20 garlic cloves, peeled

1 tablespoon sea salt

1 tablespoon red chile powder

One 14-ounce can crushed tomatoes

1 cup plain whole-milk yogurt (see page 86)

2 teaspoons garam masala (see page 69)

Fresh whole herbs (such as cilantro or mint) for garnish

The national fruit of Sri Lanka and the official fruit of the southern Indian states of Kerala and Tamil Nadu, jackfruit is known as "kathal" in Hindi, derived from Sanskrit, meaning "the fruit of a thorn." Its sweet flavor resembles banana and pineapple. The first time I made jackfruit at Pondicheri, I invited the servers to taste it with me, and one, a native of Mexico, exclaimed "Oh, you made barbacoa!" When made with ghee, it can fool the best of us into thinking they are eating meat. A soaring international demand made India the world's biggest grower and exporter of jackfruit. The weight of an average jackfruit is around five pounds, so look for the smallest one you can find. Do not discard the seeds, as they also have tremendous flavor. Freeze the left-over pulp and seeds for another use or just double the recipe and freeze the masala for a later use. When picking a jackfruit, a fresh bright-green ripe one will have yellow sweet fruit pulp, while older ones may have tougher pulp. Feel free to substitute frozen jackfruit.

Peel the jackfruit and cut it in half. Remove the seeds—they may pop out easily, and if the coating around them appears slightly tough, discard the shell. Save the seeds for another use.

Heat the ghee in a large stockpot over high heat and pop the black pepper-corns, cumin seeds, and coriander seeds (see page 40). Immediately add the onions, kari leaves, garlic, and jackfruit (pulp). Cover, decrease the heat to low, and simmer for 45 minutes to 1 hour, stirring every 10 to 12 minutes. The onions will reduce and caramelize and the jackfruit will soften. Taste the jackfruit; if it is still tough, add 1 cup water and continue cooking, covered, for another 30 minutes.

Stir in the red chile powder and tomatoes and cook for 2 to 3 minutes, or until the fat has risen to the top, then add the yogurt. Bring to a simmer and cook for another 10 to 12 minutes, or until cooked through. Then sprinkle with the garam masala and turn the heat off. Let the jackfruit rest for an hour or two, garnish with herbs, and serve.

Variation

Jackfruit Biryani: Keep the jackfruit masala in a separate large saucepan. Rinse 1½ cups basmati rice in a large pot and soak in water to cover by a couple of inches for 2 to 3 hours. Drain. Add 3 cups water, ½ teaspoon ground turmeric, ¼ cup ghee, and 2 teaspoons sea salt and bring to a boil over high heat. Cover, decrease the heat to low, and simmer for 10 minutes, then turn the heat off. Meanwhile, warm up the jackfruit and immediately spoon the rice on top. Garnish with cashews, raisins, and/or pistachios and let the mixture rest for 10 to 12 minutes. Fold gently and serve.

punjabi cauliflower

Despite being one of the smaller northern states of India, with half of its original territory now belonging to Pakistan, Punjab, the land of rich buttery flavors with a bespoke love for dairy is one the most densely populated regions in the country. From its strategic position on the legendary Silk Route, Punjab became a thriving hub of not just gorgeous textiles but bountiful harvests of wheat, millet, barley, maize, sugarcane, greens, and plenty of dairy, which are the staples of the state from Vedic times. As a result of heavy influences from the ancient Indus Valley civilization, Punjab has arguably had one of the most significant contributions to the modern cuisine of India. Punjab may have been India's pride at one time, but it was also the envy of its neighbors, judging from the invasions that bore their brunt over the centuries.

Today, the food of Punjab is a mélange of Indo-Persian-Afghani-Turkish norms. From the Afghans came the tandoor, which became an integral part of the diet for making everything from breads to grilled meats. The Punjabis incorporated fresh and dried fruits and exotic nuts, such as apricots, pistachios, and pine nuts that came from Persia, into aromatic slow-cooked stews and roasts. They like their foods deeply flavorful with plenty of spices, chiles, herbs, and large doses of ghee. Feel free to substitute olive oil or light sesame oil for the ghee to make a plant-based version.

Cut the entire cauliflower, including the stem, into 2-inch florets and pieces. Very finely chop the green jacket/stem parts and set aside separately. The only inedible part of the cauliflower is the core, which will need to be discarded.

In a shallow sauté pan, heat the ghee over high heat. Pop the mustard seeds (see page 40), then immediately add the onion and minced cauliflower greens. Lower the heat to medium-high and cook until the onion is translucent or just lightly browned, 8 to 10 minutes, then stir in the minced garlic, cauliflower florets, turmeric, and salt. Increase the heat to high again and cook for another 7 to 8 minutes, until the cauliflower sweats and then begins to take on some color.

Add the red chile powder, tomatoes, and ginger puree and bring to a simmer. Then decrease the heat to low, cover, and cook for 5 to 7 minutes, until the cauliflower is fork-tender and cooked through. Sprinkle the garam masala on top, turn the heat off, and let rest. Gently mix the cauliflower, garnish with cilantro, and serve.

SERVES 4

1 medium cauliflower with its leaves

⅓ cup ghee (see page 77)

1 teaspoon black mustard seeds

1 cup minced white onion

1 teaspoon Minced Garlic (page 80)

½ teaspoon ground turmeric

1½ teaspoons sea salt

1 teaspoon red chile powder

1 cup canned crushed tomatoes, or 2 cups diced fresh tomatoes

2 tablespoons Ginger Puree (page 80)

1 teaspoon garam masala (see page 69)

Chopped fresh cilantro leaves for garnish

paneer korma

SERVES 4 TO 6

1½ pounds paneer (see page 84), cut into 2 by ½-inch wedges

½ cup ghee (see page 77)

½ cup thick Greek-style plain yogurt

1 teaspoon black cumin seeds, lightly crushed

1 teaspoon coriander seeds, lightly crushed

1 tablespoon minced garlic

½ cup toasted ground almonds (see Note)

2 teaspoons ground white pepper

2 cups heavy cream

2 tablespoons Ginger Puree (page 80)

3 to 4 drops vetiver essential oil (see page 72; optional)

1 teaspoon rose water (optional)

2 teaspoons sea salt

½ teaspoon ground cinnamon

½ teaspoon ground mace

3 or 4 silver foil leaves (optional)

Chopped pistachios or sliced almonds for garnish

Korma has its roots in Mughlai cooking and can be traced back to the sixteenth century in the city of Lucknow, the capital of the northern state of Uttar Pradesh. It was here in the artistic and cultural hub of the Mughal Empire, that korma was perfected. Classically, a korma is a curry or stew of vegetables cooked with yogurt, cream, and spices. This is a reinterpretation of the white korma topped with silver leaf said to be served by Shah Jahan at the inauguration of the Taj Mahal. A few drops of vetiver (khus) and a bit rose water add a mysterious aroma to the curry but are not essential to the recipe, nor is the silver foil leaf that finishes the dish. Both can be purchased over the internet. When toasting the almonds, make sure to get them to a nice dark brown. And let the temperature of the yogurt remain low for it to be just at a simmer so as not to curdle it. This curry may be meatless, but it is as decadent as can be. Please note that the flavor of toasted ground almonds is different from almond flour.

Preheat the oven to 400°F.

Coat the paneer wedges in 2 to 3 tablespoons of the ghee and 2 to 3 tablespoons of the yogurt and then spread on a baking sheet. Roast in the oven for 10 to 15 minutes, until the edges are lightly browned. Remove from the oven and set aside.

Heat the remaining ghee in a small stockpot over high heat and pop the cumin seeds and coriander seeds (see page 40). Add the garlic, cook for a few seconds. Then add 1 cup water, the ground almonds, white pepper, heavy cream, ginger puree, vetiver and rose water (if desired), and salt. Bring to a boil, then decrease the heat to low, cover, and simmer for 4 to 5 minutes, until the sauce is smooth and fragrant.

In a small bowl, whisk the remaining yogurt with the cinnamon and mace and gently add it to the sauce, keeping the heat on the lowest setting. Slide the roasted paneer in and simmer, covered, for another 4 to 5 minutes, or until the paneer is heated through. Turn the heat off and let it rest. Just before serving, spread the silver leaf, if desired, on top and garnish with nuts.

Note: To toast and grind almonds, place whole almonds on a baking pan and toast in a 400°F oven for 10 to 12 minutes, or until dark brown. Then let cool and grind in a coffee grinder.

smoked eggplant

Originally from India, eggplant, also known as aubergine or brin-jal, is a berry by botanical definition. In terms of flavor, substantial, meaty eggplant could not be further away from a berry. I have yet to meet an eggplant dish I do not like, and during my years as the chef-owner of Indika restaurant, I was forced to rein in an eggplant obsession when a cook pointed out that we had eggplant nine different ways on the menu, from pakora to pickle to raita. Eggplant is notorious for needing a lot of oil during cooking, and smoking over an open flame is one of the best ways to avoid this. This "burns" off the outer skin, turns it almost molten inside, and results in a smoky, delicious pulpy interior. This recipe is inspired by the Punjabi baingan bhartha, which essentially translates to "spiced eggplant hash." To ripen the plantains, place them in a brown paper bag in a warm part of your kitchen for a few days.

Smoked eggplant is best served warm as a main course with roasted vegetables or as a dip, spread, or side dish. Eat it with steamed rice or roti. Or spread it on warm toast the next morning, throw on a poached or fried egg, and enjoy it for breakfast.

Lightly oil the eggplants and place them directly over two burners of your stove over high heat. If your burners are electric, you will need some kind of grate or rack to place the eggplants on. You can also cook the eggplants on an outdoor gas or electric grill. Char the eggplants on all sides, turning them with tongs. They will blacken and crackle on the outside and soften and smoke on the inside. To ensure that the eggplants are cooked all the way through, do not rush this part—the flesh should feel soft when prodded with a fork or table knife. Let the eggplants rest for 2 to 3 minutes, then discard the burnt skin by pulling it off in strips. If some parts are resistant, use a paring knife to cut them out. Mash or chop the inside pulp with a knife and set aside. While the eggplants are smoking, if using the plantains, char them until the peels are black on all sides. Set aside separately.

Heat the oil in a large saucepan over high heat and pop the cumin seeds (see page 40), then immediately add the onion and cook until sweaty. Lower the heat and cook until the onion softens and caramelizes slightly, 15 to 20 minutes. Stir in the minced garlic, cook for 1 minute, then add the mashed eggplant, turmeric, red chile powder, black pepper, ginger puree, and salt. Cover and simmer for another 5 to 6 minutes for the flavors to meld. Extract the plantain pulp, fold it in along with the garam masala, turn the heat off, and serve.

SERVES 4

2 large purple eggplants

2 unpeeled ripe plantains (optional)

¼ cup olive oil

1 teaspoon cumin seeds

1 cup minced white onion

1 teaspoon Minced Garlic (page 80)

½ teaspoon ground turmeric

1 teaspoon red chile powder

1 teaspoon freshly ground black pepper

2 tablespoons Ginger Puree (page 80)

1½ teaspoons sea salt

1 teaspoon garam masala (see page 69)

aviyal

SERVES 4 TO 6

ROASTED VEGETABLES

1 pound carrots, cut into 1-inch chunks or wheels

3 tablespoons melted coconut oil

1 tablespoon Ginger Puree (page 80)

1 teaspoon freshly ground black pepper

1 teaspoon sea salt

½ bunch asparagus, cut into 2-inch pieces

8 ounces green beans, cut into 2-inch pieces

1 large zucchini, cut into ½-inch wheels

SAUCE

⅓ cup melted coconut oil

1 teaspoon black mustard seeds

15 to 20 kari leaves, chopped

Pinch of asafetida

2 tablespoons Ginger Puree (page 80)

1 tablespoon Caramelized Onion Puree (page 82)

1 serrano chile, minced

One 14-ounce can coconut milk

1 teaspoon sea salt

CHILI OIL

2 tablespoons coconut oil

2 teaspoons chile powder

Aviyal is a simple South Indian curry of mythical proportions and the subject of many a legend. In its most basic iteration, it is a creamy ginger and coconut stew of seasonal vegetables. Some say that it was invented by one of the Pandava brothers (central figures in the epic Mahabharatha) on a forest exile. Others say it was invented in a hurry in a royal kitchen to please a king who wanted to feed more people than possible.

The first time I had aviyal was at a homestay in Cochin, Kerala. Kerala is a small southern state of India known for its spectacular natural beauty, fragrant curries, and coastal seafood. I arrived late one night to a beautiful blissful home surrounded by palm trees and the salty smell of the ocean. The gracious hostess had set aside a cream-colored warm curry for me to enjoy before I went to bed. It was paired with lemon rice flecked with peanuts and coconut, and I devoured every bit of it. After some trial and error, we created our version of aviyal at Pondicheri. Aviyal remains one of Pondicheri's most popular curries, and every time I eat it, I can almost taste the ocean air and feel the breeze in the palm trees that surrounded that homestay in Kerala.

For a seafood version, add 1 pound peeled small shrimp to the stew just before the asparagus, adjust the salt accordingly, and cook for 2 to 3 minutes, until the shrimp is cooked through.

To roast the vegetables: Preheat the oven to 350°F.

In a large bowl, combine the carrots, coconut oil, ginger puree, black pepper, and salt and toss to coat. Spread out on a baking pan, cover tightly with foil, and roast for 20 minutes, or until tender. Check by running a knife through one or two pieces. Take the foil off and add the asparagus, snap peas, and zucchini. Turn the heat off and let the pan rest in the oven for another 15 to 20 minutes.

To make the sauce: While the vegetables are roasting, heat the coconut oil in a large stockpot over high heat. Pop the mustard seeds (see page 40), then add the kari leaves and asafetida and cook for a few seconds. Immediately add the ginger puree, onion puree, and chile; lower the heat to medium; and cook for just a few seconds. Add the coconut milk, salt, and 2 cups water and bring the mixture to a boil. Lower the heat, cover, and simmer for 10 to 15 minutes.

To make the chili oil: Heat the coconut oil in a small pan over high heat. Once shimmering, stir in the chile powder and turn off the heat.

Slide the vegetables into the sauce and simmer for a minute or two. Garnish with the chili oil and serve.

saag

Saag is the heavenly spinach and mustard green puree native to the Punjab region of India. In restaurants, menus typically include saag with paneer, but my advice is to drop the paneer. Our bodies will absorb the nutrients of the greens better without the extra dairy. In homes in Punjab, saag is cooked long and slow until it turns dark green. I prefer mine just barely cooked to preserve the bright emerald-green color. Serve it with roasted butternut squash or other vegetables of your choice.

I have honed this recipe over the years and I will usually enjoy a version of it at least two times a week. When my friend Emmy Vest was the executive chef of NASA, she used my saag recipe to create food for astronauts for their outer-space missions. I love it smooshed onto toast with a fried egg on top, simply with roti, cooked with shrimp or fish, and stirred into pasta or noodles with diced cherry tomatoes. I have made saag with everything from fennel to collard greens, kale, and rainbow chard (prep just like the mustard greens). It keeps in the refrigerator for up to 3 days without losing its bright green color and can be frozen for up to 3 months.

SERVES 4 TO 6

3 bunches spinach

1 bunch mustard greens

¼ cup olive oil

1 tablespoon Minced Garlic (page 80)

¼ cup Ginger Puree (page 80)

¼ cup Caramelized Onion Puree (page 82)

1 medium serrano chile, thinly sliced

¼ cup dried fenugreek leaves

2 teaspoons sea salt

1 teaspoon garam masala (see page 69)

½ cup heavy cream

2 to 3 tablespoons ghee (see page 77)

Discard the bottom 2-inch stems of the spinach bunches. Cut out the large central veins of the mustard green leaves and, finely chop the leaves. Set aside.

Heat the oil in a large stockpot over medium heat until hot. Add the minced garlic and cook for a few seconds, until it turns white or light golden brown. Quickly add the ginger puree, onion puree, chile, fenugreek leaves, and salt. Cook for a few minutes, then add the spinach and mustard greens, increase the heat to high, cover, and cook until wilted, 1 to 2 minutes. Immediately turn the heat off.

Stir the garam masala into the greens and let rest, uncovered, for 10 to 15 minutes to cool slightly. Preserve any of the liquid the greens may have given off, transfer to a food processor or blender, and process until smooth yet evenly grainy. (If using a blender, make sure not to overblend. If you are not serving right away, refrigerate or freeze the saag. Transfer the saag to a pot over medium-high heat, stir in the heavy cream, drizzle with the ghee, and serve.

Variation

Plant-Based Saag: Replace the heavy cream with ⅓ cup ground sesame seeds or cashews or ⅓ cup tahini, and instead of the ghee, top the finished dish with ¼ cup extra-virgin olive oil.

stuffed karela

SERVES 4

1 pound (5 to 6) karela

1 tablespoon sea salt, plus
1 teaspoon

2 tablespoons cane sugar

Juice of 1 lemon, plus more
as needed

1 large sweet potato

¼ cup coconut oil, plus melted
coconut oil for brushing and drizzling

1 teaspoon coriander seeds

1 cup minced white onion

2 tablespoons chickpea flour

1 teaspoon red chile powder

1 tablespoon Ginger Puree (page 80)

¼ cup chopped toasted cashews

¼ cup sesame seeds

Pomegranate seeds for garnish

Fresh herbs (such as mint, basil, or
nasturtium blossoms) for garnish

Because of their health benefits, there is an emerging interest in eating bitter foods such as dandelion greens, fresh fenugreek, and karela, also known as bitter melon. As a kid, even I detested karela. But once I learned how to balance its flavor, I came to understand its magic.

Karela are bright-green knubby-looking vegetables found in Indian grocers. The Chinese bitter melon is very similar in flavor and can be found in Asian grocery stores. Karela is best eaten in small portions with caramelized onions, sweet potato, or sweet corn to offset its bitterness. Add the peel of the karela to roti dough.

Using a vegetable peeler, peel the karela, reserving the peel for another use (see headnote). Slice them in half. Prepare a brine by combining 4 cups water with the 1 tablespoon salt, sugar, and lemon juice. Immerse the peeled karela in the brine and set aside at room temperature for about 4 hours, or cover and refrigerate overnight—this will temper the bitterness. Remove from the brine and rinse off any excess. Remove the seeds from the karela and finely chop the seeds.

Place the sweet potato in a medium saucepan and add water to cover. Bring to a boil over high heat, then cover, decrease the heat, and simmer for 10 to 15 minutes, or until soft and cooked through. Turn the heat off and let the sweet potato rest in the water for another 30 minutes. Remove from the water, peel, and mash. (This can be done a day or two before completing the recipe.)

Preheat the oven to 350°F.

Heat the coconut oil in a heavy-bottom saucepan over high heat. Pop the coriander seeds (see page 40), then immediately add the minced karela seeds and onion. Decrease the heat to medium and cook for 5 to 8 minutes, stirring frequently, until the karela seeds are soft and the onion has sweated and turned slightly golden brown. Add the chickpea flour and cook for a minute or two, until it turns slightly darker and emits a toasty fragrance. Turn the heat off and add the red chile powder, ginger puree, and 1 remaining teaspoon salt. Stir in the mashed sweet potato, cashews, and sesame seeds and stuff into each karela to fill to the top.

Place the stuffed karela on a baking sheet cut-side up. Brush or drizzle the karela with melted coconut oil. Cover the sheet with aluminum foil and place in the oven. Bake for 15 to 20 minutes, or until golden brown and soft, then take the foil off and continue baking for another 10 to 15 minutes, until the karela is cooked through. Drizzle lemon juice on top, drizzle with more coconut oil, if desired, garnish with pomegranate seeds and herbs, and serve.

oondhiya

Oondhiya, a rich fall and winter harvest stew shimmering with copious amounts of spiced oil, is the pièce de résistance of Gujarati cuisine. Too daunted to make it herself, every year around that time, my mother would start asking friends and neighbors as to who makes the best oondhiya in the city. She would then commission families or groups of women who would deliver to our home a large vat of oondhiya, fragrant with tender fenugreek dumplings, ginger and cilantro, little purple eggplant, purple yams, and special flat beans (called papdi) peeking out from a thick covering of spice-scented oil. Our entire and extended family would feast on it for 2 to 3 days until we could eat no more—we would eat it on its own, with rotis or pooris (puffy warm balloon breads) or rice.

Over years of living in America, I missed oondhiya so much that I started adapting it to suit what I could find locally during the fall, using good olive oil as a base. It is supremely decadent and fairly time-consuming but well worth the effort, and I suggest throwing an oondhiya party! It will keep in the refrigerator for up to 5 days. Tuver is a deeply delicious special green pigeon pea native to Gujarat, and easily available at Indian grocers in frozen bags, however, feel free to replace it with green peas.

To make the oondhiya masala: Combine the olive oil, cilantro, mint, coconut, serrano, garlic, ginger, sesame seeds, lime juice, and salt in a small food processor and pulse until evenly ground. If the mixture appears dry, add 2 to 3 tablespoons of water. (Refrigerate for up to 4 days.)

To roast the vegetables: Preheat the oven to 400°F.

Peel the carrots or yam and cut into large 1-inch chunks. Cut the small eggplants in half or cut the Japanese eggplant into four or five equal large pieces. In a large bowl, combine the eggplant, carrots, potatoes, salt, ajwain seeds, black pepper, peas, and olive oil, then spread on a baking pan and cover tightly with foil. Roast in the oven for 30 minutes, then check the vegetables. The eggplant should be soft and slightly caramelized, and the starch vegetables should be cooked through. Set the vegetables aside—they are best made the day you are making the oondhiya.

recipe continues

GENEROUSLY SERVES 6 TO 8

OONDHIYA MASALA

½ cup olive oil

1 bunch cilantro (bottom few inches discarded)

2 cups loose mint leaves

½ cup shredded coconut

2 serrano chiles

8 to 10 garlic cloves

One 3- to 4-inch piece ginger, sliced

2 tablespoons ground sesame seeds or peanuts or tahini

Juice from 1 lime

1 teaspoon sea salt

ROASTED VEGETABLES

3 or 4 medium carrots, or 1 large purple yam

4 or 5 small purple, or 1 large Japanese eggplant (roughly 8 ounces total)

1 pound tiny pearl potatoes

1 teaspoon sea salt

1 teaspoon ajwain seeds

1 teaspoon black pepper

1 cup green peas (preferably tuver)

¼ cup olive oil

FENUGREEK DUMPLINGS

1 cup chopped fresh fenugreek, or ½ cup dried leaves

2 cups chickpea or millet flour

½ cup whole sesame seeds

1 serrano chile, minced

1 tablespoon Ginger Puree (page 80)

2 teaspoons coriander seeds, lightly crushed

¼ teaspoon baking soda

1 teaspoon sea salt

¼ cup olive oil

2 cups frying oil (rice bran, peanut, or sunflower oil)

1 pound green beans, trimmed and cut into 2-inch chunks

1 cup green peas (preferably 'tuver')

¼ cup olive oil

1 bunch cilantro (bottom 3 inches of stems removed), minced

2 to 3 tablespoons shredded coconut

Handful of pomegranate seeds

To make the fenugreek dumplings: In a large bowl, using your fingers, combine the fenugreek, flour, sesame seeds, serrano, ginger puree, coriander seeds, baking soda, salt, and olive oil. Add just enough water (roughly ¼ cup) to bring the mixture together into a mass. Refrigerate this mixture for a couple of hours or overnight.

When ready to fry the dumplings, in a shallow sauté pan or a wok, warm the frying oil over low heat. Drop in little teaspoonfuls of batter and fry on all sides until cooked through—this may take 3 to 4 minutes per batch. Remove the dumplings with a slotted metal spoon or tongs and drain on paper towels. The dumplings are best made fresh.

In a large shallow Dutch oven or saucepan over medium heat, gently combine the entire masala with the roasted vegetables, green beans, peas, olive oil, and about ¾ cup water. Simmer the mixture until the beans and peas are cooked yet remain bright green—3 to 4 minutes. Add the dumplings gently, turn the heat off, and sprinkle with cilantro, coconut, and pomegranate seeds just before serving. Eat warm or at room temperature.

SERVES 4 TO 6

2 russet potatoes, roughly 1 pound each, unpeeled and diced into 1-inch pieces

½ cup coconut milk

¼ cup Ginger Puree (page 80)

2 teaspoons sea salt

⅓ cup light sesame oil

¼ teaspoon fenugreek seeds

1 teaspoon black mustard seeds

Generous pinch of asafetida

20 kari leaves

1 cup minced red onions

2 serrano chiles, minced

½ cup sesame seeds, pumpkin seeds, or sunflower seeds

Juice of 1 lemon

Handful of whole herbs (such as cilantro or mint) for garnish

Here is a simple rustic rendition of the potato mash popular in South India and usually eaten with dosas. It's delicious as a side dish with scrambled eggs in the morning, with roasted meats, or with a curry. While the recipe calls for sesame oil, feel free to substitute ghee, coconut oil, or olive oil.

In a large saucepan, combine the potatoes, coconut milk, ginger puree, 1½ teaspoons of the salt, and 1 cup water and bring to a boil over high heat. Decrease the heat, cover, and simmer for 15 to 20 minutes, until the potato chunks are fork-tender and all the water has been absorbed.

In another large saucepan, heat the oil over high heat. Pop the fenugreek seeds and mustard seeds (see page 40), then add the asafetida and kari leaves and cook for a couple of seconds. Immediately add the onions and cook for 4 to 5 minutes, until the onions are slightly softened but still crunchy. Stir in the chiles and remaining ½ teaspoon salt. Fold this mixture over the potatoes and stir it in gently. Sprinkle the sesame seeds over the mash, squeeze lemon juice on top, garnish with fresh herbs, and serve.

mushroom masala mac 'n' cheese

My introduction to macaroni and cheese was in the 1980s, when I arrived in America. It was the box variety, which at the time tasted delicious. I played around with many variations of this American classic, from learning how to make a good béchamel to figuring out which spices pair well with cheese. Once my taste buds morphed to appreciate sophisticated cheese, I began to enjoy sharp Cheddar, raclette, and Gruyère—all of which pair beautifully with cumin, nigella seeds, and black pepper. The addition of chickpea flour to this dish may be unusual but lends a tremendous depth of flavor. The entire dish can be prepared a day ahead and baked just before serving.

Preheat the oven to 325°F. Grease a large baking dish.

To cook the mushrooms: Heat the oil in a large frying pan over high heat. Add the mushrooms, salt, and pepper and cook for 5 to 7, until cooked through and almost all the liquid has been absorbed. Set aside.

To make the cream masala: Heat the ghee in a stockpot over low heat. Add the chickpea flour and cook, stirring, until golden brown, 2 to 3 minutes. Do not leave unattended, as chickpea flour can burn easily. Add the garlic, black pepper, nigella seeds, cardamom, cumin, and salt and continue cooking for another minute. Add the heavy cream, increase the heat to bring it to a boil, and then turn the heat off.

In a large bowl, combine the cooked pasta with the cream masala, 2 cups of the grated cheese, the mushrooms, chiles, and herbs. Spread onto the prepared baking dish, top with the remaining ½ cup cheese, and bake for 40 to 45 minutes, until the top is bubbly and golden. Let the pasta rest for 10 to 15 minutes. Garnish with more herbs and serve.

SERVES 4 TO 6

MUSHROOMS

¼ cup olive oil

6 cups sliced mushrooms (such as oyster, chanterelle, or portobello)

2 teaspoons sea salt

2 teaspoons freshly ground black pepper

CREAM MASALA

2 tablespoons ghee (see page 77)

2 tablespoons chickpea flour

1 tablespoon Minced Garlic (page 80)

2 teaspoons freshly ground black pepper

2 teaspoons ground nigella seeds (kalonji)

1 teaspoon ground green cardamom seeds

1 teaspoon toasted crushed cumin seeds

2 teaspoons sea salt

2 cups heavy cream

4 cups macaroni or shell pasta, cooked according to package directions

2½ cups grated cheese (such as Gruyère, raclette, or sharp Cheddar)

2 serrano chiles, minced

½ cup chopped mixed fresh herbs (such as a mix of oregano, basil, chives, rosemary, or sage), plus more for garnish

Legumes

Grown for human consumption over three thousand years ago, lentils have a well-documented ability to thrive in unfavorable conditions to feed entire civilizations. First cultivated in the Middle East, it is believed that the South Americans introduced India to lentils. Today, India is one of the biggest producers of roughly fifty varieties of lentils and beans and consumes half of the lentils produced in the world. From the tangy light sambhar made with toor lentils of the south to the rich, creamy black urad dal the Punjabis favor, legumes or dal is the staple of every region of India and remains the most nutritious and affordable source of protein. *Dal* is often translated as "lentils" but actually refers to a split version of dried lentils, beans, or peas. Every Indian identifies with the dish dal, which is simply curried lentils or beans. A version of dal is served as an essential accompaniment alongside fancy hotel banquets and in the homes of people from all walks of life.

Most dals start with soft-cooked lentils stewed in an aromatic broth of ginger, garlic or onions, and spices. There are literally hundreds of varieties of dal preparations in India, from soupy to thick stews. Carrots, zucchini, and ripe or green mango can be grated into a dal, or chunks of tomato or squash can be added toward the end. Tender cuts of meats can be stewed with dals. Or a can of coconut milk is added for a creamy and hearty version.

Soups as we know them in Western cuisine do not really exist in traditional Indian cuisine. There are, however, dozens of light lentil-based broths like the tangy rasam of the south, made with toor dal, asafetida, and kari leaves, and the Gujarati tomato kadhi, a tomato lentil broth with pops of mustard seeds and kari leaves that can be enjoyed as a first course or soup.

Lentils are filled with fiber, protein, and minerals, but let's face it, they are a gas-inducing food. They are astringent in flavor, so they can be heavy and drying to our bodies and interfere with our digestive fire. However, when cooked correctly and paired with the right spices, such as ginger, asafetida, or fennel to offset the drying properties, lentils can be a most nutritious and easily absorbed and digested food.

Rinse and soaking: Rinse all lentils and beans at least two times by simply placing the lentils in a bowl, pouring tap water on top to cover them, and stirring them for a few seconds with your fingers. Pour most of the water out and repeat once or twice more. While it is unusual to find debris or small rocks, if you do spot any, discard them. The rinsing does the initial job of removing some of the hard indigestible protein and residues. Next, whether it is split lentils like toor, mung, or channa dal, lentils need to be soaked for a minimum of 4 hours. This loosens up impurities in their skin, which will be discarded with the soaking water. You want to be careful to not soak lentils for more than 8 hours at room temperature or they may start to ferment, especially during warmer seasons. Storing soaked lentils in the refrigerator overnight is one way to prevent fermentation. With larger pulses, like whole toor dal or black urad dal, or large beans, like chickpeas or black beans, a minimum 12-hour overnight soak yields best and fastest-cooking results. They will double in size, so be sure to use a large enough container with plenty of water.

Cooking: Fill the cooking pot with two to three times as much water as the lentils. As soon as they come to a boil, a foamy residue will rise to the top. This foam is filled with impurities, so, at the very least, use a slotted spoon to skim the residue and discard. Or better still, discard that water by simply pouring it into the sink and adding fresh water. For larger beans, you may need to use a large strainer or colander. This ensures that almost all the foamy residue on the lentils has been removed and, just as important, they will be much gentler on the stomach and easier to digest. It's an extra step that profoundly minimizes gas problems associated with beans. The next most important part of cooking pulses is to cook them thoroughly. Most lentils or beans acquire a creamy quality when cooked long enough—they are not separate from the water they are cooked in and will appear to have fully integrated. This is the stage to look for. To ensure they are cooked, when pressed between a finger and thumb, the lentils or beans should be soft with no hint of hardness.

Soak

Remove scum

Simmer

Pop

sprouted mung

1 cup mung beans

½ teaspoon ground turmeric

1 teaspoon sea salt

Juice of 2 lemons

1 teaspoon red chile powder

Sprouted mung has so many uses—it can be added to salads, chaats, soups, or plain yogurt or just eaten with rice as a light snack.

Soak the mung beans in a bowl with 3 cups water at room temperature for 4 hours or in the refrigerator overnight. Drain.

Spread the mung beans on a flat, shallow pan so they have with plenty of space around them and pour in 1 to 2 cups water, enough to keep the mung beans moist without drowning them. Place the pan near a window or in a warm place in the kitchen for another day. If the ambient temperature is warm, the beans may appear to have a few tails, or sprouts, and yes, they are perfectly edible. This is what you are looking for. Discard any water and cover with 1 to 2 cups fresh water. By the second day, the beans should have more white tails.

Drain the lentils; transfer to a saucepan; and combine with 2 to 3 cups water, the turmeric; and salt and bring to a boil over high heat. Lower the heat and simmer for 4 to 5 minutes, or until beans are cooked through but not mushy. Then turn the heat off and drain. Rinse with water to stop the cooking. Place in a container, toss with the lemon juice and red chile powder, and keep refrigerated for up to 2 weeks.

Pulse Chart

toor

split toor

OTHER NAMES: arhar dal, tuver dal, split pigeon peas

USES: smooth, velvety, best when pureed

whole toor

OTHER NAMES: sabit toor, akha toor

USES: dal stews

mung

yellow split mung

OTHER NAMES: mung or moong dal

USES: simple dals or dal purees

split mung with skin

OTHER NAMES: mung chilka

USES: dals and salads

whole mung

OTHER NAMES: green mung, green gram

USES: sprouting, salads, stuffings

masoor

masoor split dal

OTHER NAMES: orange masoor, red lentils, pink lentils

USES: simple dals or dal purees

masoor whole

OTHER NAMES: kali masoor, sabut masoor, brown lentils

USES: dals, salads

urad

white split urad

OTHER NAMES: white urad

USES: dosa batters, lentil dumplings, dal

white split urad with skin

OTHER NAMES: urad chilka

USES: dosa batters, lentil dumplings, dal

whole black urad

OTHER NAMES: kali dal, black lentils

USES: sprouting, Punjabi dal, stews

channa

channa dal

OTHER NAMES: split gram

USES: dense, rich, great for thick stews

chickpea

OTHER NAMES: garbanzo, kabuli channa, Bengal gram

USES: curries, stews, hummus, chaats

black chickpea

OTHER NAMES: desi channa, kala channa

USES: curries, stews, soups, chaats

chickpea flour

OTHER NAMES: besan, gram flour, garbanzo bean flour

USES: crepes, mithai, roux for a curry

beans

red beans

OTHER NAMES: rajma

USES: bean purees, salads, stews, soups

black-eyed peas

OTHER NAMES: lobhia

USES: bean purees, salads, stews, soups

val

OTHER NAMES: navy beans

USES: bean purees, salads, stews, soups

dal soup

Out of the fifty or so lentils grown in India, toor dal, with its velvety consistency when pureed, is one of the best lentils to make soups with. Toor, in the pigeon pea family, is used as a base for the famous sambhar served with dosas in the south of India and for the simple aromatic Gujarati dal. This soup is a combination of the two, and no matter what time of the year, it serves as a wonderful vehicle for seasonal vegetables and greens. Enjoy this soup as a light lunch, a first course, or, more traditionally, with rice or roti.

Rinse the dal two or three times in cold tap water, add water to cover by a couple of inches, and soak for 5 to 6 hours. Drain.

In a large saucepan, combine the drained dal with 4 cups water and bring to a boil over high heat. Discard any scum that may arise—scum contains impurities that can make lentils and beans hard to digest. (Alternatively, drain the dal, add 4 cups fresh water, and bring to a boil again.) Add the turmeric, cloves, and salt and bring to a boil. Lower the heat to low, cover the pot, and simmer for about 1 hour, checking every 15 to 20 minutes to make sure the water has not evaporated. The dal are done when they are cooked to a soft, fall-apart doneness; it's better to err toward overcooking than undercooking.

Toward the end of cooking, blend the dal into a smooth puree using a whisk or an immersion blender. The consistency should be fairly soupy—it will thicken after you add the vegetables. Add the ginger puree, cubed vegetables, jaggery, and peanuts (if using) and cook, covered, for 10 minutes, or until the vegetables are soft but hold their shape.

When ready to serve the soup, in a small frying pan, heat the oil over high heat and add the garlic. Cook for a few seconds, until the garlic has turned light golden brown, then pop the mustard seeds and fenugreek seeds (see page 40). Turn the heat off, add the kari leaves and red chile powder, and pour this mixture into the dal and simmer for 2 to 3 minutes, or until incorporated. Just before serving, stir in the greens until wilted, then add the herbs and lemon juice.

Variations

Instead of mustard seeds, try a cumin seed or fennel seed pop.

Instead of using garlic, try a pinch of asafetida just before adding the mustard seeds and fenugreek seeds.

When in season, add 2 cups diced fresh tomatoes after you turn the heat off and stir until the tomatoes soften but still hold their shape.

Add 1 cup diced green or unripe mango to the dal along with the other vegetables.

SERVES 4

1 cup toor dal

½ teaspoon ground turmeric

3 or 4 whole cloves

2 teaspoons sea salt

2 tablespoons Ginger Puree (page 80)

2 cups seasonal vegetables cut into 1-inch cubes (such as butternut squash, zucchini, fennel, or carrots)

1 tablespoon jaggery

2 tablespoons whole peanuts (optional)

¼ cup olive oil

8 small garlic cloves, sliced

1 teaspoon black mustard seeds

¼ teaspoon fenugreek seeds

20 kari leaves

2 teaspoons red chile powder

2 cups chopped greens (such as spinach, watercress, or kale)

½ cup loosely chopped fresh herbs (such as cilantro, parsley, or basil)

Juice of ½ lemon

SERVES 4

½ cup masoor dal
(red or orange lentils)

½ cup green split mung beans
with skin

½ cup channa dal

1 teaspoon ground turmeric

2 large cinnamon sticks

2 teaspoons sea salt

⅓ cup ghee (see page 77)

8 garlic cloves, sliced

1 teaspoon cumin seeds

1 teaspoon fennel seeds

¼ teaspoon fenugreek seeds

20 kari leaves

1 cup minced green onions,
white and green parts

1 cup canned crushed tomatoes,
or 2 cups diced fresh tomatoes

2 tablespoons Ginger Puree (page 80)

2 serrano chiles, minced

1 teaspoon garam masala
(see page 69)

1 cup chopped fresh herbs (such
as cilantro, parsley, or basil)

This is the dal that's eaten with rice, roti, or even toasted bread. It can go from being a slightly soupy light dal to a rich, thick, creamy satisfying stew. To get a huge bang for your buck, add root vegetables at the beginning of cooking or a piece or two of meat. One whole skinless bone-in chicken leg will add tremendous flavor, as will 3 to 4 ounces stewing meat of any sort. The meat may fall apart into the dal at the end. Three different lentils cook slightly differently to make for an interesting combination of flavors and textures—masoor will cook the fastest and turn into mush, while the skin of split mung is stewing away and will add texture even when cooked through, and channa dal will take the longest to cook and may remain chunky. It is important to cook all the lentils until soft and creamy before proceeding to the next stage.

Rinse the masoor dal, split mung beans, and channa dal two or three times in cold tap water, add water to cover by a couple of inches, and soak for at least 5 hours or up to overnight. Drain.

In a large saucepan, combine the drained dal with 4 cups water and bring to a boil over high heat. Discard any scum that may arise—scum contains impurities that can make lentils and beans hard to digest. (Alternatively, drain the dal, through a colander or strainer if needed, into the sink, add 4 cups fresh water, and bring to a boil again. While doing this, the skin of the split mung will rise to the top and might get thrown away, but that's okay.) Add the turmeric, cinnamon sticks, and salt and bring to a boil. Lower the heat to low, cover the pot, and simmer for about 1 hour, checking every 15 to 20 minutes to make sure the water has not evaporated. The dal are done when they are cooked to a soft, fall-apart doneness; it's better to err toward overcooking than undercooking.

In a separate pan, heat the ghee over high heat and add the garlic. Immediately pop the cumin seeds, fennel seeds, and fenugreek seeds (see page 40). Add the kari leaves and green onions, decrease the heat to medium-high, and cook until the green onions are translucent, 8 to 10 minutes. Add the tomatoes, ginger puree, and chiles and cook for 5 to 7 minutes, until the tomatoes begin to disintegrate. Pour the mixture into the soup and simmer, covered, for 5 to 6 minutes, or until incorporated. Stir in the garam masala and herbs and serve.

tomato rasam

SERVES 4 TO 6

After the India–Pakistan partition in 1947, my mother lived in Bangalore for a few years before she married my father and moved to Gujarat in the western part of India. During her time in southern India, she learned how to speak fluent Tamil, a native language, and developed a passion for local cuisine that she continued to explore for years. We often ate idlis—steamed rice cakes—for breakfast with her favorite coconut chutney. Rasam, an iconic sour, spicy, sweet soup, was one of her favorites. The beauty of rasam, which in Tamil means "essence" or "juice," can embody whatever flavor one puts in it. In the summer, we had tomato rasam with chunks of tart green mango; in the winter it would be paired with tamarind or other sour fruits. What unites all rasams is the use of toor dal, the split pigeon peas, and while the consistency might seem almost watery, the soup has a delicious sour punch with assertive fragrant spices and fleeting hints of sweetness. In season, try using 2 to 3 cups chopped heirloom tomatoes in place of canned tomato puree.

Rinse the toor dal two or three times in cold tap water, add water to cover by a couple of inches, and soak for at least 4 hours or up to overnight. Drain.

In a small saucepan, combine the drained dal with 2 cups water and bring to a boil over high heat. As soon as it comes to a boil and scum starts to rise, pour the water out along with the scum. Add 2 cups fresh water, the turmeric, red chile powder, and jaggery and bring to a boil again. Cover with a tight-fitting lid, lower the heat to low, and simmer for 45 minutes to 1 hour, until the dal is completely cooked through. Toor dal is small but notoriously slow at cooking all the way. Turn the heat off and let rest for 15 to 20 minutes. Whisk the dal until smooth or use an immersion blender to puree the mixture.

Add the tomato puree, ginger puree, salt, and 2 cups water to the saucepan and bring to a boil. Lower the heat to low and simmer for 15 to 20 minutes, or until smooth and bright red in color.

Using a mortar and pestle or small hammer, pound the channa dal, black peppercorns, fenugreek seeds, cumin seeds, coriander seeds, and mustard seeds until they are mostly crushed. (Alternatively, use a clean coffee grinder; pulse them quickly so they don't grind all the way.)

Heat the coconut oil in a small frying pan over high heat. Pop the pounded masala (see page 40), add the kari leaves, and immediately add to the soup. Simmer for another 10 to 12 minutes, or until the spices soften.

Add the lemon juice to the soup, garnish with the herbs, and serve.

Ingredients

⅓ cup toor dal

½ teaspoon ground turmeric

1 teaspoon red chile powder

1 tablespoon jaggery

1 cup canned tomato puree

1 tablespoon Ginger Puree (page 80)

1½ teaspoons sea salt

1 teaspoon channa dal or urad dal

½ teaspoon black peppercorns

¼ teaspoon fenugreek seeds

½ teaspoon cumin seeds

½ teaspoon coriander seeds

½ teaspoon black mustard seeds

¼ cup coconut oil

20 kari leaves

Juice of 2 lemons

Small handful of fresh herbs (such as cilantro, basil, or parsley)

mushroom bean stew

SERVES 4 TO 6

1 cup dried beans (black, white, red, or channa)

¼ cup olive oil

5 or 6 garlic cloves, sliced

1 teaspoon fennel seeds

1 teaspoon crushed green cardamom seeds

1 cup minced white onion

1½ cups minced shiitake mushrooms

2 celery stalks, sliced ½ inch thick

2 cups diced (½-inch) vegetables (such as squash, brussels sprouts, potatoes, cauliflower, or carrots)

1 teaspoon red chile powder

1 teaspoon freshly ground black pepper

1 tablespoon sea salt

One 28-ounce can crushed tomatoes

2 cups chopped (bite-size) wild mushrooms (see headnote)

½ cup chopped fresh herbs (such as cilantro, basil, oregano, or mint)

At home, I often cook a version of this soup on cold days. I use whatever beans I have at hand—my pantry is usually stocked with black, white, and red beans and chickpeas. They key is to remember to soak them the night before; this makes cooking so much faster. Large white cannellini, which have a relatively thin skin, melt in your mouth and work really well in this recipe, but they are delicate, so take care not to overcook them. Regarding the wild mushrooms, shiitake, trumpet, and maitake are best, but cremini or portobello can be used as well.

Rinse the beans two or three times in cold tap water, add water to cover by a couple of inches, and soak overnight. Drain.

In a large saucepan, combine the drained beans with 4 cups water and bring to a boil over high heat. Discard any scum that may arise—scum contains impurities that can make beans hard to digest. (Alternatively, drain the beans, through a colander or strainer if needed, into the sink, add 4 cups fresh water, and bring to a boil again.) Decrease the heat to low, cover, and simmer for 1 hour, or until the beans are tender.

Meanwhile, in a small frying pan, heat the oil over high heat. Add the garlic and pop the fennel seeds and cardamom seeds (see page 40). Immediately add the onion, decrease the heat to medium-high, and cook for 4 to 5 minutes, until the edges of the onion are golden brown. Add the shiitake mushrooms, celery, and diced vegetables and cook for 2 to 3 minutes, or until cooked through. Lower the heat to low, add the red chile powder, black pepper, salt and cook for just a few seconds, then add the tomatoes. Bring to a simmer and let simmer for another 4 to 5 minutes, until the oil appears at the edges or surface. Add this mixture to the pot of beans. If the mixture is too thick, add more water. Increase the heat to medium-high and bring the soup to a boil, then lower the heat to low, cover, and simmer for 10 to 15 minutes, until the vegetables are tender. Add the wild mushrooms and cook for another 3 to 5 minutes, until they have cooked through. Turn the heat off and, if you have the time, let the soup rest for 30 minutes to 1 hour to allow the flavors to marry and mellow. Garnish with the herbs and serve.

sai bhaji

SERVES 4

½ cup channa dal

2 green onions, white and green parts, thinly sliced

1 celery stalk, cut into ½-inch pieces

1 bulb fennel, cut into ½-inch pieces, fronds reserved

1 large carrot, grated

1 small sweet potato, skin on, grated

10 garlic cloves, peeled

¼ cup Ginger Puree (page 80)

1 large serrano chile, minced

1 teaspoon ground turmeric

1 teaspoon freshly ground black pepper

2 teaspoons ground cumin

2 teaspoons sea salt

1 teaspoon ground green cardamom seeds

¼ cup olive oil, or 3 to 4 tablespoons butter or ghee (see page 77)

1 bunch spinach

1 bunch dandelion greens

1 cup chopped fresh fenugreek leaves (see headnote)

1 cup chopped fresh cilantro leaves

1 large tomato, cut into ½-inch pieces

Basmati rice, roti (see page 239), or parathas (see page 240) for serving

Sai bhaji, which simply means "green vegetable," is an age-old staple from the province of my vanished homeland, Sindh. Not the most attractive of dishes but delicious when made right, sai bhaji is popular because it's a one-pot dish, commonly enjoyed during the winter, and it's easy to prepare. It is also highly nutritious with an abundance of vegetables and can be prepared with a minimum of fat. As with most Indian stews, every family has its own version, but for the most part, it consists of channa dal slow-cooked with root vegetables, leafy greens, herbs, and aromatic spices. I have mixed memories of sai bhaji as a child. Depending on the vegetables at hand and time available, my mother would fuss over it all day and lay out a luscious stew with notes of fennel, cardamom, and ghee for dinner. Other times it was bottom-of-the-refrigerator vegetables rushed into a pressure cooker, and it tasted more like vegetable gruel. I had abandoned cooking it for years, but lately I have been finding ways to bring back the magic of sai bhaji using local seasonal vegetables. Late winter and early spring are the best times to make sai bhaji, when fresh fennel and fenugreek, which I consider integral to this dish, are in season. Fresh fenugreek should be available at most Indian grocers during winter; if not, use dried. Feel free to substitute any vegetables.

Soak the channa dal in water to cover by a couple of inches for 2 to 3 hours. Drain.

In a large saucepan, combine the drained channa dal with the green onions, celery, fennel, carrot, sweet potato, garlic, ginger puree, chile, turmeric, black pepper, cumin, and salt. Add 4 cups water and bring to a boil. Lower the heat to the lowest setting, cover, and simmer for 1 to 1½ hours, checking every 10 to 15 minutes, making sure it is not sticking to the bottom and adding more water if needed. It's done when the vegetables are softened and cooked through and the dal dissolves into the stew, becoming almost gelatinous and creamy. Stir in the cardamom seeds and oil.

Meanwhile, discard the bottom 3 to 4 inches of the spinach and dandelion greens and chop the leaves. Just before serving the stew, stir in the spinach, dandelion greens, fenugreek, cilantro, tomato, and fennel fronds. Enjoy with basmati rice, roti, or parathas.

red beet soup

As a kid, I hated the taste of beets. But as an adult, I love beets and their visually stunning color when cooked correctly. Over the years, I have prepared about ten different beet soups, all of which I liked but did not love. When I made this one for my first restaurant, Indika, I did a small dance around the kitchen. I knew I had achieved beet-soup nirvana. Even though there is only a small amount of chickpea flour, I have included this recipe in the lentil section because it is a significant change to the flavor of the soup. The chickpea roux along with the coconut milk mellows the earthy, slightly medicinal taste of the beets and brings out their sweetness. This soup is satisfying on its own, topped with your favorite melting cheese, or even as a sauce for grilled fish.

In a large saucepan, heat the ¼ cup oil over medium-high heat. Add the chickpea flour, lower the heat to medium and cook, stirring frequently, for 4 to 5 minutes, until you have a golden brown roux that gives off a nutty aroma. Add the beets, ginger, red chile powder, coconut milk, salt, and 3 to 4 cups water and bring to a boil. Decrease the heat, cover, and simmer for 15 to 20 minutes, until the beets are cooked through. Take care not to overcook the beets or their bright color will be lost. Turn the heat off and allow the soup to rest for a few minutes.

Transfer the soup to a blender and blend until smooth. (At this point the soup may be chilled and kept in the refrigerator for 2 to 3 days.) Return the soup to the saucepan and bring to a simmer, adding water if the soup is too thick.

In a small sauté pan, heat the remaining 2 tablespoons coconut oil over high heat, pop the mustard seeds (see page 40), and add the kari leaves. Gently fold into the soup. Serve the soup garnished with the pumpkin seeds, sesame seeds, coconut, and herbs.

SERVES 4 TO 6

¼ cup coconut oil, plus 2 tablespoons

¼ cup chickpea flour

3 large or 4 small (about 1½ pounds) red beets, peeled and cut into ½-inch cubes

One 3-inch piece unpeeled ginger, sliced

1 teaspoon red chile powder

1 cup coconut milk

2 teaspoons sea salt

1 teaspoon black mustard seeds

20 kari leaves, minced

1 tablespoon pumpkin seeds

1 tablespoon sesame seeds

Grated or chopped fresh coconut for garnish

Fresh herbs (such as, purslane leaves, cilantro, or mint) for garnish

seafood mulligatawny

¼ cup toor dal

One 3-to 4-inch piece fresh turmeric

2 cups cauliflower florets

1 large carrot, cut into 1-inch pieces

One 3- to 4-inch piece ginger, roughly chopped

1 or 2 serrano chiles

2 teaspoons sea salt

One 14-ounce can coconut milk

¼ cup ghee (see page 77)

Generous pinch of asafetida

1 teaspoon black mustard seeds

20 kari leaves

2 large celery stalks, cut on the diagonal into 1-inch pieces

8 ounces French green beans, cut into 1-inch pieces

6 large scallops

8 ounces small shrimp, peeled and deveined

1 pound fresh mussels or clams

1 teaspoon garam masala (see page 69)

Juice of 1 lemon

½ cup chopped fresh cilantro

Legend has it that during colonial times in India, when a British officer in South India once asked his cook to prepare a soup as a starter, the cook was confused. The closest thing to a soup that the Tamil cook knew was a watery rasam (broth) made with black pepper or chiles, lentils, tamarind, and water, which in Tamil is called a molo tuny, or pepper water. The ingenious cook added some rice, a few vegetables, and a bit of meat and transformed this broth into what became known as mulligatawny. Mulligatawny soup was one of the earliest dishes to emerge from the new hybrid cuisine that local cooks developed in India to please the British, combining British concepts of how food should be presented with Indian spices. Most fancy hotels in India serve this soup, and I honestly have never had a restaurant version that I liked. This version has a velvety consistency and is hearty with vegetables and filled with flavor. The soup can be also be made with chicken or just vegetables and can be served with plain rice or warm crusty bread. The broth keeps in the freezer for up to 3 months.

Rinse the dal two or three times in several changes of water, add water to cover by a couple of inches, and soak for 5 to 6 hours. Drain.

In a large saucepan, combine the drained dal with 4 cups water and bring to a boil over high heat. Discard any scum that may arise—scum contains impurities that can make lentils hard to digest. (Alternatively, drain the dal, through a colander or strainer if needed, into the sink, add 4 cups fresh water, and bring to a boil again.) Add the turmeric, cauliflower, carrot, ginger, chiles, and salt and bring to a boil. Lower the heat, cover, and simmer for 30 to 45 minutes, until the dal is dissolved to a mushy consistency and the vegetables are cooked through. Turn the heat off and let the soup rest. Puree in a blender, in batches if needed, until smooth and pour the soup back into the pot. Add the coconut milk, and if the soup is too thick, ½ to 1 cup water.

Heat the ghee in a small frying pan over high heat. Pop the asafetida and mustard seeds (see page 40), add the kari leaves, and immediately scrape them into the soup. Stir in the celery and green beans, then add the scallops, shrimp, and mussels and cook for 2 to 3 minutes, until the vegetables are still bright green and the seafood is almost cooked through—it will continue to cook in the hot soup. Add the garam masala, lemon juice, and cilantro and serve.

Seafood and Meat

There has never been a better time than the present to reexamine our relationship to animals and sea creatures. History books show that even hunter-gatherers ate meat occasionally, but never has it been eaten in such large amounts and without care for its provenance like it is now in the West. In the last century, political and corporate greed led to the unconscionable advent of factory farming where animals and fish became regarded as commodities and not lives. Indiscriminate long-line commercial fishing kills hundreds of thousands of sea turtles, dolphins, birds, sharks, and other untargeted fish every year in the United States alone. Despite how popular freshwater fish and crustaceans are in many coastal parts of India, like Mumbai, Kolkata, and the coast of Malabar, overfishing has depleted the world's oceans of more than 90 percent of large fish. This combined with factory-farm fishing; meat and seafood subsidies; and air and water polluted with methane, oil spills, and microplastics warrant a careful reset in our eating habits.

Emerging moral examinations of eating meat have become a battle cry in the interest of spiritual practices and environmentalism. On a personal note, while I am by no means a strict vegetarian, I have drastically reduced my meat consumption and have resolved to eat small quantities only on very special occasions and only when I know it has been raised using regenerative and humane practices. I think a middle ground of eating less meat or using meat for flavoring may be one of the best ways forward to help our impact on the environment.

Contrary to most beliefs, at one time, Indian Hindus did eat beef, and the country was not always the haven for vegetarianism it is today. In epic tales from the Mahabharat, the holy Indian scripture created during pre-Vedic times, the gods sit down to gargantuan meals of roasted meat. It was believed that powerful environmental essences from the soil were transferred from plants to herbivores and then to humans. Despite warnings that beef was "heavy, hot, unctuous, and difficult to digest," ancient Ayurvedic texts considered beef broth to be one of the first effective medicines, in particular for people with active occupations. Kings and rulers who relied heavily on meat-filled diets led the way, as did hunters and warriors who dealt decisively with the burdens of government. However, there were early signs of a growing unease about the killing of cows and other animals. There's a passage in the Mahabharat where a cow complains about the wanton carnage committed on her relatives.

This general positive attitude toward meat was challenged around the fifth century BCE, when Buddhism and Jainism, with their fascinating and tremendously inclusive philosophy, were founded. The Indian epics, originally oral folklore, were reinterpreted and documented by religious scholars, who adjusted the narrative, resulting in the cow becoming revered as a sacred animal and banned from slaughter and consumption. Buddhism and Jainism both promoted the practice of vegetarianism as a way of demonstrating compassion.

Around the eleventh century, invaders from Turkey, Persia, and Afghanistan began to settle in India in search of gold and wealth and established themselves as landed aristocracy. They regarded food as pleasure and often clashed with the solemn Ayurvedic approach of the Indians, who believed that food was an integral part of people's relationship with their surroundings and the divine. Indians attempted to keep their bodies in balance with the environment by adjusting their diets to the climate. Their beliefs were looked down upon by the pleasure-driven foreigners. It was in the kitchens of northern and eastern India that the mismatched culinary cultures came together to produce a synthesis of nonvegetarian foods. A hybrid cuisine flourished, with the creation of famous dishes like korma, a creamy preparation with nuts; meat kebabs; roghan josh, a spicy Kashmiri meat stew; and biryani, a fragrant layered rice and meat dish with nuts and dried fruits. In addition, when the Portuguese invaded the western and southern parts of India in the fourteenth century, mass Christianization and newly imposed religious beliefs led locals to also take to eating meat.

While a third of Indians remain vegetarian, meat is now a status symbol, and for the wealthy, food has become more about aspiration than tradition.

mustard scallops

SERVES 4

12 large scallops

2 tablespoons mustard oil

½ teaspoon ground turmeric

1 teaspoon lightly crushed fennel seeds

1 teaspoon freshly ground black pepper

2 teaspoons sea salt

2 tablespoons yellow mustard seeds (rai kuria)

2 tablespoons white poppy seeds

4 tablespoons ghee (see page 77)

Small pinch of fenugreek seeds

1 teaspoon black mustard seeds

1 tablespoon Minced Garlic (page 80)

1 small boiled potato, peeled and mashed

2 teaspoons red chile powder

½ cup canned tomato puree

1 tablespoon Ginger Puree (page 80)

2 tablespoons jaggery

From the Tropic of Cancer running just south of Kolkata, the eastern state of Bengal is an extraordinarily fertile land with rice paddies, dense groves of coconut and palm trees, fields bursting with greens and vegetables, and numerous rivers, ponds, and lakes teeming with fish. Bengalis are lovers of fish, in particular freshwater fish. Even the crustaceans that Bengalis adore—crabs, prawns, and scallops—are harvested from lakes, rivers, and their subsidiaries, not from the open sea. As a child, I developed a distaste for fish after being dragged by my mother to fish markets where the stench of fish ran high. Fishmongers, usually women with saris tucked into their laps, would squat on blocks of large concrete surrounded by freshly caught fish sitting on ice blocks, hawking their wares. My mother would always tell me to eat more fish if I wanted to become smart like the Bengalis, who are renowned for their scholarly, literary, and artistic accomplishments. If you cannot find white poppy seeds, substitute ground sesame seeds or tahini. Replace the scallops with jumbo peeled shrimp or flounder or kingfish steaks if you prefer. (*See the recipe photo on page 193.*)

Place the scallops in a medium bowl. Add the mustard oil, turmeric, fennel seeds, black pepper, and 1 teaspoon of the salt and stir to coat. Cover and refrigerate to marinate for at least 2 hours or up to overnight.

In a small grinder, grind the yellow mustard seeds and poppy seeds until smooth with flecks of graininess. Heat a large, heavy-bottom saucepan over high heat. Add 1 tablespoon of the ghee, add the scallops, and sear on each side for 1 minute each—this is not to cook them entirely but just to give them a little color. Transfer the scallops from the pan to a plate and set them aside while you prepare the sauce. No need to wipe or clean the pan unless there are burnt bits and pieces that need to be discarded.

Heat the remaining 3 tablespoons ghee in the same pan over high heat and pop the fenugreek and black mustard seeds (see page 40). Add the ground seeds, the garlic, boiled potato, and red chile powder and cook for 2 to 3 minutes, until the fat has risen to the top or is bubbling at the edges, then add 2 cups water. Bring to a boil, then lower the heat, cover, and simmer for 5 to 6 minutes, until again the mixture is well incorporated. Add the tomato puree, ginger puree, jaggery, and remaining 1 teaspoon salt and continue cooking until the sauce turns a reddish golden color with drops of fat shimmering at the top.

Slide the scallops into the sauce, cook for a minute or two, until cooked through, and serve.

chile masala shrimp

Completely unrelated to Indian black peppercorns, Sichuan pepper-corns, or prickly ash, as they are sometimes called, have been used in China for thousands of years. There are a few related varieties in parts of Kashmir and Nepal, like triphal and timur, but these are much milder than the assertive head-spinning Sichuan peppercorns. I encountered Sichuan peppercorns in a New York restaurant many years ago, and the instant mouth-numbing tingling I experienced blew my mind at first. However, it coated my mouth in such a way that I was unable to taste much for a few hours after, and this taught me to use the peppercorns judiciously. Now it is a flavor I crave frequently, especially during cold winter months when I want to keep my digestive juices flowing. This recipe is a foray into Indo-Chinese cuisine, and I love the tofu version (see variation, below) just as much. (*See the recipe photo on page 95.*)

Place the shrimp in a large bowl. Add the sesame oil, 1 tablespoon of the garlic, the turmeric, and salt and stir to coat. Cover and refrigerate for at least 2 hours or up to 2 days.

Heat the sesame oil in a large wok or saucepan over high heat. Pop the cumin seeds (see page 40), then add the kari leaves and cook for a couple of seconds. Immediately add the onion and the remaining 1 teaspoon minced garlic, lower the heat to low, and cook until translucent. Increase the heat to high, then add the carrots and cook for a minute or two. Decrease the heat again, cover, and simmer for 5 to 7 minutes, until the carrots are softened.

Turn the heat up to high; add the shrimp, celery, bell pepper, ginger puree, and peanuts; and cook for 1 to 2 minutes, until the celery remains bright green, the shrimp are opaque, and the vegetables are still crisp. Add the vinegar, Sichuan peppercorns, whole red chiles, and garam masala and lower the heat. Simmer for another minute, then turn the heat off. Garnish with sesame seeds and cilantro and serve.

Variation

Tofu or Cauliflower Chile Masala: Replace the shrimp with 1 pound firm or extra-firm tofu or oven-roasted cauliflower. With tofu, drain, marinate, and bake the whole block at 350°F for 15 to 20 minutes, or until it has golden brown edges, then cool and cut into cubes. Marinate the cauliflower exactly the same way as the shrimp, spread on a baking sheet, then roast in a 350°F oven for 15 to 20 minutes, or until golden and cooked through.

SERVES 4

1 pound medium shrimp, peeled and deveined, with tails on

2 tablespoons toasted sesame oil

2 tablespoons Minced Garlic (page 80)

1 teaspoon ground turmeric

1 teaspoon sea salt

⅓ cup toasted sesame oil

1 teaspoon cumin seeds

15 to 20 minced kari leaves

1 cup minced white onion

2 large carrots, sliced ½-inch thick on the diagonal

2 celery stalks, sliced ½ inch thick on the diagonal

1 red bell pepper, cut into ½-inch pieces

2 tablespoons Ginger Puree (page 80)

¼ cup chopped toasted peanuts

2 tablespoons rice wine vinegar

1 teaspoon crushed Sichuan peppercorns

10 to 12 whole red chiles

1 teaspoon garam masala (see page 69)

Sesame seeds for garnish

Chopped fresh cilantro for garnish

coconut crab dip

The first time I saw live lobsters or soft-shell crabs was at Café Annie, the first and only restaurant I worked for in Houston, Texas. At first, I was horrified seeing them squirm and move about in the boxes. Watching the fish guy spear the live critters and then drop them in hot water made my heart pound. Unfortunately, this did not prevent me from tasting the crab hours later. I do recognize that whether it's a giant king crab leg or pristine jumbo lump crabmeat, most of us omnivores love crab. Whether it's stuffed into a samosa, tossed in a crisp cold salad, or fried into a cake, enjoying crab is a no-brainer. This warm bubbly crab dip combines the best of good South Indian cooking and can become a lovely party appetizer. Serve it with warm bread, small dosas, naans, rotis, or parathas.

Preheat the oven to 400°F.

To make the crab: In a large bowl, gently combine the crabmeat with the grated coconut, coconut milk, lemon juice, and salt and set aside.

To make the masala: In a medium frying pan, heat the oil over high heat. Pop the mustard seeds (see page 40), then add the kari leaves and cook for a couple of seconds. Immediately add the garlic and leeks, decrease the heat to medium-high, and cook for 4 to 5 minutes, until the leeks are translucent. Lower the heat; add the red chile powder, tomatoes, and salt; and simmer for 5 to 7 minutes, until the fat in the masala has risen to the top or to the edges, it is an orange red in color, and thick, chunky, or semidry. The time will vary based on the water content of the tomatoes. If the tomatoes start to stick to the bottom of the pan, add a few tablespoons water. Turn the heat off and stir in the garam masala.

Spread the tomato masala evenly on the bottom of a baking dish. Place the coconut-crab mixture on top, letting the edges of tomato masala peek out. Bake for 10 to 12 minutes, until bubbly, and top with fresh herb springs. Serve with a crispy dosa, uthappams, naan, or crusty bread.

SERVES 4

CRAB

1 pound fresh jumbo crabmeat

½ cup fresh or frozen grated coconut

½ cup coconut milk

Juice of ½ lemon

1 teaspoon sea salt

TOMATO MASALA

3 tablespoons coconut oil

1 teaspoon black mustard seeds

15 to 20 kari leaves

8 to 10 garlic cloves, sliced

2 cups sliced leeks, white and green parts

1 teaspoon red chile powder

1 cup canned ground tomatoes, or 2 cups diced fresh tomatoes

1 teaspoon sea salt

½ teaspoon garam masala (see page 69)

Fresh herb sprigs for garnish

Dosas (see page 99), uthappams, naan (see page 245), or crusty bread for serving

kerala crawfish stew

I learned about crawfish, also known as crayfish, freshwater lobsters, or mudbugs, when I moved to Texas. Southerners' enormous consumption of crawfish betrays the love they have for the little crustacean. Coinciding with Lent, crawfish season is kicked off by spring currents, when the tiny crustaceans come out of their burrows and Cajuns and Creoles gather for giant crawfish boils. Fresh wild crawfish is available for a short season and makes a delicious curry with flavors of southern India.

In a shallow stockpot, heat the coconut oil over high heat. Pop the mustard seeds (see page 40), then immediately add the kari leaves and onion. Turn the heat down to low, cover the pot, and cook for 5 to 7 minutes, until the onion turns light golden brown, watching carefully so they don't burn.

Add the minced garlic, crushed tomatoes, and red chile powder; turn the heat down to low; cover; and cook for 2 to 3 minutes, or until the fat appears at the edges. Add the ginger, coconut milk, and 1 cup water; turn the heat up; and bring to a boil. Lower the heat to low, cover the pot, and simmer for 10 to 12 minutes, or until the flavors have melded—the fat from the coconut oil may rise to the top.

Gently slide in the crawfish tails along with the garam masala and cook for 1 minute to warm through. Turn the heat off. Stir in the lime juice, garnish with the herbs and coconut, and serve.

SERVES 4

¼ cup coconut oil

1 teaspoon black mustard seeds

15 to 20 kari leaves, minced

1 cup minced white or yellow onion

1 tablespoon Minced Garlic (page 80)

1 cup canned crushed tomatoes

1 teaspoon red chile powder

2 tablespoons Ginger Puree (page 80)

One 14-ounce can coconut milk

1 pound cooked crawfish tail meat

¼ teaspoon garam masala (see page 69)

Juice of 1 lime

½ cup chopped fresh herbs (such as cilantro or parsley)

Sliced fresh coconut for garnish

patra fish

SERVES 6 TO 8

2 whole fillets, or 6 to 8 steaks
firm fish (see headnote), weighing
1½ to 2 pounds total

1 teaspoon sea salt

GREEN MASALA

1 bunch cilantro, leaves and stems

1 cup loose fresh mint leaves

1 serrano chile

2 tablespoons Ginger Puree (page 80)

2 teaspoons Minced Garlic (page 80)

½ cup grated or chopped
fresh coconut

1 teaspoon garam masala
(see page 69)

½ teaspoon sea salt

Juice of 1 lemon

¼ cup olive oil

1 large banana leaf (see headnote)

Grated fresh coconut for garnish

1 lemon, cut into slices

Fish wrapped in banana or other leaves and steamed is common through India's fish-eating communities. Bengalis wrap fish in a mustard marinade, and Parsi cooks marinate fish in an aromatic green chutney before steaming it in banana leaves. However, the fish can also be wrapped in edible leaves like mustard leaves, hoja santa, or fig leaves. When Islam was established in Persia (erstwhile Iran), Zoroastrian fire temples were destroyed and its followers faced religious persecution and were forced to leave their homeland. India, known for its religious tolerance and inclusivity, welcomed the refugees. A large contingent of Parsis were granted permission to land in Gujarat, thus founding the Parsi (Gujarati term for Persian) community in India. They assimilated into Indian culture and flourished under British colonial rule by showing an uncommon aptitude for Western education and sensibilities. They became the local titans of trade and commerce and used their tremendous influence to endow schools, colleges, and hospitals for the poor.

Today, Mumbai is home to the largest Parsi population in the world. I spent most summers at the Mumbai home of a Parsi friend, Jena, where I experienced firsthand the interesting cuisine that had developed from combining Indian spices, herbs, and pulses with Persian luxuries like nuts and dried fruits. I would know we were having patra fish for dinner when the herby aroma of the green chutney and the sounds of ritual grinding on the stone would waft up the stairway. Sometimes it was local kingfish, other times it was carp or mackerel. Any firm seasonal fish like snapper or halibut will do well, and while the recipe calls for either steaks or fillets, patra fish is traditionally made with thick fish steaks. If you are unable to locate banana leaf, use only parchment paper instead.

Rub the fish with the salt and set aside.

To make the green masala: Discard the bottom 3 inches from the cilantro stems, rinse, and squeeze lightly to remove excess water. Roughly chop and set aside.

Combine the mint, chile, ginger puree, minced garlic, coconut, garam masala, salt, lemon juice, and oil in a food processor and process until roughly chopped. Add the cilantro, a few stems at a time, and continue processing until the mixture is evenly chopped.

recipe continues

Preheat the oven to 400°F. Place a shallow baking pan with hot water on the bottom rack of the oven (this will create steam in the oven). Make sure there is always water in this pan as the fish bakes.

Pass the banana leaf over a hot gas flame or, using tongs, hold over an electric burner on high for a second or two to soften it. Lay the fish pieces over the center of the banana leaf. Spread enough of the masala to coat the top generously and evenly. Flip the pieces over and repeat. Fold the leaf over like a package and cover the entire package in parchment paper. Place on a baking sheet and bake for 10 to 12 minutes, until the fish is almost cooked through, then remove the fish from the oven and let it rest for 10 minutes. It will finish cooking during this time. Open the parchment package, garnish with grated coconut and slices of lemon, and serve immediately.

roasted wild quail

Considered a jewel of the local ecosystem, the Gir National Park lays near the southern part of Gujarat, the state I grew up in. It is filled with wild flora and fauna, including the Asiatic lion, nilgai, deer, antelope, Bengal fox, cheetahs, tigers, and about thirty varieties of birds and reptiles. My two older brothers would often accompany my uncle, who ran the forest division, on early-morning hunting expeditions. Usually on the hunt for a deer but not always finding one, they would often return home with teetar, a local gray partridge. The birds were small and lean with delicious flavorful meat, and my mother would stuff and braise them with spicy nut masalas to overcome the gamy flavors. When I moved to Texas, local wild quails came close to the flavors of teetar.

Hunting has a long and sordid history in India. Religious animal sacrifice is a custom prevalent even today, and during the Aryan times, sacrificing feral horses or tigers was common. The emperors would also hunt tigers and lions as a show of masculinity. This was followed by British colonial masters, who hunted to find the prized elusive Bengal tiger and raided many forests to clear land to grow varied plants. Today, the Gir Forest is a fiercely protected sanctuary and a popular heritage tourist spot in Gujarat. In Texas, quail hunting is very popular and many a customer would send me their prize quails to cook at Indika. This pine nut–stuffed quail was a fixture on our menu for over ten years and, needless to say, very popular with the hunting populace of Texas. The jaggery amchur masala turns into something like a glaze on the skin of the birds. The saffron yogurt can be served on the side or drizzled over the roasted birds.

To make the quail masala: In a small bowl, combine the minced garlic, amchur, jaggery, garam masala, black pepper, oil, and salt. Rub the quail with the garlic mixture and set aside in the refrigerator for up to 24 hours to marinate while you prepare the stuffing.

To make the stuffing: Preheat the oven to 300°F. Spread the pine nuts on a baking sheet in an even layer and toast in the oven for 7 to 8 minutes, until light golden in color. Transfer to a plate to cool. Add the onion puree, fenugreek leaves, red chile powder, garam masala, and salt to the pine nuts and stir to combine.

recipe continues

SERVES 4

QUAIL MASALA

1 tablespoon Minced Garlic (page 80)

1 tablespoon amchur (dried mango powder)

2 teaspoons jaggery

1 teaspoon garam masala (see page 69)

1 teaspoon freshly ground black pepper

2 to 3 tablespoons olive oil

1 teaspoon sea salt

4 whole semiboneless quail

QUAIL STUFFING

¾ cup pine nuts

½ cup Caramelized Onion Puree (page 82)

2 tablespoons dried fenugreek leaves

2 teaspoons red chile powder

1 teaspoon garam masala (see page 69)

1 teaspoon sea salt

Saffron Yogurt (recipe follows) for serving

Divide the stuffing into four equal portions and stuff each quail with one portion. Secure the opening of the quail cavity closed with toothpicks.

Increase the oven temperature to 400°F. Grease a baking sheet, place the quails on the sheet, and roast for 10 minutes. Lower the oven temperature to 350°F and roast for another 10 minutes, or until clear juices start trickling out. Turn the oven off and allow the quail to rest in the oven for another 20 minutes without opening the oven door. Remove from the oven and serve with saffron yogurt.

Saffron Yogurt: Combine 2 cups plain thick whole-milk yogurt (see page 86) with a generous pinch of saffron, 1 teaspoon sea salt, and 1 teaspoon sugar or honey in a medium bowl and stir to mix. Cover and refrigerate for at least 3 hours or up to 4 days ahead to infuse into the yogurt.

oxtail nihari

SERVES 4 TO 6

4 pounds oxtail

1 tablespoon Minced Garlic (page 80)

1 tablespoon sea salt, plus
1 teaspoon

1 tablespoon freshly ground
black pepper

¼ cup ghee (see page 77)

8 to 10 whole cloves, lightly crushed

1 teaspoon green cardamom seeds,
lightly crushed

½ cup chickpea flour

½ cup Caramelized Onion Puree
(page 82)

⅓ cup Ginger Puree (page 80)

1 teaspoon ground turmeric

1 tablespoon red chile powder

1 tablespoon toasted ground cumin

1 teaspoon garam masala
(see page 69)

Julienned ginger for garnish

Fresh chopped herbs (such as
cilantro or mint) for garnish

On one of my annual trips to India and in an attempt to cheer up my father after my mother's passing, he and I went on a trip to Jaipur. We stayed at the iconic Rambagh Palace Hotel, and while I enjoyed the utter warmth and luxury, after a few days I was restless and asked our driver, Rahim, to take us to his favorite street-food vendors. With a glint in his eye, he asked me if I would like to join him for breakfast the next morning. I accepted his invitation with much anticipation. The next morning, Rahim drove us to a very different part of the city; the streets were much smaller and packed with shops and street-cart vendors. He parked the car across from what looked like an extremely crowded restaurant with dozens of men and women milling about waiting for their food, mostly day laborers, some squatting on the sidewalk and eating hurriedly, and some on inverted boxes or large cans. My father took one look at the surroundings and refused to get out of the car. I covered my head with a scarf and jumped out, and Rahim led me up the steps to the restaurant. There were two giant vats of nihari, a slow-cooked spiced beef-shank stew, bubbling while men in loincloths gently stirring the pots with six-foot ladles. One pot of nihari could feed over a hundred people. Right next to the nihari was a massive tandoor buried into the ground, where a man was expertly making stacks of naans. Rahim walked up to one of the cooks, said something in rapid-fire Urdu, then led us to an empty table at the back of the restaurant. We sat down, and within three minutes, large bowls of the famous nihari with a stack of naans appeared.

No silverware or napkins in sight, I tore a naan with my hands, dipped it into the nihari, and started eating. Surrounded by the deeply stained concrete room with high ceilings that had been around for decades or more, I took a deep breath and tears of joy started flowing from my eyes. I felt transported to a previous era, enveloped in the devastatingly intoxicating aroma and flavors of beef shank nuanced with clove, cardamom, and ginger simmered for days. The simplicity and beauty of the entire operation left me speechless, and this became one of my top food memories. One curry, one bread, three men who cooked it, and hundreds of people who ate it every morning. The legend of this place, which had no visible name, was that the nihari had what is called a taar, an unbroken string of flavor over decades. It was made each night using a portion from earlier that day to start the new batch,

recipe continues

concentrating the flavors, and simmered throughout the night to serve for next morning's breakfast. I finished the entire bowl of nihari, licked my fingers clean, and jumped up to give Rahim a hug of gratitude.

To this day, when I prepare nihari, I am transported to that concrete room with men in loincloths stirring vats of aromatic nihari. I may not be able to replicate that flavor with decades of taar, but I will never stop trying.

Preheat the oven to 400°F.

In a large, deep roasting pan, coat the oxtail with the minced garlic, 1 tablespoon salt, and black pepper and then spread it out. Roast for 45 minutes, then lower the oven temperature to 250°F.

Meanwhile, heat the ghee in a small stockpot or Dutch oven over high heat. Add the cloves, cardamom seeds, and chickpea flour and cook for 3 to 4 minutes, stirring constantly, until a nutty fragrant aroma emits. Add the onion puree, ginger puree, turmeric, red chile powder, cumin, and remaining 1 teaspoon salt. Then add 4 to 5 cups water and bring to a boil.

After the oxtail has been roasted, pour the mixture over it, seal it tightly with foil, and place it back in the oven for 4 to 6 hours, or lower the oven temperature to 200°F and leave it overnight. The meat should be falling off the bone. Stir in the garam masala, let the stew rest on the counter until cooled to the touch, and refrigerate for 1 to 2 hours or overnight before serving. Garnish with julienned ginger and fresh herbs.

homestyle butter chicken

My first few years in North America were spent starstruck with local culture and in blissful ignorance of many destructive practices prevalent around me, like factory farming. On the rare occasion when we ate chickens in India, since women were not allowed into meat shops, my father would haul them back alive, screaming and clucking in a shopping bag. They would run around in our backyard until D-Day arrived. My mother would calmly pick up a hapless chicken, and with a swift flick of her wrist, twist the neck of the poor bird and hand it over to our family cook to prepare for dinner. It took me a few trips to India to realize that those scrawny chickens we ate growing up had much more depth of flavor than the plump chickens of the American supermarket.

Today, butter chicken, aka chicken tikka masala (aka CTM) is hands down the most popular Indian restaurant dish. The word *tikka* has its origins in Persian; it simply means "bits or pieces," and *chicken tikka* refers to spiced and roasted boneless chunks of chicken. In 2001, Robin Cook, then the foreign minister, announced CTM as the new national dish of Great Britain as a shining example of multiculturalism. Critics immediately responded by condemning it as a British invention and yet another demonstration of the British facility to reduce foreign foods to their most unappetizing form. While there is some controversy about the origins of the dish, the most likely story is that the modern version was created during the early seventies by an enterprising Indian chef near London. In a quick attempt to fix a dry chicken tikka sent back by an upset customer, he whipped together a can of Campbell's tomato soup, cream, and spices to provide a sauce for the offending chicken. Of course, this unknown chef, who received no credit for his ingenuity, inadvertently went on to invent a dish that Britons now eat upward of twenty tons of in a week. While originally dismissed as "mongrel cuisine," in the hands of a skilled cook, butter chicken has evolved with periodic improvisations as a popular curry known all over the world.

When my children were young, butter chicken made with bone-in chicken pieces was a regular meal we enjoyed with great gusto, especially when their friends came over. Today, I consider butter chicken, or CTM, as gateway cuisine—once you get a good handle on it, there are so many more delicious and fragrant stews to explore. This recipe calls for boneless chicken, but the best flavor is achieved with bone-in chicken legs. If using bone-in meat, increase the cooking time as needed.

recipe continues

SERVES 4 TO 6

MARINATED CHICKEN

2 pounds boneless skinless chicken thighs, trimmed and cut into 2-inch pieces

½ cup plain thick Greek-style yogurt

2 tablespoons olive oil

1 tablespoon Minced Garlic (page 80)

1 teaspoon red chile powder

1 teaspoon ground cumin

1 teaspoon ground nigella seeds (kalonji)

1 tablespoon sea salt

SAUCE

4 tablespoons unsalted butter, plus 1 to 2 tablespoons for finishing (optional)

2 tablespoons Ginger Puree (page 80)

1 tablespoon Minced Garlic (page 80)

1 tablespoon red chile powder

1 teaspoon sea salt

1 cup canned tomato puree

2 cups heavy cream

3 tablespoons dried fenugreek leaves

1 teaspoon garam masala (see page 69)

At my restaurant, I created a more complex and wildly popular version of butter chicken and named it Chicken 25, a reference to its twenty-five seasonings and spices. To make Chicken 25, halve the amount of cream and add 2 tablespoons Caramelized Onion Puree (page 82) and 2 tablespoons ground white poppy seeds to the sauce and a generous pinch of saffron to the chicken marinade. If you don't have poppy seeds, use toasted ground almonds or cashews.

To marinate and roast the chicken: Place the chicken in a large bowl. Add the yogurt, oil, garlic, red chile powder, cumin, nigella seeds, and salt. Cover and refrigerate for at least 2 hours or up to overnight.

Preheat the oven to 450°F and grease a baking sheet.

Spread the marinated chicken over the baking sheet, place in the oven, and roast for 15 to 20 minutes, until the chicken appears firm with clear juices flowing. Set aside.

To make the sauce: In a wide heavy-bottom saucepan, heat the butter over high heat. Add the ginger puree and garlic and cook for a few seconds, until the garlic turns white. Add the red chile powder, salt, tomato puree, and heavy cream and bring to a boil. Lower the heat and simmer for 10 to 12 minutes—the mixture will turn pinkish red. Add the fenugreek leaves and garam masala and continue to simmer for another 5 to 7 minutes, or until fragrant.

When the chicken has finished roasting, add it to the simmering sauce along with any juices from the pan and continue cooking for another 10 to 12 minutes, or until the meat is tender and the fat rises to the top. It you want the curry to be more saucy, add ½ to 1 cup water. Turn the heat off and let the curry rest for 10 to 15 minutes. Stir in the additional 1 to 2 tablespoons butter, if desired before serving.

Variations

Dairy-Free Option: Replace the butter with olive oil and the heavy cream with coconut milk.

Biryani Option: Cook 2 cups rinsed and presoaked basmati rice seasoned with whole spices, like a stick of cinnamon, mace, or whole cardamom, in 3 cups chicken stock. In a large shallow Dutch oven or saucepan, spread the hot rice over the warm Chicken 25 and let it rest for 10 to 12 minutes. Add nuts and dried fruit of your choice. Fold the rice and chicken carefully with a spatula before serving.

SERVES 4 TO 6

LAMB

½ cup plain whole-milk yogurt
(see page 86)

¼ cup grated ripe or green papaya

3 tablespoons mustard oil

1 tablespoon freshly ground
black pepper

1 tablespoon ground cinnamon

1 tablespoon Minced Garlic (page 80)

Generous pinch of saffron

2 teaspoons sea salt

4 lamb hind shanks

MASALA

¼ cup ghee (see page 77)

1 teaspoon lightly crushed
green cardamom seeds

1 teaspoon lightly crushed
fennel seeds

½ teaspoon lightly crushed
fenugreek seeds

½ cup Caramelized Onion Puree
(page 82)

2 teaspoons ground cumin

1 to 2 tablespoons Kashmiri
chile powder

1 cup coconut milk

1 cup plain whole-milk yogurt
(see page 86)

¼ cup Ginger Puree (page 80)

2 medium parsnips, peeled and
cut into 1-inch wheels

2 large carrots, cut into 1-inch
wheels

1 teaspoon garam masala
(see page 69)

2 teaspoons rose water

2 tablespoons amchur
(dried mango powder)

The food culture of Kashmir has been heavily influenced by trespassing foreigners, starting with the Persian invasion, followed by Alexander the Great, the Turks, and Central Asians. Timur, one of the best-known nomadic leaders of Central Asia, invaded India during the fifteenth century, and in his wake came skilled woodcrafters, calligraphers, weavers, architects, and cooks from Samarkand (now located in Uzbekistan). The descendants of these cooks, the wazas, are the master chefs of Kashmir. A wazwan is an unforgettable sumptuous thirty- to thirty-five-course feast usually reserved for special occasions, like weddings. Roghan josh, a Kashmiri specialty often served at wazwans, is a blending of Persian and Indian cultures. This decadent, rich preparation of lamb is great for holidays and best made the day before or the morning of for the flavors to really come together.

To prepare the lamb: In a large storage container, combine the yogurt, papaya, mustard oil, black pepper, cinnamon, garlic, saffron, and salt. Add the lamb and toss to coat. Cover and refrigerate for at least 2 hours or up to overnight.

Preheat the oven to 450°F.

Spread the shanks on a large, deep baking pan and roast uncovered for 10 to 15 minutes, until the shanks are slightly caramelized and browned.

Meanwhile, to make the masala: In a medium saucepan, heat the ghee over medium heat. Add the cardamom seeds, fennel seeds, and fenugreek seeds. Stir in the onion puree, cumin, and chile powder; cook for a few seconds; then add the coconut milk. Simmer for just 2 to 3 minutes to incorporate the spices in the coconut milk, then add 2 cups water and bring to a boil. Stir in the yogurt and ginger puree and pour the mixture around the roasted shanks. Place the parsnips and carrots around the shanks.

Cover the top or seal the pan with foil, lower the oven temperature to 250°F, and roast for 2 hours, or until the meat is tender and falling off the bone. The sauce should have thickened around the shanks, but if it appears too watery, take the foil off and place the pan back in the oven for another 15 to 20 minutes, or until the sauce has thickened.

Turn the oven off, and stir in the garam masala, rose water, and amchur. Leave in the oven for another 10 to 15 minutes for the flavors to meld. This dish is best eaten an hour or two after it has been prepared or the next day.

goa pork

In May 1498, six years after Columbus had crossed the Atlantic, three Portuguese vessels, in continued search of a maritime route from Europe to the East, anchored off the coast of Calicut on the Malabar Coast of India. Under the command of Vasco da Gama, a well-known fearless explorer, the Portuguese conquistadors had crossed to Africa around the Cape of Hope and triumphantly sailed across the Arabian Sea to India, succeeding in a mission that Columbus had famously failed at. The local Hindu ruler welcomed da Gama and his men, and the crew ended up staying in Calicut for three months. Not everyone welcomed their presence, though, especially Muslim traders, who clearly had no intention of giving up their trading grounds to Christian visitors. After returning with ships loaded with spices and newfound intelligence, King Manuel of Portugal welcomed the returning mariners as heroes. They were paraded through the streets of Lisbon, and Vasco da Gama was the toast of the town. Plans were made to return to India to outflank the Muslims and Hindus and establish a Christian colony. The Portuguese returned to India, seized control of the sea route from the Venetians, usurped the Middle Eastern traders, and thus began their ruthless domination of the East Indies trade that was to last through most of the sixteenth century. It is by means of the Portuguese that the chile pepper, which they had found in Brazil, made its way into India and in no time became essential to the South Indian diet and soon the rest of India. Even Ayurvedic physicians, who rarely incorporated foreign foods into the cosmic world of health and healing, embraced chiles wholeheartedly. This stew is a cross between vindaloo and xacuti (pronounced "shakuti"), both of which are fiery meat stews traditionally made with pork. The mushroom variation is just as delicious, so do give that one a try too. *(See the recipe photo, right, opposite.)*

Trim and cut the pork into 2-inch pieces. (If using pork on the bone, leave the bones in to add flavor to the sauce.) Place in a large bowl, and add the mustard oil, minced garlic, turmeric, and 1 teaspoon of the salt. Cover and refrigerate to marinate for at least 4 hours or up to overnight.

In a small dry frying pan, toast the coriander seeds, mustard seeds, black peppercorns, cardamom, cloves, and ajwain seeds over medium heat for 2 to 3 minutes, until fragrant. Add the red chiles and cook for a few more seconds. Turn the heat off and let the spices cool for a few minutes.

recipe continues

SERVES 4 TO 6

2 pounds pork leg or shoulder, with or without bone

2 tablespoons mustard oil

1 tablespoon Minced Garlic (page 80)

½ teaspoon ground turmeric

2 teaspoons sea salt

1 tablespoon coriander seeds

1 teaspoon black mustard seeds

2 teaspoons black peppercorns

1 teaspoon green cardamom seeds

½ teaspoon whole cloves

½ teaspoon ajwain seeds

8 to 10 whole dried red chiles

½ cup Caramelized Onion Puree (page 82)

One 3-inch piece unpeeled ginger, roughly chopped

One 14-ounce can coconut milk

¼ cup coconut oil

2 cups chopped (2-inch pieces) carrots

1 cup baby potatoes

Fragrant chopped herbs (such as cilantro, mint, oregano, or basil) for garnish

In a blender, combine the spice mixture with the onion puree, ginger, coconut milk, and remaining 1 teaspoon salt and blend until smooth and speckled medium brown in color.

In a wide heavy-bottom saucepan, heat the coconut oil over high heat. Add the marinated pork and cook for 5 to 6 minutes, making sure it has color on all sides. Add the pureed masala, rinse out the blender bowl with 1 to 2 cups water, and pour it into the curry. Increase the heat to high, bring to a boil, then lower the heat, cover, and simmer for 30 to 45 minutes, until the curry is a smooth rich brown in color Now add the carrots and potatoes and continue simmering until the pork is tender and the vegetables are cooked through, another 30 to 45 minutes. Garnish with herbs and serve.

Variation

Mushroom Option: Cut 6 portobello mushrooms into 2-inch chunks and swap them for the pork; cut the cooking time for the sauce in half. Make the sauce with the carrots and potatoes and slide the mushrooms in at the very end before serving.

vindaloo ribs

Nowhere in the world did European settlements have more impact than the Portuguese colonial empire in India. Within less than a hundred years of the Portuguese establishing themselves in India, two-thirds of the population of Goa was Christian as a result of brutal mass conversions to Catholicism. A new cuisine emerged: meats, potatoes, tomatoes, and vinegars native to Portugal were combined with the Arab influence of dried fruits, nuts, tamarind pulp, shredded coconut, and aromatic spice masalas. Vindaloo is a Goan adaptation of the Portuguese dish carne de vinho e alhos, or meat cooked in wine, vinegar, and garlic. Add to this coconut, black pepper, cinnamon, and red chiles, and vindaloo was born. Pickled onions make a great side to the ribs. (*See the recipe photo, left, on page 214.*)

To make the pickled onions: Peel the onion, cut it in half, and then thinly slice it. Place it in a container with the beet, star anise, red chiles, black cardamom, cinnamon, red wine, salt, and 2 cups water. Cover and refrigerate for 2 to 3 days for the onions to turn a deep magenta pink and infuse with the flavor of the spices. Discard the spices and store the onions in a little bit of the brine.

To marinate and roast the ribs: Place the entire rib rack on a baking sheet. In a small bowl, whisk together the red wine, mustard oil, minced garlic, black pepper, cloves, and salt. Rub all over the ribs and marinate bone-side down in the refrigerator for at least 2 hours or up to overnight.

Preheat the oven to 450°F.

Place the ribs bone-side up in the oven and roast for 45 minutes.

Meanwhile, to make the masala: In a small bowl, whisk together the coconut milk, red chile powder, jaggery, ginger, turmeric, cumin, and salt.

Take the ribs out of the oven, flip them over to bone-side down, and lower the oven temperature to 250°F. Place the potatoes around the ribs and pour the sauce over the ribs and potatoes. Cover with foil, making sure to tuck the corners tight, and bake for 1½ to 2 hours, until the meat is tender and sliding off the bone.

Turn the oven off and remove the foil from the sheet. Sprinkle with the amchur and garam masala and let the ribs rest in the oven for another 30 minutes. Serve with the pickled red onions.

SERVES 5 OR 6

PICKLED ONIONS

1 large red onion

1 small beet, peeled and sliced

2 star anise pods

6 whole red chiles

4 black cardamom pods

2 large cinnamon sticks

½ cup red wine

2 teaspoons sea salt

MARINATED RIBS

1 rack baby back ribs (2 to 3 pounds)

2 tablespoons red wine

2 tablespoons mustard oil

1 tablespoon Minced Garlic (page 80)

1 tablespoon freshly ground black pepper

¼ teaspoon ground cloves

1 tablespoon sea salt

MASALA

½ cup coconut milk

2 tablespoons red chile powder

1 tablespoon jaggery

1 tablespoon ground ginger

½ teaspoon ground turmeric

1 tablespoon toasted ground cumin

1 teaspoon sea salt

1 pound small potatoes, cut in half if large

1 tablespoon amchur (dried mango powder)

1 teaspoon garam masala (see page 69)

sayel goat

SERVES 4 OR 5

2 pounds goat chops (10 to 12 chops)

¼ cup melted ghee (see page 77)

2 cups minced white onions

1 teaspoon ground turmeric

1 tablespoon Minced Garlic (page 80)

1 tablespoon lightly crushed
coriander seeds

1 teaspoon lightly crushed green
cardamom seeds

1 teaspoon freshly ground
black pepper

2 teaspoons sea salt

2 tablespoons Ginger Puree (page 80)

1 tablespoon red chile powder

1 teaspoon ground cardamom

1 teaspoon garam masala
(see page 69)

Despite the geographic proximity of Sindh, the land my parents were from, and Gujarat, the province I was born and raised in, the contrast of the two cuisines, almost unrecognizable if set side by side, delighted me. Acquiring meat in the strictly vegetarian state of Gujarat was no easy feat. Women were not allowed in butcher shops. My dad, like most men of that time and culture, was absent from any home duties except to go buy meat. But Saturday mornings, he would travel to the other end of the city to a butcher shop. Goat was our red meat because my mother would not allow beef in the house.

I use goat chops in this recipe and make it in the oven for ease, but lamb chops would be an excellent substitute. If you prefer not using chops, goat meat on the bone would be just as flavorful. (*See the recipe photo, upper left, on page 190.*)

Preheat the oven to 400°F.

Place the goat chops in a large shallow baking pan. Mix together the ghee, onions, turmeric, garlic, coriander seeds, crushed cardamom, black pepper, and salt and place around over the chops. Cover tightly with foil and bake for 30 minutes. Lower the oven temperature to 250°F and continue baking for about another hour, checking on the chops every 20 minutes to make sure they do not dry out. The meat should be soft and almost falling off the bone. The onions will transform into a thick masala coating. Add a few tablespoons water if the chops appear dry.

While the chops are still warm, stir in the ginger puree, red chile powder, ground cardamom, and garam masala. Turn the oven off and let the chops rest in the oven for 10 to 12 minutes before serving.

kerala beef fry

The state of Kerala, where cardamom and black pepper grow in the wild, is on a narrow strip of land overlooking the southern tip of the Indian subcontinent. Few areas in the world boast more ideal conditions for growing spices. It's a lush green land teeming with people and filled with lakes, rivers, streams, backwaters, and coconut trees. The Arabian Sea's white beaches fringe Kerala to the west while the Western Ghats, with their impenetrable tropical forests and eternal grasslands, define its eastern boundary.

The origins of the beef fry, a slow-cooked fragrant roast that is first boiled, then "fried" in its own fat with other seasonings, can be traced as far back as 52 CE, when the famous Saint Thomas the Apostle, the one who questioned Jesus, was believed to have arrived in Kerala and started a community of Syrian Christians (aka Malabar Christians) in India. *Syrian* does not refer to Syria the country but to the medieval language spoken by Saint Thomas and Jesus himself. Kerala is still filled with the saint's namesake churches, prayers and ceremonies are still performed in his name, and modern Christians believe that Saint Thomas baptized their forefathers, thereby starting a lineage of Christians as far back as almost two thousand years ago. Kerala fry can easily be prepared with lamb or chicken; however, decrease the cooking time for chicken. (*See the recipe photo, bottom left, on page 190.*)

Cut the beef into 2-inch chunks against the grain. Place the beef in a large shallow saucepan, add 2 cups water, the turmeric, black peppercorns, coriander, cumin, shallots, garlic, grated coconut, and 2 teaspoons of the salt and bring to a boil over high heat. Decrease the heat to low, cover, and simmer for 1 to 1½ hours, or until the beef is tender and the shallots and garlic have dissolved into the liquid.

Heat the oil in a small frying pan over high heat. Add the kari leaves, onion, bell pepper, and red chiles. Lower the heat to medium and cook for 3 to 4 minutes, until vegetables are seared with brown edges. Then add this mixture to the beef along with the garam masala, ginger, and remaining 1 teaspoon salt. Fry for another 7 to 8 minutes, until the beef is dry and coated with the masala. Garnish with fresh coconut and cilantro and serve.

SERVES 6

2 pounds boneless chuck roast

1 teaspoon ground turmeric

1 tablespoon crushed black peppercorns

1 tablespoon coriander seeds, lightly crushed

1 teaspoon toasted ground cumin

4 shallots, sliced

10 to 12 garlic cloves, cut into long slices

½ cup grated fresh coconut, plus more for garnish

3 teaspoons sea salt

¼ cup coconut oil

20 kari leaves

1 red onion, cut into 1-inch pieces

1 red bell pepper, cut into 1-inch pieces

10 to 12 whole red chiles

1 teaspoon garam masala (see page 69)

2 tablespoons freshly julienned ginger

2 tablespoons chopped fresh cilantro

bheja masala on toast

¼ cup ghee (see page 77), plus more as needed

½ teaspoon cumin seeds

½ cup minced white onion

1 teaspoon Minced Garlic (page 80)

½ cup grated raw potatoes

1½ teaspoons ground turmeric

1 teaspoon red chile powder

1 teaspoon sea salt

¼ cup plain whole-milk yogurt (see page 86), if needed, plus more for serving

2 whole goat brains, deveined and rinsed

Pinch of garam masala (see page 69)

2 teaspoon amchur (dried mango powder)

Crusty sourdough bread, or stuffed parathas (see page 242) or rotis (see page 239)

½ cup chopped fresh cilantro

Ignorance can be bliss, and for years on Sundays, I would look forward to my father bringing back two or three whole goat brains for our family to enjoy for breakfast. My mother would carefully pry out all the red veins from the organs, rinse them out completely, make a rich masala with onions, potatoes, and/or tomatoes; place the bheja on top; and simmer it with the masala until done. My brothers and I would fight over the brains and the crisp pan-seared parathas until one day when my brothers decided to take me out of the game. They held up an anatomy book at the breakfast table and unhurriedly explained to me exactly what part of the goat I was eating. I had not made the brain-to-body connection until then and ran to my room crying. Mission accomplished—that day I stopped eating bheja, and it took me almost ten years after that anatomy lesson to start enjoying it again.

We served bheja masala on the menu at Indika and Pondicheri for years. My servers tell me they would enjoy watching the expression on people's faces when they saw it on the menu, ranging from startled surprise to an outright visceral outrage. One food writer even accused me of putting it on the menu for "shock" purposes. Little did she know that even though I barely eat meat these days, I still crave organ meat, including goat brain. Look for goat brain in Middle Eastern or Pakistani halal meat shops.

Heat the ghee in a medium saucepan or frying pan over high heat. Pop the cumin seeds (see page 40), then immediately lower the heat, add the onion, garlic, potatoes, and ½ cup water and cook, covered, for 10 to 12 minutes, stirring frequently, until the potatoes are soft and the onions are just translucent. Add the turmeric, red chile powder, and salt and, if the mixture gets stuck to the bottom of the pan, ¼ cup yogurt to deglaze it. The water or yogurt is just there to make sure neither the onions nor potatoes burn and to prevent the mixture from drying out. The mixture should be thick and saucy before adding the brains. Gently add the brains, lower the heat to low, cover, and simmer for 5 to 7 minutes, until the brains appear firm and done. Sprinkle the garam masala and amchur on top and let the bheja masala rest for 10 minutes. Pan-sear slices of sourdough bread in ghee in a frying pan or saucepan and serve the bheja masala on the toast topped with the cilantro with a side of yogurt. Alternatively, serve it with stuffed parathas or rotis.

Condiments

India boasts an enormous world of condiments. First there are chutneys. Just like chaat, the word *chutney* is derived from the Hindi word *chatna*, which means "to lick." Seasonal stone fruit chutneys, like peach, plum, and mango, can be preserved for up to a year and brighten up a simple meal. South Indian chutneys, like peanut chutney and sesame chutney, are some of my absolute favorites.

The pickles of India, to be eaten in small portions with caution because of their intense seasoning, bear no resemblance to American brined pickles and are usually oil-, sugar-, and/or salt-based with intense piquant, spicy flavors. The Punjabi parsnip pickle was one I learned from the lovely host of a home I stayed at in New Delhi many years ago.

Raita (pronounced *rai tuh*) is a savory, mildly spiced yogurt vegetable or fruit salad. Eaten in small portions alongside a meal to cool off the heat of chiles or spices, raitas also work as palate cleansers. I favor the lighter corn raita or apple raita with chicken or seafood dishes, and the eggplant raita with red meat. The banana raita is particularly tasty with seafood stews or curries.

At the simplest end of the condiment spectrum are the instant relishes. I usually start with radishes and add sweet seasonal fruits, like mango, pineapple, or pomegranate seeds. A cumin seed or mustard seed pop, a squeeze of lemon juice, a dash of salt and the relish is ready in minutes. My mother had a pickle and chutney fetish. At any given time, we would have twelve to fifteen pickles and chutneys in the house. Now, every time I visit India, I hunt down the oldest aunties of my extended family and friends and plead with them to share their favorite pickle and chutney recipes. Most of them know the ingredients off the top of their head because they have been honing their recipes for years.

grapefruit chile chutney

In a small saucepan, combine the orange juice, sugar, red chile powder, ginger puree, and salt and bring to a boil over high heat. Lower the heat to medium and simmer until reduced by two-thirds, 8 to 10 minutes. Remove from the heat and let cool.

Peel the grapefruits, remove the segments, and gently stir into the cooled juice mixture.

In a small frying pan, heat the oil over high heat until it is just shy of smoking. Fry the garlic until light golden in color and pop the mustard seeds (see page 40), and fry the kari leaves. Immediately pour the hot oil over the grapefruit-orange mixture and carefully stir to combine. Refrigerate until ready to use. This chutney is best used the day it is made.

MAKES ABOUT 2 CUPS

2 cups fresh orange juice

½ cup cane sugar

1 teaspoon red chile powder

1 tablespoon Ginger Puree (page 80)

2 teaspoons sea salt

2 large pink grapefruits

3 tablespoons olive oil

3 to 4 garlic cloves, sliced

1 teaspoon black mustard seeds

20 kari leaves

mango chutney

MAKES ABOUT 3 CUPS

3 medium or 2 large firm mangoes

½ cup cane sugar

1 teaspoon red chile powder

1 teaspoon sea salt

2 tablespoons Ginger Puree (page 80)

1 cinnamon stick

4 or 5 green cardamom pods

2 tablespoons mustard oil

1 teaspoon nigella seeds (kalonji)

10 to 12 kari leaves, minced

Peel and cut the mangoes into ½-inch chunks. In a medium saucepan, combine the mangoes, sugar, red chile powder, salt, ginger puree, cinnamon, cardamom pods, and ½ cup water and bring to a simmer over low heat. Simmer for 10 to 15 minutes, until the mangoes turn translucent. Turn the heat off.

In a small frying pan, heat the mustard oil over high heat. When the oil is just shy of smoking, pop the nigella seeds (see page 40), add the kari leaves, and immediately stir into the chutney. Let the chutney cool before eating. It keeps in the refrigerator for up to 1 month.

peanut chutney

MAKES ABOUT 2 CUPS

1 tablespoon channa dal or urad dal

1 cup toasted peanuts

One 3-inch piece ginger, roughly chopped

Juice of 1 lemon

½ cup fresh orange juice or water

1 teaspoon freshly ground black pepper

1 teaspoon sea salt

2 teaspoons red chile powder

¼ cup peanut oil or light sesame oil

1 teaspoon black mustard seeds

10 to 12 kari leaves

In a small bowl, cover the dal with water, mix for a few seconds, and then drain most of the water out. Repeat twice, then soak in water to cover by a couple of inches for 3 to 4 hours. Drain.

In a food processor, combine the soaked and drained dal with the peanuts, ginger, lemon juice, orange juice, black pepper, and salt and process until smooth with flecks of graininess. Transfer to a bowl and sprinkle the red chile powder on top.

Heat the oil in a small frying pan over high heat. Pop the mustard seeds (see page 40), then add the kari leaves and cook for a couple of seconds. Add the hot oil to the bowl, spreading it over the red chile powder so it cooks slightly. Stir to combine. The chutney can be used as a sandwich spread or an accompaniment and will keep in the refrigerator for up to 1 week.

roasted cherry tomato chutney

In a medium saucepan, heat the mustard oil over high heat. Pop the cumin seeds and fenugreek seeds (see page 40), then add the kari leaves and cook for a couple of seconds. Immediately add the onions and garlic and cook for 2 to 3 minutes, or until wilted, then add the red chile powder, salt, and two-thirds of the cherry tomatoes. Lower the heat to low, cover, and simmer for 15 to 20 minutes, until the tomatoes are soft and cooked through and the chutney has thickened. Slice the remaining tomatoes in half, add to the chutney, and cook for another 4 to 5 minutes, just until heated through. Add the kishmish after the chutney has cooled, then store the chutney in the refrigerator for up to 1 month.

MAKES 3 TO 4 CUPS

¼ cup mustard oil

1 teaspoon cumin seeds

¼ teaspoon fenugreek seeds

20 kari leaves

1 cup minced red onions

20 garlic cloves, peeled

2 teaspoons red chile powder

1½ teaspoons sea salt

1 pound cherry tomatoes

½ cup kishmish (green raisins) or brown raisins

cranberry apple chutney

In a medium saucepan, combine the cranberries, apples, ginger puree, orange juice, red chile powder, cardamom seeds, sugar, and salt and cook over high heat until the mixture starts to bubble. Lower the heat to low, cover, and simmer for 15 to 20 minutes, until the fruit has cooked through and the chutney has thickened slightly. Remember, it will thicken as it cools in the refrigerator. Let cool completely. Store the chutney in the refrigerator for up to 1 month.

MAKES ABOUT 4 CUPS

One 14-ounce package fresh cranberries

2 large red apples, peeled, cored, and cut into ¼-inch cubes

2 tablespoons Ginger Puree (page 80)

1 cup fresh orange juice

2 teaspoons red chile powder

½ teaspoon crushed green cardamom seeds

1 cup cane sugar

2 teaspoons sea salt

coconut chutney

2 cups grated or chopped
fresh coconut

½ cup sesame seeds, peanuts,
or cashews

One 3-inch piece ginger,
roughly chopped

2 serrano chiles, chopped

1½ teaspoons sea salt

Juice of 1 lemon

1 cup coconut water or water

3 tablespoons mustard oil

1 teaspoon black mustard seeds

10 to 12 whole kari leaves

Pinch of asafetida

A few whole red chiles

In a blender, combine the coconut, sesame seeds, ginger, serranos, salt, lemon juice, and coconut water and blend until smooth.

In a small frying pan, heat the mustard oil over high heat. Pop the mustard seeds (see page 40), then add the kari leaves, asafetida, and red chiles and cook for a couple of seconds. Immediately fold the spices into the chutney. Let cool completely. Store the chutney in the refrigerator for up to 1 week.

stone fruit chutney

In a medium saucepan over high heat, combine the stone fruits, turmeric, sugar, ginger puree, cinnamon, cardamom pods, vinegar, salt, and 1 cup water. Bring to a boil over high heat, then lower the heat and simmer for 10 to 15 minutes, until the fruits have softened and the mixture has thickened.

In a small frying pan, heat the oil over high heat. Pop the mustard seeds, coriander seeds, and cumin seeds (see page 40). Immediately turn the heat off, add the red chile powder, and stir the spiced oil into the chutney. Let cool completely. Store the chutney in the refrigerator for up to 1 month.

MAKES ABOUT 4 CUPS

4 cups pitted and chopped (1-inch pieces) stone fruits (peaches, plums, or apricots)

1 teaspoon ground turmeric

1 cup cane sugar, or ½ cup jaggery

2 tablespoons Ginger Puree (page 80)

1 or 2 cinnamon sticks

A few green cardamom pods

2 tablespoons distilled vinegar or lemon juice

1 teaspoon sea salt

2 tablespoons light sesame oil or mustard oil

1 teaspoon black mustard seeds, lightly crushed

1 teaspoon coriander seeds, lightly crushed

1 teaspoon cumin seeds, lightly crushed

1 tablespoon red chile powder

Note: If you're using ripe sweet fruit, reduce the sugar; for raw fruit that is slightly sour and less sweet, you may need more sugar.

masala garlic ghee

Preheat the oven to 350°F and set an oven rack to the middle position.

Leaving the papery skins on, slice the garlic heads in half horizontally. Place in a shallow baking pan and add the shallots. Sprinkle on the cardamom seeds, black peppercorns, coriander seeds, and salt. Pour ½ cup of the oil over the ingredients. Cut the butter into small pieces and distribute around the ingredients. Cover the pan with a heavy lid or wrap with foil and pinch the edges tightly.

Place the baking pan in the oven and bake for 45 minutes to 1 hour, or until golden brown and soft. Check halfway through to make sure the garlic is not burning. Lower the oven temperature to 250°F and continue baking for another 20 to 30 minutes, or until caramelized. Pour the remaining ½ cup oil over the ingredients and sprinkle with the herbs. Serve with rolls, warm bread, or crudités. The garlic masala ghee will keep in the refrigerator for up to 2 weeks.

Variation

Plant-Based Version: Swap the butter for more olive oil or coconut oil.

SERVES 4 TO 6

1 whole head elephant garlic, or 3 large heads smaller garlic

3 shallots, peeled

2 teaspoons green cardamom seeds, lightly crushed

2 teaspoons black peppercorns, lightly crushed

1 tablespoon coriander seeds, very lightly crushed

2 teaspoons sea salt

1 cup extra-virgin olive oil

½ cup unsalted butter

1 cup chopped mixed fresh herbs (such as basil, parsley, mint, rosemary, oregano, or sage)

Bread rolls, warm bread, or crudités for serving

radish jalapeño pickle

1 bunch French breakfast radishes

3 jalapeño chiles

½ cup whole toasted cashews

2 tablespoons olive oil

½ teaspoon cumin seeds

10 kari leaves

1 teaspoon red chile powder

1 teaspoon sea salt

Juice of 1 lemon

Juice of 1 orange

2 tablespoons maple syrup

Slice the radishes in half lengthwise and put them in a bowl. Slice the jalapeños into thin diagonal wheels, add them to the radishes, then add the cashews.

Heat the oil in a small frying pan over high heat. Pop the cumin seeds (see page 40), then add the kari leaves and cook for a couple of seconds. Immediately add the red chile powder, salt, lemon juice, orange juice, and maple syrup. Pour the hot oil over the radish mixture and toss to combine. Refrigerate for a few hours for the flavors to mellow before serving. Store in the refrigerator for up 1 week.

punjabi parsnip pickle

MAKES ABOUT 6 CUPS

1 tablespoon sea salt, plus 1 teaspoon

2 pounds parsnips, peeled and cut into 2-inch chunks

½ cup peanut oil or light sesame oil, plus more for topping off

2 teaspoons Minced Garlic (page 80)

2 tablespoons Ginger Puree (page 80)

2 teaspoons red chile powder

½ teaspoon ground turmeric

1 tablespoon ground yellow mustard seeds

1 cup distilled vinegar

½ cup jaggery

Pour 6 cups water into a large saucepan and add the 1 tablespoon salt. Bring to a boil over high heat. Add the parsnips and blanch them for 3 to 5 minutes, until slightly softened but still crisp. Drain, then lay the parsnips on a tray or sheet pan with paper towels to let them air dry completely—this will take several hours.

In a medium frying pan or saucepan, heat the oil over high heat. Add the garlic and ginger puree, then immediately turn the heat off. Add the red chile powder, turmeric, mustard seeds, and remaining 1 teaspoon salt. Add the vinegar and jaggery, turn the heat back to high, and bring to a boil. Immediately pour the mixture over the vegetables and stir well to combine the ingredients. Pack into a jar or jars and top with a ¾- to 1-inch layer of oil. (This also works as a barrier against bacterial contamination.) Cover the jar tightly and let the pickle sit out for 2 to 3 days, then store in the refrigerator for up to 2 months.

banana raita

In a large bowl, combine the yogurt, bananas, cumin, peanuts, and salt.

In a small frying pan, heat the oil over high heat. Pop the mustard seeds (see page 40), then fry the kari leaves and red chile powder. Stir the hot oil into the raita. The raita needs to be stored in the refrigerator and is best used within 2 days. (*See the recipe photo, bottom right, on page 235.*)

MAKES ABOUT 4 CUPS

2 cups plain whole-milk yogurt (see page 86)

4 ripe but firm bananas, cut into ½-inch wheels

2 teaspoons toasted ground cumin

¼ cup chopped toasted peanuts

1 teaspoon sea salt

2 teaspoons olive oil

1 teaspoon black mustard seeds

10 to 12 kari leaves, chopped

½ teaspoon red chile powder

apple cucumber raita

In a large bowl, combine the yogurt, cumin, and salt and whisk for a few seconds, until smooth. Fold the cucumbers, apple, onion, and cilantro into the yogurt. Chill the raita and store in the refrigerator until ready to serve. The raita needs to be stored in the refrigerator and is best used within 2 days.

MAKES ABOUT 4 CUPS

2 cups plain whole-milk yogurt (see page 86)

2 teaspoons toasted ground cumin

1 teaspoon sea salt

4 or 5 small Persian cucumbers, cut into ½-inch cubes

1 large green apple, cored and cut into ½-inch chunks

1 small red onion, minced

¼ cup chopped fresh cilantro

smoked eggplant raita

MAKES ABOUT 3 CUPS

2 medium purple eggplants

Olive oil for rubbing the eggplants

2 cups plain whole-milk yogurt
(see page 86)

2 tablespoons minced red onion

¼ cup toasted walnuts, chopped

1½ teaspoons sea salt

1 teaspoon freshly ground
black pepper

Handful of fresh cilantro leaves,
minced

1 tablespoon mustard oil

½ teaspoon cumin seeds

Pomegranate seeds for garnish

Rub the eggplant with olive oil all over and, using medium to high heat, char all sides directly over your stove's burners, turning with tongs, until visibly burnt and crackled and the entire eggplant is cooked on the inside. This can take anywhere from 8 to 10 minutes depending on whether you are working with an electric or gas stove; however, I do not recommend smoking eggplants in the oven. Remove from the heat, let the eggplant cool for a few minutes, then peel off the skin—most of it should come off easily, but you may need a knife to cut some of it off.

Place the eggplant pulp in a large bowl and stir in the yogurt, onion, walnuts, salt, black pepper, and cilantro.

In a small frying pan, heat the mustard oil over high heat. Pop the cumin seeds (see page 40), immediately pour the hot oil over the raita, and fold it in. Garnish with pomegranate seeds. This raita needs to be stored in the refrigerator and is best used within 2 days.

corn mint raita

MAKES ABOUT 4 CUPS

2 ears fresh corn

2 cups plain whole-milk yogurt
(see page 86)

1 small red onion, minced

3 tablespoons chopped fresh
mint leaves

2 teaspoons toasted ground cumin

1 teaspoon sea salt

Grill the ears of corn for 2 minutes on each side or boil in a large pot of boiling water for 2 to 3 minutes, until crisp-tender. Remove the kernels, placing them in a large bowl, and add the yogurt, onion, mint, cumin, and salt. The raita needs to be stored in the refrigerator and is best used within 2 days.

Breads

In the sixties and seventies, every neighborhood in India had a grain mill. Most homes stored large barrels of wheat, millet, or other grains and they would regularly take them to the mill to be ground. My perennially untrusting mother would make weekly trips to the grain mill, standing over it carefully watching the grains she had brought go through the machine to ensure we brought home finely milled, pure whole-wheat flour.

Rotis (also called chapati and phulkas) and parathas are the quintessential unleavened flatbreads of India—every region has their own version. Since I discovered that the dough can be the perfect vehicle for vegetables or vegetable peelings, I never make a plain roti. You can add anything from grated carrots, zucchini, and beets to greens, like spinach and kale. Spices, like crushed cumin or coriander seeds, and all kinds of finely chopped herbs add a delicious touch to rotis. Parathas, laminated crispy flatbreads usually made from roti dough, are more decadent and might even require a nap after eating.

Naans, usually made in large commercial tandoors, were and continue to be restaurant food. For me, the best way to eat a naan is straight out of a tandoor or regular oven. You will need a pizza stone, or you could buy a simple 18-inch ceramic tile from a hardware store for a few bucks.

While flatbreads remain the mainstay of breads in India, I am excited to report that ambitious young bakers all over the country are experimenting with wild sourdough breads made with ancient grains, like ragi, finger millet, amaranth, and sorghum, and flavored with spices such as turmeric and ginger.

simple roti

This is the simplest version of a roti; however, the variations are endless. Replace ½ cup of the roti flour with ground flax seeds, ground chia seeds, almond meal, millet flour, or any other flour of your choice. This may require an adjustment in water, but the best way to learn how to make rotis is practice and getting a feel for the dough that makes a perfect roti. Just remember to keep the dough soft and pliable.

Roti flour is much more finely milled than supermarket whole-wheat flour, which does not work very well for rotis. Roti flour can be bought at Indian grocery stores or online; if you can't find it, whole-wheat pastry flour is a good substitute.

In a medium bowl, combine the roti flour, salt, and ½ cup water. Using your fingers, palm, and fist, knead the mixture, adding more water if needed, until the ingredients are evenly mixed and the mixture comes together into a soft ball that's malleable and pliable—if it appears dry, add a couple more tablespoons water, and if it is too wet and sticky, add a small sprinkling of roti flour. Pour the olive oil into the bowl and knead it into the dough until you have a smooth ball. Cover the dough loosely with a clean kitchen towel and set aside at room temperature for 20 to 30 minutes or in the refrigerator for up to 2 days.

Divide the dough into eight equal smooth balls.

Heat a frying pan or griddle over medium-high heat. Dab the ball of dough in a little flour and, using a rolling pin, roll it out into a 7- to 8-inch circle. Immediately place on the hot pan, and while it is cooking, roll out the next roti. As soon as the first side is slightly cooked, flip the roti over and cook until brown bubbles appear on the top of the entire surface of the second side. Flip the roti over again to finish cooking it. It can also be finished directly on the flame using tongs for a quicker turnaround. Smear the roti with a bit of ghee or oil, crush it with your fingers (to keep it soft), and keep wrapped in a warm towel while you cook the rest.

recipe continues

1½ cups roti flour or whole-wheat pastry flour, plus more if needed

1 teaspoon sea salt

2 tablespoons olive oil, plus more if needed

Ghee (see page 77) for topping the rotis

Note: Half-cook the rotis for freezing. Cook the rotis on both sides until half cooked, with a few light brown bubbles appearing on the surface, and the dough does not appear raw. Cool and freeze them with a small piece of parchment paper in between each for up to 3 months. To bring them back, either flame them directly or finish them on a skillet over medium-high heat.

Variations

Adding vegetable peelings or gratings to roti dough makes it infinitely more exciting and tasty. Carrot roti is a favorite, and other vegetables can be used in the same way. Grated daikon, rutabaga, turnips, potatoes, or a combination also make a delicious roti.

Carrot Roti: Add 2 cups loosely packed coarsely grated carrots, 1 tablespoon dried fenugreek leaves, ½ teaspoon ground turmeric, and 1 teaspoon freshly ground black pepper to the flour, salt, and water when you make the roti dough. (*See photo on page 238.*)

Beet Roti: Add 2 cups raw or roasted beets when you make the roti dough.

Spinach or Kale Roti: Add use 3 cups chopped raw or steamed kale or spinach leaves when you make the roti dough.

Cauliflower Roti: Add 2 cups grated raw cauliflower and ½ teaspoon ajwain seeds. Grated or finely chopped roasted cauliflower also makes a delicious addition to rotis.

Herb Roti: Add 2 cups chopped fresh herbs, like fenugreek, cilantro, sage, or oregano, to the roti dough.

parathas

To make a paratha, take a ball of roti dough (see page 239), dab it into dry flour, and roll it out into a 6-inch circle. Smear oil or ghee on one half and fold the other side over into a half-moon. Smear oil or ghee on one half of the half-moon and fold the other half over into a triangle of sorts. Dab it into dry flour and roll the paratha out into a triangle.

Cook the paratha on a skillet or frying pan over high heat on both sides first, then decrease the heat to low, smear 1 to 2 tablespoons oil on both sides, and cook them through until crisp. This will take several minutes on each side, so do not rush them.

Roll

Fold once

Fold twice

Pan-fry

241

stuffed paratha

MAKES 6 PARATHAS

POTATO FILLING

2 cups cooked mashed or grated potatoes

1 cup minced fresh cilantro leaves and stems

1 serrano chile, minced

1 green onion, white and green parts, minced

1 teaspoon ajwain seeds

2 teaspoons amchur (dried mango powder)

2 teaspoons toasted ground cumin

1 teaspoon sea salt

PARATHAS

1 recipe simple roti dough (see page 239)

Roti flour for dusting

Ghee (see page 77) or vegetable oil for brushing

To make the potato filling: Place the potatoes in a medium bowl. Add the cilantro, chile, green onion, ajwain seeds, amchur, cumin, and salt and mix until thoroughly combined. Cover and refrigerate until you are ready to roll the parathas.

To roll the parathas: Heat a large skillet or a frying pan over medium heat while you make the first stuffed paratha.

Divide the roti dough into six equal parts. Using a little roti flour to dust, roll each one out to a 6-inch circle. Spread about 1 teaspoon ghee or vegetable oil over the top. Mound about ½ cup of the filling in the center. Gently pick up one of the edges of the paratha dough and seal it together at the top, covering the entire filling inside. Pinch off any excess dough you may have at the top. Too much overlapping dough will cause it to cook unevenly. Flatten the pocket into a thick disc. Very gently, while using minimal pressure, roll the paratha out into a 6-inch round that's about ¼ inch thick. This can be done with soft pressure of the palm of your hand.

Immediately transfer the paratha to the hot skillet. Cook for 2 to 3 minutes on each side, until it is light golden in color. At this point, you can leave the parathas half finished by taking them off the skillet and cooling while you continue with the other parathas.

When you're ready to finish cooking the parathas, spread 1 tablespoon ghee or oil on each side of a paratha. Cook the parathas until medium golden in color and cooked to a crisp on each side, adding a little more ghee if they appear dry. Depending on the thickness of the skillet and intensity of heat, this can take up to 5 minutes for each paratha. Remove from the pan. These are best eaten straight from the pan, but, if necessary, cover the paratha with a cloth towel or napkin to keep warm, and repeat with the remaining parathas. Serve immediately.

Stuff

Seal

Flatten

Pan-fry

243

royal naan

Originating in ancient Egypt and brought to India via the Persians, naan is the one of the most popular breads to rise out of the Mughal Empire in India. Created and sustained by military warfare and founded in the 1500s by Babur, the Mughal Empire ruled over northern parts of India for hundreds of years. In the wake of these Muslim invaders sweeping down the Khyber Pass, the cuisine of northern India went through a huge shift. The tandoor, a giant clay or concrete oven often built into the ground that could withstand temperatures of over 600°F, had arrived in India. Skewered kebabs and a variety of breads emerged from this new cuisine. Naan became the most popular of breads, and this version, in particular, harkens back to its royal heritage with the aroma of rose water, saffron, and vetiver. Used in desserts and certain curries, vetiver, aka khus, is a fragrant grass native to India. It is sold as an extract in Indian grocery stores and can be replaced with vanilla or almond extract. Naan dough can be made the day before, but give it 2 to 3 hours of proofing time at room temperature before baking.

Soak the saffron in the hot milk for 30 minutes or overnight in the refrigerator.

In a large bowl, whisk the warm saffron milk, yeast, sugar, khus (if desired), rose water, and eggs. Add the all-purpose flour, roti flour, semolina flour, cardamom seeds, black pepper, and salt and mix until a dough comes together into a ball that's soft and slightly sticky. Coat the dough with olive oil. Lay a clean kitchen towel over the bowl and let the dough rise at room temperature for 2 to 3 hours, until it doubles in size. If not using immediately, refrigerate in the same bowl or a large storage container (as it will rise) until you're ready to make the naans.

Adjust an oven rack to the lower part of the oven and set a ceramic tile (see page 237), pizza stone, or inverted baking sheet in the center of the rack.

Preheat the oven to as hot (at least 500°F) as it will get for at least 1 hour; preferably 2 hours.

Divide the risen dough into ten equal balls, punching down slightly as you go. Cover the balls with a clean kitchen towel and let rest for 1 hour, or until they have doubled in size.

recipe continues

¼ teaspoon saffron strands

1¼ cups warm milk

1 teaspoon active dry yeast

1 tablespoon cane sugar

1 teaspoon khus, or 4 or 5 drops vetiver (optional)

1 teaspoon rose water

2 large eggs

3 cups all-purpose flour or bread flour

1 cup roti flour or whole-wheat pastry flour

2 tablespoons semolina flour

1 teaspoon ground green cardamom seeds

1 teaspoon freshly ground black pepper

2 teaspoons sea salt

Olive oil for coating the dough

Sesame seeds, fennel seeds, or cumin seeds for sprinkling

Ghee (see page 77) for spreading

Using a few drops of oil, use your fingers to press each ball into an oval about 7 inches long and about 4 inches wide. Or gently roll it out using a rolling pin. Sprinkle some seeds on top.

Quickly lay four to six naans on the hot tile with 1 inch in between each. Immediately close the oven and bake the naans for 2 to 3 minutes. Open the oven and, using tongs, remove the naans. The bottom part will be golden in color, but if the top is not, quickly flame the naans over the burner of a gas stove. Smear ghee on the naans while hot. Repeat with the remaining dough.

Naans, like most bread, are best eaten fresh, but if you need to make them ahead of time, let them cool on a wire rack in a single layer so they do not steam from the bottom. To reheat them, sprinkle a few drops of water on each, lay them directly on the oven racks in a preheated 450°F oven, over a grill, or directly over a gas flame, turning them with tongs and working quickly so as not to burn the edges. They can be left at room temperature for a day or frozen in an airtight plastic bag for up to 6 months.

naan pickle pizza

I started making naan pizzas for my children when they were young. With regular trips to Indian grocery stores, I stocked store-bought naans in the freezer and was able to make pizzas in a pinch using store-bought pasta sauces and any melting cheese I had in hand. Over the pandemic, a local farmer asked us to find a way to use hundreds and hundreds of pounds of fennel bulbs that he was unable to sell to other restaurants, then gorgeous heirloom tomatoes, eggplant, peppers, and so on. At one time, we featured different varieties of peppers in more than half the dishes on the menu. Knee-deep in produce that needed to be used and I was determined not to waste, we made curries, soups, and salads and finally turned to pickles and chutneys. When I was making family meal one day, I spread fennel pickle on a bunch of naans, topped them with Gruyère cheese, and baked them in the oven. The pickle pizza was born! Now I make naan pizzas at home with store-bought pickles and chutneys from time to time. At the restaurant, we have a weekly Friday pickle pizza special featuring seasonal homemade Indian pickles or chutneys.

Mango Chutney (page 226) will work well. If you prefer to use store-bought chutneys or pickles, try to pick brands that are made in India. If they are too salty, add minced tomato, 1 sliced green onion, or 2 tablespoons minced red onion. Hot lime, lemon, mango, or "mixed" pickle work really well, as do mango "chundo" or chutney. Fragrant herbs, like oregano, lemon balm, mint, and cilantro, are delicious with assertive Indian pickles. Sharp cheeses, like feta, goat, or Cheddar, will work better than mild ones, like mozzarella. (*See the recipe photo on page 236.*)

Royal Naan (page 245) or store-bought naan

¼ cup Roasted Cherry Tomato Chutney (page 227) for each naan

½ cup grated cheese (such as raclette, Gruyère, fresh mozzarella, or another melting cheese) for each naan

Fresh whole herbs (such as cilantro, basil, oregano, or mint) for topping

Preheat the oven to 500°F and let the oven stay at that temperature for at least 1 hour. (If making royal naans, let them cool for a minute or two, then follow the below directions to make pizza.)

Spread the chutney evenly on top of the baked naan, followed by the cheese. Place directly on the middle rack of the oven on top of a hot ceramic tile (see page 237) or pizza stone. Bake for 3 to 4 minutes, until the cheese is melted and bubbly. Top with herbs and serve.

masala biscuit

A *biscuit* in India can refer to anything from a cookie or cracker to a savory puff pastry. The first evidence of coal-fired Indian biscuits can be traced back to the arrival of Mughals in the sixteenth century. The tradition of biscuits continued with the Dutch and the French, reaching its peak popularity during the British Raj. The most popular biscuit in Kolkata is the projapoti ("butterfly" in Bengali), a version of the palmier topped with salt and sugar that came to Bengal via the French in the sixteenth century. It is believed that the Parsis took it upon themselves to become the custodians of breads and bakeries in India, and it was they who brought the biscuit to the masses. In the tiny streets around Jama Masjid, the majestic mosque in the heart of Old Delhi, carts filled with large mountains of nankhatai (cardamom biscuits) abound.

Here is a recipe adapted from an American Southern biscuit with the addition of spices and one very special dried herb, moringa. *Moringa oleifera*, or miracle drumstick tree as we call it in India, is arguably the world's most nutritionally dense plant. This ancient tree native to India is revered in Ayurveda for its tremendous health benefits. The bright green leaves are a rich source of antioxidants and an excellent source of vitamins and minerals.

In a large bowl, combine the flour, moringa powder, baking powder, baking soda, sugar, and salt. Stir in the green onions, herbs, and chile. Add the cold butter and mix it into the flour with your fingers, lightly breaking it up into smaller pieces. This should take no more than a minute or two, and you want chunks of butter to remain in the dough. Stir in the sour cream to make a shaggy dough.

Transfer the dough to a work surface. Pat it together into a rectangle and fold it over like a book. Gently roll it into a larger rectangle, turn it 90 degrees, and fold it over like a book again. For a third time, roll it out into a rectangle, roll the rectangle into a log, and wrap it in parchment paper or plastic wrap. Refrigerate the log for a couple of hours but no longer than 12 to 14 hours, or the bright green color of the moringa will start to fade.

Preheat the oven to 350°F.

Cut the log into ten thick discs. (Instead of baking now, at this point, the discs can be frozen for up to 3 months.) Set them on a baking sheet 2 to 3 inches apart and bake for 20 to 25 minutes, until golden brown on the outside. Let cool slightly and serve drizzled with warm ghee or melted butter.

MAKES 10 BISCUITS

2½ cups all-purpose flour

2 tablespoons dried moringa powder

2 teaspoons baking powder

½ teaspoon baking soda

2 tablespoons cane sugar

2 teaspoons sea salt

1½ cups sliced green onions, white and green parts

½ cup chopped fresh herbs (such as mint, cilantro, basil, or parsley)

1 serrano chile, minced

10 tablespoons (1¼ sticks) cold unsalted butter, sliced

1¼ cups sour cream or Greek-style yogurt

Warm ghee (see page 77) or melted butter for serving

corn semolina bread

MAKES 8 WEDGES OR
4-INCH SQUARE PIECES

BREAD

2 cups fresh corn kernels

1 cup semolina flour

2 tablespoons chickpea flour

1 cup chopped fresh fenugreek, or
2 tablespoons dried fenugreek leaves

½ cup chopped fresh cilantro

½ teaspoon ground turmeric

1 teaspoon red chile powder

1½ teaspoons sea salt

1 teaspoon baking powder

½ teaspoon baking soda

½ cup plain whole-milk yogurt
(see page 86)

1 tablespoon Ginger Puree (page 80)

¼ cup olive oil

¼ cup raw peanuts, chopped
(optional)

1 teaspoon black mustard seeds

Pinch of asafetida

15 to 20 kari leaves

1 tablespoon raw sesame seeds

1 tablespoon raw pumpkin seeds

YOGURT SAUCE

1 cup plain whole-milk
Greek-style yogurt

1 tablespoon cane sugar

½ teaspoon sea salt

Pinch of red chile powder

2 tablespoons mustard oil

4 garlic cloves, sliced

1 teaspoon cumin seeds

20 kari leaves, chopped

Gujarat is famous around the country for savory snacks with a telltale lingering sweet finish. From snack mixes made from crispy chickpeas or lentils to fried rice and potato flakes and the popular long, thick chickpea wafers known as fafda that are usually eaten with a hot green chile pickle, a snack shop may have upward of thirty varieties of snacks. There is a whole family of steamed breads, including khaman, dhokla, and handvo, made from fermented lentil batters, usually eaten with herb chutneys, that could make small meals on their own.

This is a savory snacking bread loosely inspired by the handvo, a bread usually baked in a shallow pan and filled with seasonal vegetables. This bread is best enjoyed with a pickle, chutney, or slightly sweetened yogurt. Chickpea flour can be replaced with any lentil flour. To make a gluten-free version, replace the semolina with cornmeal. The bread can be baked in a cast-iron skillet or a cake pan.

To make the bread: Preheat the oven to 350°F. Grease an 8-inch cake pan or cast-iron skillet.

In a large bowl, combine the corn, semolina flour, chickpea flour, fenugreek, cilantro, turmeric, red chile powder, salt, baking powder, baking soda, yogurt, and ginger puree. Stir to mix and set aside.

Heat the olive oil in a small frying pan over high heat. Add the peanuts and cook for a minute or two to fry them, then pop the mustard seeds (see page 40), add the asafetida and kari leaves and cook for a couple of seconds, then turn the heat off. Fold the mixture into the semolina mixture.

Add 1 cup hot tap water (around 120°F) to the mixture and stir until evenly mixed. Pour into the prepared baking pan and sprinkle the sesame seeds and pumpkin seeds on top. Bake for 30 to 45 minutes, until the edges pull back a little and the top appears set. It is better to slightly overbake than underbake the bread. Let the bread rest for 10 to 15 minutes before loosening it from the pan.

While the bread is in the oven, make the yogurt sauce: In a small bowl, whisk the yogurt with the sugar and salt. Sprinkle the red chile powder on top. Heat the mustard oil in a small frying pan over high heat. Add the sliced garlic and cook until the edges are golden, just a few seconds. Pop the cumin seeds (see page 40), then add the kari leaves and cook for a couple of seconds. Gently stir the mixture into the yogurt.

Cut the bread into wedges or large chunks and serve with a dollop of yogurt sauce on top.

Rice

In India, rice is revered as more than a grain. It is said in the Vedas that the entire universe is held within each grain. A grain endures the seven stages of life, from seed to sprout to seedling, young plant, mature plant, flowering plant to fruitful plant. Consuming rice is believed to create a cosmic connection with divinity, and religious ceremonies and celebrations will usually include rice. It is the first food given to a baby and the last to honor the dead. The tradition of tossing rice at newlyweds originated in India, and a wedding is the only time an Indian willingly tosses away the kernels. Countless varieties of rice are used in India, from the short-grain ponna rice to the sturdy South Indian rose matta rice, but none is more venerated than the aged basmati. Grown along the Himalayan foothills, considered the queen of rice (*bas* means "fragrance" and *mati* means "queen"), basmati rice has long, slender grains and a delicate nutty aroma that makes it ideal for pilafs and biryani.

Basmati rice is unpolished rice, meaning it still retains some of its nutrient-rich exterior bran layer, which is also why it cooks best after soaking. Unlike the popular sticky rice native to many Asian countries, Indians love their rice separate, not stuck together. The key to perfect basmati rice is to treat it gently while rinsing and cooking—the kernels are long and delicate and will break if mishandled. Rinsing simply means combining the rice with double the amount water in a bowl, stirring it with your fingers for a few seconds, holding a hand over the rice, and discarding most of the water into the sink. It is best to repeat this process once or twice. For cooking presoaked basmati rice, the usual proportions of rice to water are 1:2; however, this may need to be adjusted slightly based on the brand and quality of rice you choose. To preserve the flavors within the rice, it is best to use a pot with a tight-fitting lid. All the recipes in this book were made with extra-long grain (often called platinum quality) basmati. Minimize stirring the rice during cooking to maintain each kernel's integrity, and refrain from stirring immediately after cooking. It's the resting phase of 10 to 12 minutes that promotes the magic of flavor and flakiness. Sometimes at the end of cooking, you may notice a few tablespoons of water at the bottom of the pot, or the rice may appear wet. As it rests, the rice will absorb most of the liquid. If it doesn't, use a little less water the next time you cook that variety of rice. If using brown basmati rice, the ratio of rice to water for cooking is 1:3 and the cooking time will more than triple. The same proportions of white rice can be applied to white quinoa; however, quinoa does not need to be soaked.

I almost never cook plain white rice, as the simple addition of a whole cinnamon stick, a few strands of saffron, a few pods of green or black cardamom, or a combination of whole spices can brighten up a pot of rice. At the very least, I add a bit of ground turmeric or slices of fresh turmeric or ginger to a pot of rice. I like to treat rice as a vehicle for added nutritional flavors, like coconut, vegetables, citrus, beans, spices, herbs, nuts, and seeds. Determined to eat as many local vegetables as I can, I instinctively find myself either lightly sautéing hearty greens, like kale or Swiss chard, or simply folding or tossing delicate torn lettuce leaves into warm rice or quinoa pilafs. Leftover roasted vegetables make a great addition to freshly cooked rice, as do pumpkin seeds, sunflower seeds, and sesame seeds. Pomegranate pilaf (see page 258) makes a stunning statement on a holiday table (be mindful to keep the lid off to maintain the bright color of the beet during the resting phase). The gorgeous stems of rainbow chard may be beautiful enough to use in flower arrangements, but there are so many reasons to incorporate chard into our daily diet. During medieval times, when food was truly used as medicine, chard, a descendant of the wild beet, was used to alleviate chronic pain, allergies, and constipation.

The last recipe in this section is the quintessential khichri (see page 261), a wholesome peasant stew of rice and lentils with a world of possibilities and a resident favorite of urban yogis. Brown basmati rice or rose matta rice works best here, as it develops a creamy texture after long and slow cooking. During the winter, hearty grains like whole sorghum, millet, or buckwheat can be added to khichri. In its simplest and gentlest form, khichri is a stew of rice and mung dal topped off with ghee. It's what my mother would feed me when I was sick as a child, and it is the daily meal of choice during panchakarma, the traditional Ayurvedic cleanse. The ghee coats the intestines and makes for easy passage. Like all my rice dishes, I consider khichri another vehicle for seasonal wholesome vegetables, like grated carrots or turnips, chopped celery, warm spices, and herbs.

spice-infused rice

SERVES 4

1 cup white basmati rice

2 tablespoons light sesame oil, olive oil, coconut oil, or ghee (see page 77)

Whole spices (such as a cinnamon stick, whole mace flowers, cloves, green or black cardamom, and/or star anise)

1 teaspoon sea salt

Rinse the rice in tap water two or three times. After the last rinse, soak the rice in twice the amount of water for at least 30 minutes or up to 2 hours. Drain.

In a medium saucepan, combine the drained rice with 2 cups water, the oil, whole spices, and salt and bring to a boil over high heat. Lower the heat to low, cover, and simmer for 7 to 8 minutes, until the water has been absorbed completely. Turn the heat off and let the rice rest for 10 to 12 minutes. Stir gently with a fork before serving. (*See the recipe photo, bottom left, on page 252.*)

lemon rice pilaf

SERVES 4

1 cup white basmati rice

2 tablespoons light sesame oil

1 teaspoon black mustard seeds

10 to 12 kari leaves

1 serrano chile, minced (optional)

1 teaspoon ground turmeric

1 or 2 cinnamon sticks

Zest and juice of 2 lemons

½ cup chopped toasted peanuts

½ cup currants or raisins

1 teaspoon sea salt

Rinse the rice in tap water two or three times. After the last rinse, soak the rice in twice the amount of water for at least 30 minutes or up to 2 hours. Drain.

In a medium saucepan, heat the oil over high heat and pop the mustard seeds (see page 40), then add the kari leaves and cook for a couple of seconds. Immediately add the drained rice, chile, turmeric, cinnamon sticks, lemon zest and juice, peanuts, currants, salt, and 2 cups water and bring to a boil. Lower the heat to low, cover, and simmer for 7 to 8 minutes, until the water has been absorbed completely. Turn the heat off and let the rice rest for 10 to 12 minutes. Stir gently with a fork before serving.

saffron citrus rice pilaf

Soak the saffron in 2 cups of warm water for 2 to 3 hours before preparing the rice.

Rinse the rice in tap water two or three times. After the last rinse, soak the rice in twice the amount of water for at least 30 minutes or up to 2 hours. Drain.

In a medium saucepan, heat the ghee over high heat and pop the black cumin seeds (see page 40), then add the kari leaves and cook for a couple of seconds. Immediately add the drained rice, saffron with its soaking water, mace, orange zest, kishmish, and salt and bring to a boil over high heat. Lower the heat to low, cover, and simmer for 7 to 8 minutes, until the water has been absorbed completely. Turn the heat off and let the rice rest for 10 to 12 minutes. Stir gently with a fork before serving. (*See the recipe photo, center right, on page 252.*)

SERVES 4

Generous pinch of saffron

1 cup white basmati rice

3 tablespoons ghee (see page 77)

1 teaspoon black cumin seeds

10 to 12 kari leaves

1 or 2 mace flowers

Zest of 2 oranges

½ cup kishmish (green raisins), brown raisins, or currants

1 teaspoon sea salt

mushroom mace rice pilaf

Rinse the rice in tap water two or three times. After the last rinse, soak the rice in twice the amount of water for at least 30 minutes or up to 2 hours. Drain.

In a medium saucepan, warm the oil over medium heat and pop the fennel seeds (see page 40). Fennel seeds tend to burn easily, so make sure the oil is not too hot. Add the mushrooms and leeks and cook for 5 to 7 minutes, until they have wilted and taken on a little color. Add the drained rice, black pepper, mace, turmeric, figs, salt, and 2 cups water and bring to a boil over high heat. Lower the heat to low, cover, and simmer for 7 to 8 minutes, until the water has been absorbed completely. Turn the heat off, add the peas without stirring, and let the rice rest, for 10 to 12 minutes. Stir gently with a fork before serving. (*See the recipe photo, top left, on page 252.*)

SERVES 4

1 cup basmati rice

3 tablespoons olive oil

1 teaspoon fennel seeds

2 cups chopped mushrooms (crimini, maitake or shiitake)

1 cup sliced leeks (white and light green parts) or minced white onions

1 teaspoon freshly ground black pepper

1 teaspoon ground mace

½ teaspoon ground turmeric

8 to 10 dried figs, thinly sliced

1 teaspoon sea salt

½ cup frozen peas, thawed

swiss chard rice pilaf

SERVES 4

1 cup white basmati rice

1 large cinnamon stick

½ teaspoon ground turmeric

1 teaspoon freshly ground
black pepper

½ teaspoon red chile powder

1½ teaspoons sea salt

1 large bunch Swiss chard

4 tablespoons olive oil

1 teaspoon black mustard seeds

1 cup minced leeks (white and
light green parts) or white onions
(optional)

1 tablespoon Minced Garlic (page 80)

¼ cup toasted pumpkin seeds

2 to 3 tablespoons chopped fresh
herbs (such as parsley or cilantro)

Juice of 1 lemon or lime

Rinse the rice in tap water two or three times. After the last rinse, soak the rice in twice the amount of water for at least 30 minutes or up to 2 hours. Drain.

In a medium saucepan, combine the rice with 2 cups water, the cinnamon stick, turmeric, black pepper, red chile powder, and 1 teaspoon of the salt and bring to a boil over high heat. Lower the heat to low, cover, and simmer for 7 to 8 minutes, until the water has been absorbed completely. Let the rice rest for 10 to 15 minutes.

While the rice is resting, mince the chard stems and tear the leaves into bite-size pieces. In a medium frying pan, heat 2 tablespoons of the oil over high heat and pop the mustard seeds (see page 40). Add the leeks, minced garlic, and remaining ½ teaspoon salt and cook for 2 to 3 minutes, until the leeks and chard stem pieces have wilted. Gently fold this mixture into the rice along with the torn chard leaves, pumpkin seeds, and remaining 2 tablespoons oil. Garnish with the herbs and lemon juice. Serve warm or at room temperature. *(See the recipe photo, far right, opposite.)*

pomegranate rice pilaf

SERVES 4

1 cup white basmati rice

¼ cup mustard oil

1 teaspoon cumin seeds

1 small red beet, peeled and cut
into thick slices

3 cups pomegranate juice

1 teaspoon red chile powder

2 large cinnamon sticks

1½ teaspoons sea salt

½ cup fresh pomegranate seeds

¼ cup toasted pine nuts

Rinse the rice in tap water two or three times. After the last rinse, soak the rice in twice the amount of water for at least 30 minutes or up to 2 hours. Drain.

In a medium saucepan, heat the oil over high heat. Pop the cumin seeds (see page 40), then immediately add the beet, pomegranate juice, red chile powder, cinnamon sticks, and salt and bring to a boil. Lower the heat, cover, and simmer for 5 to 7 minutes, or until the mixture is a deep red in color, then increase the heat to high. Add the rice, bring to a boil again, then lower the heat, cover again, and simmer for 7 to 8 minutes, until the water has been absorbed completely. Turn the heat off, take the lid off, and let the rice rest for 10 to 12 minutes. (Leaving the lid off while resting secures the bright pink color of the pilaf.) Discard the beet and gently stir the pilaf with a fork. Garnish with the pomegranate seeds and pine nuts and serve. *(See the recipe photo, near left, opposite.)*

quinoa cabbage pilaf

SERVES 4

1 cup white quinoa

Zest and juice of 1 orange

½ teaspoon ground turmeric

1 teaspoon freshly ground
black pepper

1½ teaspoons sea salt

2 tablespoons olive oil

1 teaspoon black mustard seeds

10 to 12 kari leaves

½ small purple cabbage, cored
and thinly sliced

½ cup toasted dried coconut

⅓ cup chopped toasted peanuts

2 cups chopped fresh cilantro
(roughly 1 whole bunch)

In a medium saucepan, combine the quinoa, orange zest and juice, turmeric, black pepper, 1 teaspoon of the salt, and 2 cups water and bring to a boil over high heat. Lower the heat, cover, and simmer for 7 to 8 minutes, until the water has been absorbed completely. Let the quinoa rest for 15 to 20 minutes.

In a medium frying pan, heat the oil over high heat and pop the mustard seeds (see page 40). Add the kari leaves and cook for a couple of seconds, then add the sliced cabbage and remaining ½ teaspoon salt. Cook until the cabbage wilts, no more than a minute or two. Fold the cabbage into the quinoa along with the toasted coconut, peanuts, and cilantro. Serve warm or at room temperature. (*See the recipe photo on page 255.*)

caramel coconut rice pilaf

SERVES 4

1 cup white basmati rice

2 tablespoons cane sugar

1 or 2 cinnamon sticks

4 or 5 whole cloves, crushed

1 teaspoon red chile powder

3 tablespoons coconut oil

1 cup coconut milk

1 teaspoon sea salt

1 cup chopped fresh herbs (such as
basil, cilantro, or parsley)

Rinse the rice in tap water two or three times. After the last rinse, soak the rice in twice the amount of water for at least 30 minutes or up to 2 hours. Drain.

In a medium saucepan, without stirring, heat the sugar over high heat until it turns dark golden brown and caramel in color. Add the drained rice, cinnamon sticks, cloves, red chile powder, coconut oil, coconut milk, salt, and 1 cup water and bring to a boil over high heat. Lower the heat, cover, and simmer for 7 to 8 minutes, until the water has been absorbed completely. If the rice appears dry, add another ¼ cup water. Turn the heat off and let the rice rest for 10 to 12 minutes. Fold in the chopped herbs and stir gently with a fork before serving.

khichri

In a medium bowl, rinse the rice and dal together in tap water two or three times. After the last rinse, soak the rice and dal in twice the amount of water for 4 hours or overnight in the refrigerator. Drain.

In a large saucepan or Dutch oven, combine the rice and dal mixture with 2 cups water and bring to a boil over high heat. Discard the water along with any foam or residue that rises. Add 4 cups fresh water, turmeric, black pepper, cloves, carrots, and salt. Bring to a boil over high heat, then lower the heat to the lowest setting, cover, and simmer for about 1 hour, stirring every 15 to 20 minutes, until the mixture is completely integrated, creamy, and smooth and the carrots have dissolved into the rice-dal mixture, adding more water if needed.

In a small frying pan, heat the ghee over high heat. Pop the cumin seeds (see page 40), then stir the hot oil into the khichri. Fold in the greens; as they start wilting, turn the heat off. Let the khichri rest for 10 to 15 minutes. Stir in the herbs, drizzle ghee on top, and serve with any desired toppings.

SERVES 4

1 cup brown basmati rice

½ cup channa dal

1 teaspoon ground turmeric

1 teaspoon freshly ground black pepper

4 or 5 whole cloves, lightly crushed

2 cups grated carrots

1½ teaspoons sea salt

3 tablespoons ghee (see page 77), plus more for drizzling

1 teaspoon cumin seeds

4 cups chopped greens (such as spinach, watercress, kale, or mustard greens)

1 cup loosely packed fresh herb leaves

Optional toppings: poached or fried eggs, nuts, dried fruits, fresh herbs

Drinks and Desserts

Despite living in one of the hottest regions of India their whole life, my parents drank slightly cooled room-temperature water with no ice cubes. They never missed a chance to extol the virtues of room-temperature water. Ice-cold water is considered a shock to the system, as our internal body temperature usually hovers around 98°F. Every morning, my mother would fill filtered water into a clay urn with a spigot, which would help cool the water. The ice was reserved for the weekend evenings when my father would indulge in a Scotch and soda. For our bodies to properly digest food without diluting our digestive juices, my brothers and I were not allowed to drink water during dinner or, at the very most, we could sip a tiny bit of water. I didn't give it much thought at the time, but in hindsight, I am grateful to them for helping me form good habits. Even lassis and juices are best consumed on their own, not with a meal, for optimal nutrient absorption.

Many years ago, I stayed at a small Ayurvedic resort in Kerala where they served only warm water to drink. I had never in my life encountered that, and I was amazed at how much this one simple change helped my daily digestion. I took to it immediately, and to this day I drink water warm. Once when I was out at a fancy restaurant for dinner, I inadvertently sent the staff in a tizzy when I requested warm water. At many Indian restaurants, including mine, room-temperature water is the default, and we happily serve up warm water if requested. That is my secret way of helping Americans build better habits.

According to Vedic texts, around 500 BC, Indians led the way in perfecting the art of extracting and refining sugar from sugarcane. Cane sugar was widely available for more than a millennium in India, where confectioners created sweet ambrosias to feed gods and mortals alike, way before the bakers of France and Vienna began showering their tortes and pies with crystallized sugar. In medieval India, sugar was used not just to make desserts; it was fermented into an alcoholic toddy. The first recorded text of a sweet in India is payasam, a South Indian rice pudding sweetened with jaggery. Around the first millennium, an ancient Greek envoy described sugar-cane as an "Indian bamboo filled with honey."

In India, religious holidays and celebrations are closely associated with sweets. A newborn's lips are often rubbed with honey or jaggery, and the first solid food fed to a child is sweet rice pudding. One of the most basic forms of worship, or puja, is to present sweet delicacies to one or few of hundreds of different deities, some who take on different incarnations or avatars. During festivals, many temple kitchens turn into temporary sweet factories to produce enough sweets to feed the thousands of streaming pilgrims.

Milk and its derivatives are undisputedly the most revered element of sweets in India, and milk, ghee, and sugar make up the holy trinity of sweets. Various combinations of jaggery and flour, nuts, and dried fruits results in hundreds of varieties of sweets. However, no region of India is as fond of sweets as Bengal; their desserts are legendary. Despite having 8 percent of the country's population, Bengalis spend 50 percent of what the entire country does on sweets. Growing up in India, with a few exceptions, like the halwa served at temples or chickpea fudge, I did not much care for the traditional cloying sweets, or mithai, as they are called. Over the years, I have come to appreciate them and understand the Indian obsession with small portions of sweets a little better.

masala chai

SERVES 4

4 cups water

1 tablespoon Ginger Puree (page 80)

8 to 10 green cardamom pods, lightly crushed

½ teaspoon black peppercorns, lightly crushed

1 cup whole milk

A few sprigs mint or basil

2 tablespoons Assam tea leaves, or 4 black tea bags

Honey for sweetening

Masala chai is the quintessential fragrant milky brew of India, and I wake up with it every morning. However, the story of how tea made its way to India is one of monopoly, adventure, and corporate espionage. The Chinese had been growing varieties of teas for thousands of years, and around the mid-nineteenth century, the British, who were colonizing India at the time, wanted to break that monopoly. After sending a botanist spy to China on a dangerous yet successful years-long mission to acquire tea seedlings and related information, the British started growing tea in the Himalayan foothills to compete with the Chinese monopoly. Tea plantations flourished in the idyllic mountains of Assam and Darjeeling in northern India, and the Brits were sending shiploads of their beloved tea back to England. However, they were unable to inspire any local interest in the teas until one day a street vendor brewed black tea from Assam with milk and aromatic spices, and the masala chai was born. Today, there are chai vendors all over the streets of India, from shopping centers to train stations. The word *chai* is derived from the Mandarin word for "tea", *cha*. At Pondicheri, we make gallons and gallons of chai each day, as it is the beverage of choice for many of our regulars. Feel free to substitute a teaspoon or two of chai masala (see page 67) for the cardamom pods and black peppercorns. In the winter, I often substitute rosemary sprigs for the mint to helps bring heat into our bodies.

In a medium saucepan, combine the water, ginger puree, cardamom (seeds and pods), and black peppercorns and bring to a boil over high heat. Lower the heat to the lowest setting, cover the pot, and simmer for 10 to 12 minutes to infuse the water with the spices. Raise the heat to high and add the milk and mint sprigs. As soon as the mixture comes to a boil, add the tea leaves, making sure it doesn't boil over. Immediately lower the heat and simmer for 20 to 30 seconds, then turn the heat off, cover, and let the tea steep for 3 to 4 minutes. Strain and enjoy with a generous dollop of honey stirred in.

Variation

Drunken Chai Option: Add 2 ounces rum and 2 tablespoons honey (or more to taste) to the chai and serve warm or chilled with ice.

lassi

Originally from northern India, lassi, a cooling summer yogurt drink, is popular not just all over India but in the rest of the world as well. The simplest lassi has cumin and salt but can be embellished with spices like black pepper and cardamom and herbs like cilantro and basil. For our body to absorb its probiotic nutrients, lassi is best consumed on its own. My father loved the sweet version with cardamom and sugar, and sometimes we'd sweeten it with the juice of fresh mango. There was also a potent cannabis-laced version of lassi called bhang, popular with pilgrims during festivals and sold by bootleggers late at night.

Hands down, my favorite day of the year during my childhood was Holi, the spring festival of colors signifying the emergence of light over darkness and good over evil. It was time for new beginnings and the end of petty grievances. For us kids, it was all about fun and play. We'd gather with neighborhood friends and go from street to street throwing colored powders on strangers on the streets. Anyone and everyone out on the streets would be fair game, friend or stranger, rich or poor, man or woman, children or elders. We'd stagger home unrecognizable at the end of the day, dripping with color and sometimes paint.

My parents, however, would sneak out to play cards with their friends late into the night and indulge on bhang lassi followed by samosas or pakoras, that being one of the few times I'd see my father wasted. Ayurvedic and Tantric practices from over two thousand years ago suggest the use of cannabis to reduce pain and as an aphrodisiac. Cannabis leaves were ground into a paste, mixed with aromatic spices, and added to drinks or foods. Here, we use aromatics and CBD oil. Adjust the drops as needed based on potency, or leave the CBD out altogether if it's not for you.

The coconut lassi is a plant-based version of mango lassi that I enjoy as dessert or embellished with rum or vodka. Canned mango puree, usually made from delicious varieties of mangoes at their peak sweetness, is available in Indian grocery stores.

lush lassi

SERVES 4

½ cup cane sugar

½ teaspoon ground green cardamom seeds

Pinch of saffron threads

1 cup water

4 cups plain whole-milk yogurt (see page 86)

4 to 6 drops CBD oil (optional)

Pinch of sea salt

Ice for serving

In a medium saucepan, combine the sugar, cardamom seeds, saffron, and water. Bring to a boil over high heat, then turn the heat off. Let cool completely. Whisk the yogurt, CBD oil (if desired), and salt into the sugar syrup. Serve on ice.

coconut lassi

SERVES 4

3 cups canned mango puree

One 14-ounce can coconut milk

1 tablespoon Ginger Puree (page 80)

½ teaspoon ground green cardamom seeds

Pinch of sea salt

In a pitcher, whisk all the ingredients together. Serve chilled.

Variation

Rose lassi: Instead of mango puree, add 1 teaspoon rose essence, ¼ cup red beet juice, and 2 cups water.

honey lime soda

SERVES 4

¼ cup honey

1 cup hot water

Juice of 4 limes

½ teaspoon sea salt

2 cans sparkling water, chilled

A few sprigs of mint, crushed

Despite having approximately 5 percent of the world's population, the United States consumes more than 17 percent of the world's energy. During the early nineties, around my first summer in Texas, I read an article about how "freezing it was in the summer." The article was referring to the rampant use of air-conditioning that most Texans are spoiled to, not just in their homes but in office buildings, grocery stores, and malls. However, summers in India can put Texas summers to shame. The temperatures can soar upward of 110°F with unrelenting humidity, and air conditioners are a luxury to most people. People usually stay indoors during the peak hours, and nimbu-pani (lemon water) is a common drink to offset dehydration. On a plane journey in India, fresh lime soda is often the first thing the airline cabin crew will offer you—it provides electrolytes and helps keep us hydrated during the flight. Here, I replace sugar with honey, which provides the necessary glucose, the salt helps push the water into our cells for proper absorption, and the potassium in the lime helps replenish our kidneys of this essential mineral.

Put the honey in a pitcher or other vessel, pour in the hot water, and mix to dissolve. Let cool. Add the lime juice and salt and divide into four glasses. Top with the sparkling water, add the crushed mint sprigs, and serve.

SERVES 4

½ cup ghee (see page 77)

½ teaspoon ground green cardamom seeds

Pinch of freshly ground black pepper

½ cup roti flour or whole-wheat pastry flour

2 tablespoons semolina flour

¾ cup cane sugar

Pinch of sea salt

2 cups whole milk

2 tablespoons toasted chopped nuts (such as almonds or pistachios)

My mother, Kamala, uprooted and traumatized by the forced exile from her homeland of Sindh, chose to go on a spiritual quest that led her on many different paths. When she first landed in Chennai from Sindh, she became a devotee of Sathya Sai Baba, a renowned local guru with a large halo of frizzy hair. When she married my father and moved to Gujarat, she identified more with the Punjabis and Sikhs than the local Gujaratis and would go to gurudwaras on the weekends. A gurdwara (translated to "at the door of God") is a place of spiritual worship and assembly for the Sikh community, and like most temples in India is welcoming to people of all faith and walks of life. Many temples in India have community kitchens run by volunteers offering free meals and sweets to the temple patrons every day. The famous Golden Temple in Amritsar, with a massive state-of-the-art facility, offers fifty thousand free meals a day. Surrounding farms donate ingredients, and volunteers run the entire operation.

My brothers and I accompanied my mother for weekend services. I would promptly fall asleep in her lap during the praying and chanting, only to awaken when seera, being served as the prashad, the sacred offering, was being passed around at the end of service. Spoiled rotten that I was, I would sit up and demand that she share her portion with me. Sometimes she would make the seera for breakfast to please my father, who had an obsessive sweet tooth. It takes minutes to make and is delicious warm, room temperature, or cold. It's decadent and best eaten in small portions or as a base for poached pears or fruit compote. (*See the recipe photo, bottom right, on page 262.*)

In a medium frying pan or saucepan, heat the ghee over medium heat. Add the cardamom seeds, black pepper, roti flour, and semolina flour and cook for 5 to 7 minutes, stirring constantly, until it turns golden brown. It is important to watch over it carefully, as it can burn fast. If you must walk away, turn the heat off. Add the sugar, salt, and milk and cook, stirring constantly, until the seera comes together, within 1 to 2 minutes. Turn the heat off and garnish with the nuts. The seera can sit out for a few hours before serving, or you can refrigerate it for up to 4 days.

sindhi churi laddu

A family portrait of the gods of India, with their bevy of avatars and incarnations, can seem bewildering, yet a deeper study of the scriptures reveals their cosmic significance. The chubby-cheeked Krishna, an avatar of Vishnu and the preserver of the universe, is renowned for his love of all things dairy, especially butter, milk, and ghee. Legend goes that to escape the murderous intent of a scoundrel uncle who had usurped his father's throne, as a baby, Krishna was deposited in a family of cowherds. There he developed a deep love for sweets, his favorite being laddus, spherical balls of sweet goodness loved by all—kids and adults, rich and poor—and the equivalent of a cookie to Americans. In religious ceremonies, laddus are served up in the name of Krishna and other gods in temples across India. There are hundreds of varieties of laddus, made from wheat, nuts, lentils, ghee, dried fruits, and more. Here is my rendition of a whole-wheat laddu called churi laddu, native to my homeland, Sindh. Instead of forming the mixture into laddus, it also can be enjoyed simply as the churi, or the crumble. (*See the recipe photo, bottom left, on page 262.*)

In a medium frying pan or saucepan, melt the ghee over low heat. Add the roti flour and cardamom and toast for 5 to 7 minutes, stirring constantly, until the flour is golden brown. The mixture will be slightly crumbly and will emanate a roasted roux aroma when it is close to being ready. Turn the heat off and let the mixture cool for a few minutes. Stir in the salt and sugar. This is the churi and can be eaten as is also. To make laddus, take 2 tablespoons of the mixture and press into a tight round ball. If it falls apart, add about 1 tablespoon ghee to the mixture and try again. Form the remaining laddus. They can be left at room temperature for a few days; refrigerate for longer storage.

MAKES 8 TO 10 LADDUS

½ cup ghee (see page 77), plus more for forming laddus as needed

1½ cups roti flour or whole-wheat pastry flour

1 teaspoon ground green cardamom seeds

Pinch of sea salt

1 cup turbinado sugar

mawa cake

**MAKES 12 LITTLE CAKES,
OR 1 LOAF CAKE**

¾ cup (1½ sticks) unsalted butter, softened

1¼ cups cane sugar

½ cup cream cheese, softened

3 large eggs

¾ cup heavy cream, plus ¼ cup for topping

1 teaspoon kewra water (see page 72)

1¾ cups all-purpose flour

2 tablespoons semolina flour

1½ teaspoons baking powder

1 teaspoon ground green cardamom seeds

1 teaspoon ground cinnamon

¼ teaspoon sea salt

One early morning not very long ago, I first tasted a mawa cake when a friend took me to B. Merwan, a famous Parsi bakery in Mumbai, for breakfast. Walking into a mountain of mawa cakes on the counter of this expansive, busy, noisy café, my senses were immediately swarmed with the sweet aroma of cardamom, warm butter, and freshly baked rolls. Hundreds of men, mostly construction workers and day laborers, sipping chai and munching on mawa cakes or bread rolls with butter, filled the room. An employee quickly shepherded us into a small side room reserved for ladies only. I was stunned, as I had never encountered a segregated café in my life before. Seeing my expression, the employee quietly whispered in my ear that women are such a rare sight at the café, they prefer to keep it separate in the interest of protecting women. I glared back at him, not wanting to make a scene. Within minutes, masala chai and mawa cakes—sweet, buttery, crumbly cakes warmly scented with cardamom—arrived. I recovered and tucked into the delicious food.

Upon returning home, I resolved to make a version of these at Pondicheri. *Mawa* means "evaporated cream"—at the restaurant we use khoya, a reduced cream product from India sold at most Indian grocers. You may replace it with clotted cream, marscapone, or crème fraîche. Here, I use cream cheese, and the results are just as delicious.

Preheat oven to 350°F and generously grease a shallow muffin tin or loaf mold with melted butter. Dust a few tablespoons all-purpose flour over the surface of the tin. Combine the butter, sugar, and cream cheese in a stand mixer fitted with the paddle attachment and mix on medium speed for 5 to 7 minutes, until creamy and almost white in color. Add the eggs, one at a time, and mix just until combined. Add the ¾ cup cream and the kewra water and mix just until fully incorporated.

In a separate bowl, combine the all-purpose flour, semolina flour, baking powder, cardamom, cinnamon, and salt and add them all once to the butter mixture, continuing to mix until the batter is smooth and homogeneous.

Scoop the batter into the prepared muffin tins or loaf mold. Bake for about 25 minutes if using muffin tins and 45 minutes to 1 hour or longer if using a loaf pan, until a toothpick inserted comes out clean or with just a few crumbs. Remove from the oven, poke a few holes in the cakes with a toothpick, and drizzle with the remaining ¼ cup cream. Allow to cool for a few minutes before serving.

temple fudge

MAKES 12 PIECES

½ cup ghee (see page 77), plus more as needed

1½ cups chickpea flour

1 cup cane sugar

1 teaspoon ground green cardamom seeds

Pinch of sea salt

Milk or water, if needed

2 tablespoons chopped toasted pistachios

1 tablespoon chopped toasted almonds

Dried rose petals or marigold petals, for sprinkling

The god Krishna's love for sweets may be legendary, but Krishna was a veritable saint compared to the gluttonous yet affable god of good fortune and success, Ganesh. Ganesh is popular all over India and easily recognized by his fat belly and elephant head. One of the legends I was told about him as a child is a time when Ganesh ate too many sweets and his stomach exploded on his way home. The laddus scattered all over the forest and the moon could not control its laughter. Ganesh, in embarrassed fury, banished the moon to eternal darkness. He eventually relented but forced the moon to wax and wane as a reminder to never laugh at a god, even a fat and jolly one. Of all the sweets in India, this chickpea fudge (aka mithai or barfi), often served in temples, is my absolute favorite. It will keep for months in the refrigerator, and the chocolate option is even more decadent.

Grease a 6 by 8-inch baking sheet and line it with parchment paper.

In a medium frying pan or saucepan, heat the ghee over medium-low heat. Add the chickpea flour, sugar, cardamom, and salt and toast the ingredients, stirring constantly, until golden brown. The mixture should look like a creamy roux; if it appears dry, add 1 or 2 tablespoons ghee. It will emit a nutty aroma within 15 to 20 minutes. At this point, do not leave the pan unattended with the heat on even for a minute—the mixture will burn. If you must walk away, turn the heat off.

If the mixture appears crumbly, add a few tablespoons milk or water to bring it back into an even mass. Remove from the heat and immediately spread onto the prepared pan until smooth. Sprinkle with the pistachios, almonds, and rose petals. Refrigerate the mithai for an hour or two for it to set. Let sit out at room temperature for 20 to 30 minutes, then cut into twelve equal pieces, cleaning the knife with each cut to keep the edges even.

Variation

Chocolate Temple Fudge Option: Set up a small saucepan filled with a small amount water and set a steel bowl on top (or use a double boiler). Make sure the bottom of the bowl doesn't touch the water. Add 1 cup chocolate chunks and ½ cup heavy cream and bring the water to a simmer. Heat, stirring frequently, until the chocolate is melted and combined with the cream. Spread on the mithai just after you spread it on the pan, before you add the pistachios, almonds, and rose petals. (*See the recipe photo, top left, on page 262.*)

saffron chocolate bread pudding

We all need a nudge or push to do something new and daring in our lives. I can credit part of that encouragement to my wonderful friends at the renowned Café Annie in Houston. In 2001, I opened my first restaurant, Indika. Robert Del Grande, a James Beard Award–winning chef and owner of Annie Café, the restaurant where I worked in the pastry division for a few years prior, had become a mentor, and his wife, the effervescent Mimi, a friend. At the opening, maybe I was just tired and not thinking straight, but I did not see the need for a dessert menu—I was going to give away crisp airy cardamom cookies at the end of lunch and dinner, which would probably reduce if not eliminate the need for dessert. Within a couple of days of opening Indika, Mimi stopped by and was aghast by that decision. She said, "What? No dessert menu?" She insisted that I have a menu soon, and I did and in hindsight, I cannot thank her enough for it. Baking pastries and navigating my way into Indian sweets has now become one of my biggest passions. One of the best desserts that evolved out of that initial scramble was bread pudding with warm Valrhona chocolate melting in between the layers of bread.

For best results and to allow the pudding to puff up, use a pan approximately 9 by 9 by 4 inches (slightly bigger is okay). Find a local bakery or grocer that makes thick plain French bread loaves, not baguettes, or use a soft white bread of your choice. Find the best-quality single-origin sustainably sourced chocolate you can. The bread pudding freezes well, and one of the best ways to serve it is to chill it after baking. The next day, slice the pudding into neat thick slabs and reheat them individually. The slices also freeze well packed in an airtight container. This bread pudding also makes a great stash for midnight sweet cravings, with a microwave the best way to reheat it. If you're planning in advance, defrost in the refrigerator for a day, then reheat in a 300°F oven for 15 to 20 minutes. (*See the recipe photo on page 265.*)

SERVES 6 TO 8

4 large eggs

1 cup cane sugar

1 teaspoon ground green cardamom seeds

¼ teaspoon sea salt

2 cups whole milk

1 cup heavy cream, plus more for serving

Generous pinch of saffron

1 loaf French bread

10 ounces dark chocolate pieces

In a medium bowl, combine the eggs, sugar, cardamom, and salt and whisk until mixed thoroughly. Add the milk and cream and, using a large-mesh strainer, strain into a container. Stir in the saffron and store the custard in the refrigerator until ready to use. It will keep for 2 to 3 days.

recipe continues

Cut the bread into 1-inch slices and line the bottom of a baking pan with two layers of the bread slices. Disregard the gaps in between the slices, as they will plump up while absorbing the custard. Cover the bread with half of the custard mixture and set it aside for 10 to 15 minutes to absorb. Spread the chocolate pieces evenly over the top, avoiding the edges to prevent the chocolate from scorching while baking. Add two more layers of bread, finishing the whole loaf. Press the bread down gently to force the custard to rise to the top. Cover tightly with foil and refrigerate for at least 3 hours or up to overnight.

Preheat the oven to 300°F.

Bake the pudding for 30 minutes to 1 hour and check to see if it looks set. Remove the foil and finish baking for another 15 to 20 minutes, until the pudding appears set but still jiggles. If serving warm, wait about 1 hour before serving.

chocolate chile cookies

Some of the best recipes happen by accident. One morning while preparing for Sunday brunch service at Indika, our ingenious pastry chef Michael Michel, upon discovering that we were out of toasted walnuts for the chocolate oatmeal cookies, substituted the spiced walnuts we used to make for a dinner appetizer. These walnuts were coated in red chile powder, cinnamon, and salt. Our regular customers were so thrilled with these cookies that they demanded we never go back to the plain one. And the chocolate chile cookie was born. Almost ten years later, despite a multitude of other cookies, the chocolate chile remains the number-one-selling cookie at the Bake Lab. If using a mild chile powder, feel free to increase the amount.

One of the best-kept professional secrets about cookie making is to freeze cookie-dough balls and bake straight from the freezer to oven. This simple hack can contain the "spread" of the cookie, resulting in a moister cookie that keeps its shape. (*See the recipe photo, bottom, on page 267.*)

Preheat the oven to 350°F.

In a large bowl, mix the flour, oats, cardamom, red chile powder, baking powder, baking soda, and salt and set aside.

Spread the walnuts on a small baking sheet, place in the oven, and toast for 3 to 4 minutes, until golden brown. Let them cool for 20 to 30 minutes to finish crisping up before adding to the dough.

In the bowl of a stand mixer fitted with the paddle attachment, mix the butter with the sugar for 2 to 3 minutes, just until it comes together (do not cream it—too much air in the cookies will make them fluffy, not chewy and gooey). Add the eggs, one at a time, and mix until combined. Add the dry ingredients and mix just the mixture is evenly distributed. Stir in the chocolate chunks and toasted walnuts.

Scoop the cookie dough into 3-ounce balls. Freeze in a freezer bag for at least 3 hours or, preferably, overnight.

Preheat the oven to 325°F.

Spread the dough balls on a baking sheet 2 inches apart and bake for 12 minutes. Press each cookie down with the back of a ladle, lid, or bowl and bake for another 2 minutes, or until cooked on the outside but a little gooey on the inside. The cookies need to rest on the baking sheet for about 30 minutes and are best warm the day they are made but can be frozen for later use. Store in an airtight container.

MAKES 12 COOKIES

1½ cups all-purpose flour

1¾ cups rolled quick oats

½ teaspoon ground green cardamom seeds

1 teaspoon red chile powder

1 teaspoon baking powder

½ teaspoon baking soda

¼ teaspoon sea salt

½ cup walnut pieces

¾ cup (1½ sticks) unsalted butter, softened

1½ cups cane sugar

2 small eggs

10 ounces dark chocolate chunks

mango rice pudding

Mango is the national fruit of India, and it would be an understatement to say that Indians love mangoes. In fact, Indians are obsessed with mangoes. During mango season, which is March through June, we eat them for breakfast, lunch, and dinner, and sometimes in between as a snack. And while we eat mangoes, we go into deep discussions about the virtues of mangoes and their varieties and where we will travel to get the next best box of mangoes. India produces 99 percent of the world's mangoes yet exports only 1 percent. When mangoes first arrive in markets, the air is thick with the perfumy, sticky-sweet aroma. People mill excitedly, trying to decide which variety to buy. During the Muslim rule, all the emperors were misty-eyed about fruits from Central Asia, like grapes, melons, and peaches, yet each one of them, from Akbar to Shah Jahan, developed a profound love for the mango.

Every mango variety has a different use. As a child, kesar was my favorite. I would massage a ripe kesar in my hands until the pulp loosened into juice, then cut a hole at the top and start sucking the juice out. Totapuri, the shape of which reminds me of a parrot's beak (*tota* in Hindi means "parrot"), with its firm, smooth pulp, is perfect in creamy desserts, and the Alphonso, known as the king of mangoes, arrives a little later and has a heady aroma and an unmistakable sweet flavor. Find the sweetest mangoes you can and make sure they are completely ripe before making this rice pudding recipe. A small yellow variety called the Ataulfo, which comes from Mexico, is my favorite mango here in the United States.

In a medium bowl, combine the rice with 2 cups tap water, stir gently for a few seconds, then drain all the water by simply holding your hand over the bowl and pouring most of the water out into the sink. Repeat and drain. Return to the bowl, add the milk, and let soak on the counter for 2 hours or overnight in the refrigerator.

In a medium heavy-bottom saucepan or Dutch oven, combine the rice with the milk, cream, sugar, and cardamom. Bring to a boil over medium-high heat, then lower the heat, cover, and simmer for 10 to 12 minutes, or until rice is opaque and cooked through. Turn the heat off and let the rice rest. There will still be liquid in the pudding, which will get absorbed by the rice over the next few hours. After the pudding has cooled to the touch, roughly 2 hours after, stir the rice, making sure to be gentle to maintain the integrity of the long grain. Refrigerate the pudding for at least 2 hours or up to overnight. Serve cold, with the mango folded in or served alongside, and top with the almonds.

SERVES 4 TO 6

½ cup white basmati rice

2 cups whole milk

½ cup heavy cream

¾ cup cane sugar

1 teaspoon ground green cardamom seeds

1 large ripe mango, peeled and cut into ½-inch cubes

¼ cup sliced toasted almonds

kulfi

SERVES 4 TO 6

3 cups whole milk

Pinch of saffron

One 14-ounce can sweetened condensed milk

1 cup heavy cream

1 teaspoon ground green cardamom seeds

½ teaspoon ground mace

1 teaspoon khus essence or a few drops of vetiver essential oil (see page 72)

4 large egg yolks

⅓ cup chopped mixed raw nuts (such as pistachios, cashews, and almonds)

Derived from the Persian word *qulfi* and originating during the sixteenth-century Persian rule in India, kulfi is a cardamom-scented and nut-laced ice cream from India. It is dense and rich, served in a slab or as a slice and not churned like most ice cream. Sold on streets, sometimes in kulfi carts fitted with long metal cone-shaped containers, it comes in dozens of flavors from simple cream to rose-scented. The traditional way to make kulfi is to simmer milk for hours until it reduces to a thick consistency. This is a simpler version with egg yolks, shortening the time usually required to reduce it to a thick consistency. At home, I find an old ice-cube tray the best mold for kulfi; it doesn't take up too much room in the freezer and you can pop the cubes out in small portions, perfect for sharing.

In a medium heavy-bottom saucepan or a Dutch oven, combine the whole milk and saffron. Place over high heat and bring to a boil, then lower the heat and simmer for 5 to 7 minutes, stirring almost continuously to prevent it from sticking to the bottom of the pan, until the milk has reduced a bit. Add the condensed milk, heavy cream, cardamom, mace, and khus and cook for another 2 to 3 minutes, until the entire mixture comes to a boil. Remove from the heat, add the egg yolks, and whisk until smooth. Add the nuts, let the mixture cool, then pour it into a mold of your choice (such as an ice-pop mold) and freeze until solid. You can also freeze it in a shallow pan or small ramekins. The kulfi will keep in the freezer for up to 3 months.

Take the kulfi out 5 to 10 minutes before serving to soften it a bit and make it easier to remove and cut.

indika cookies

MAKES 24 COOKIES

1 cup (2 sticks) unsalted butter, at room temperature

1¾ cups confectioners' sugar

1½ cups all-purpose flour

3 tablespoons semolina flour

3 tablespoons cornstarch

1½ teaspoon ground green cardamom seeds

¼ teaspoon sea salt

During the Dutch reign in India, a bakery in Surat, a small town in Gujarat, employing five Parsi (originally from Persia) men was established. When the Dutch left India, the bakery was handed over to one of the Parsi men, Mr. Dotivala, and it became the Dotivala Bakery. Today, Cyrus Dotivala, a seventh-generation Parsi, runs the bakery, making it almost 160 years old. The bakery is credited with inventing my favorite cookie, the nankathai, a crispy cardamom-scented shortbread cookie. It took me years to hone the recipe for my version of this cookie, which we served complimentary at the end of the meal at Indika. For a more celebratory cookie, dip half the cookie in melted chocolate and scatter chopped pistachios on top.

In the bowl of a stand mixer fitted with the paddle attachment, cream the butter with the confectioners' sugar at medium speed for 4 to 5 minutes, until light and fluffy.

In a separate bowl, whisk together the all-purpose flour, semolina flour, cornstarch, cardamom, and salt. Add the dry ingredients to the butter mixture and mix just until combined. Divide the dough into two parts and shape each into an 8 by 1-inch log. Roll the logs in parchment paper and refrigerate for at least 2 hours or up to overnight. At this point, the logs may be frozen for up to 6 months.

Preheat the oven to 350°F and line a baking sheet with parchment paper.

Remove the parchment paper from the cookie-dough log. If frozen, allow it to come to room temperature, then slice into ½-inch discs. If refrigerated, slice and bake the cookie dough cold. Place the cookies on the prepared baking sheet and bake for 15 to 20 minutes, until golden. Stored in an airtight container, the cookie will stay fresh for up to 3 months.

Acknowledgments

The poetic and passionate writing of Maya Tiwari first inspired me to learn about Ayurveda, and I devoured her books, one after another. To her and Dr. Deepak Chopra, I owe a huge debt of gratitude. The brilliant works of Dr. Chopra gave me a glimpse into the esoteric world of health, his teachings becoming my moral compass. A lifetime of learning and cooking culminating in writing arrives on the heels of so many thoughtful and wonderful books I have enjoyed, and for this, I thank Charmaine Solomon in her great exploration of foods from Asia, Inder Singh Kalra's definitive book on masterful Indian cooking, Tarla Dalal's prolific recipe writing from Gujarati to Indian Italian, and Suneeta Vaswani's books on regional food. Marryam Reshii's defining book on spices taught me almost everything I need to know about spices. From writings by renowned historian Dr. K. T. Achaya, I learned about the history of foods in India. Lizzie Collingham's and Michael Krondl's books on the history of the spice and sweet trade inspired me to dig deeper and deeper into colonial influences on the culture of India.

My community in Houston, from the staff at Pondicheri, almost all of whom we have turned into chai drinkers, to the customers from all walks of life who have wholeheartedly embraced my cooking and have come to make our restaurant their home away from home, I offer a heartfelt thank-you for your staunch support. To my recipe testers, Emmy and Lizzie Vest, Aila Peck, Sarah Gelb, Ben Jordan, and Sally Zike—thank you for letting me into your kitchens. I am counting on you to become dosa masters! To my yoga teacher and dear friend, Ann Hyde, who has eaten at my restaurants almost every day for fifteen-plus years and has cheered me on with great gusto. I thank my friend, Neelam Singh, lawyer by day and Ayurvedic expert by night for carefully fact checking my writings on this vast subject.

The wind beneath my wings comes from my beloved children, Ajna and Virag, my ultimate unwavering fans, who became foodies by default and were open to lapping up whatever I felt like feeding them for years. They are the ones who counseled me on what to feed American kids for breakfast—not just parathas and dosas, but crepes and pancakes, please, Mom!

The Journey of Spices

About the Author

Anita Jaisinghani is the chef-owner of Pondicheri Restaurant and Bake Lab + Shop in Houston, Texas. After obtaining a degree in microbiology and working in Canada for several years, Anita moved to Houston, Texas, where she pursued her passion for food by first selling locally made chutneys to Whole Food Market, then by going to work for Robert Del Grande at Café Annie to learn the ins and outs of the restaurant business. In 2001, she opened Indika, an award-winning restaurant with a modern take on Indian food, in Houston, which she helmed until 2015. In 2011, wanting to take food to the "street level" by showcasing regional cooking of India, Anita opened Pondicheri, an all-day café with inspiration from street and home cooking of India. With an industrial décor of pungent colors and bright Indian textiles, Pondicheri has become an unofficial Houston landmark beloved by people of all generations. Pondicheri Bake Lab + Shop, a beautiful sun-filled annex located directly above the restaurant, opened in 2014. It sells a variety of baked goods, prepared masalas, other condiments, and unique textiles from India. It is a space where Anita and her team explore creative ideas and where Anita teaches cooking classes. Anita writes a weekly recipe column for the *Houston Chronicle* and runs the recipe website India1948.com. She is a perennial student of Ayurveda and yoga, with a deep passion for food and how it relates to every aspect of our mind, body, and spirit.

Index

Additional photo credits:
Jen Duncan: Pages viii–1, 52, 55, 66, 74, 173 (top right), 207, 213,
       224, 252–253, and 275, copyright © 2022 by Jen Duncan.
       Used by permission of the photographer.
Kirby Trapolino: Pages 4–5, 8–9, 17, and 167, copyright © Kirby
       Trapolino. Used by permission of the photographer.
Lou Vest: Page 286, copyright © Lou Vest. Used by permission
       of the photographer.

Typefaces: Typeverything's Room 205 by Simon Walker,
       Grilli Type's GT Alpina by Reto Moser, Lineto's Akkurat Pro
       by Laurenz Brunner

Library of Congress Control Number: 2021949765

Hardcover ISBN: 978-1-9848-6070-5
eBook ISBN: 978-1-9848-6071-2

Printed in China

Editor: Emma Rudolph
Designer: Isabelle Gioffredi | Art Director: Emma Campion |
       Production designer: Mari Gill
Production manager and prepress color manager: Jane Chinn
Prop stylist: Summer Moore |
       Prop stylist assistant: Ajna Jaisinghani
Photo assistant: Amy Scott
Copyeditor: Leda Scheintaub | Proofreader: Mikayla Butchart |
       Indexer: Amy Hall
Publicist: David Hawk | Marketer: Brianne Sperber

10 9 8 7 6 5 4 3 2 1

First Edition